The White Row Press

WILLIAM
CARLETON

The
AUTOBIOGRAPHY

The White Row Press

WILLIAM CARLETON

The AUTOBIOGRAPHY

The White Row Press

First published 1896.
This edition published 1996
by the White Row Press
135 Cumberland Road, Dundonald
Belfast BT16 OBB

Foreword copyright © Benedict Kiely

Cover: William Carleton by Neil Shawcross 1996
All rights reserved

This book has received financial assistance from the
Cultural Traditions Group of the Community Relations Council

Printed by The Universities Press Ltd, Belfast

A catalogue record for this book is available from the British Library

ISBN
1 870132 75 0 (paper)
1 870132 80 7 (cloth)

Contents

Birthplace – McManus's misleading picture – Parentage – The legends of the elder Carleton – Mrs Carleton's songs – Catholic tolerance – Removal from Prillisk – Carleton goes to school – The hedge schoolmaster – State of education.

Mrs Dumont's school – Jack Stuart's barn – Carleton falls in love – Expulsion from school – Findramore – Pat Frayne's academy at Skelgy – Pat's anecdotes – Sam Nelson's joke – Pat's method of correction – How to obtain provisions – The egg trick.

Carleton is intended for the priesthood – Popularity of political plays – Catholics and Protestants – Performance of 'The Battle of Aughrim' – A panic – Orangeism – The yeomanry – A nocturnal visit – Removal to Nurchasy – Tulnavert school.

The altars – No chapels – Removal to Springtown – Shoes and stockings not expected – Robbing an orchard – Springs and man-traps – Carleton is caught – A whimsical magistrate – A dangerous exploit.

Fondness for nature – Another love affair – Blighted affection – Anne Duffy marries – A brutal master – Retaliation – The superstitions of the elder Carleton – His death.

Foreword

William Carleton's more-or-less official biographer, David O'Donoghue, wrote of him: 'He gave offence to every class of Irishman in one or other of his books, and all that can be done by way of extenuation or excuse is to explain the incidents which seem to have occasioned his conduct.'[1]

But considering the character of the man, and the chaotic time in which he lived, I do not know if O'Donoghue's remark can be explained as easily as all that. It is just possible that, anyway, what it needs is not explanation but the considerate contemplation that years of comparative calm should give to years of uncertainty and suffering.

For William Carleton knew the Irish people in the cabins in a time of hunger and unease and miserable change, in a time of chaos when even the strongest were not sure of their footing. He may never have been one of the strongest, never one of the most stable. But he had imagination, rich humour, a capacity for honourable tears. He went with his own people to weddings and wakes, funerals, christenings, places of prayer, places of merriment. He saw that black withering visitation of famine. All these things he remembered and wrote down. And about and because of his own people he wrote some of the world's great stories.

He had his credit for it: not much money for he was a bad man at business, not much worldly comfort, beyond the fragrance of poteen punch, or the beauty of rivers and mountains and green fields, or love and contentment around his own hearth. But he had praise from great men who were few, from small men who

---

[1] *The Life of William Carleton: Being his autobiography and letters; and an account of his life and writings, from the point at which the autobiography breaks off.* David J. O'Donoghue; with an introduction by Mrs Cashel Hoey. (Two volumes, Downey, London, 1896.)

were many, and from some he had blame and bitter words.

He came with us out of the cabins, and Charles Gavan Duffy, who had travelled a somewhat similar road, saw Carleton rising like a mountain above the men of his time. Thomas Davis, reading his stories, saw 'the moory upland and the corn slopes, the glen where the rock juts through the mantling heather and bright brooks gurgle amid the scented banks of wild herbs, the shivering cabin and the rudely lighted farmhouse', all as plain as if Carleton had used canvas and colours as Poussin did, or Teniers, or Wilkie.

For W.B. Yeats he was 'the great novelist of Ireland by right of the most Celtic eyes that ever gazed from under the brow of a storyteller'. The poet, somewhere between the Indian twilight and the Celtic twilight and the twilight of the nineteenth century, found also in the works of the novelist a clay-cold melancholy that made Carleton kin to the animals in Milton's *Paradise*, 'half-emerged only from the earth and its broodings'.

Sir Shane Leslie wrote that:

> In the Ireland before the Famine one genius only equalled O'Connell's: like him in weakness and strength, lavish of language, hysterical of emotion and more Irish than the Irish: William Carleton, novelist... All the burlesque and beauty of the old Irish life survives in his pages. In some ways he was greater than Walter Scott, who never suffered and lived with the folk he described. Alone they can be compared with each other: the Scottish laird and the Irish peasant.

II

There have been other wise voices speaking out of his own time, and out of the years after his time, to tell the people of Ireland forever how important this man is in the story of their past and to their knowledge of the present. Attentively listening to those voices one may learn in what way and under what circumstances he managed to give offence to so many of his countrymen, always remembering that the mystery of the man's soul, as of the soul of any man, is hidden as completely as anything can be. In his own chaotic and entangled soul he has mirrored all our own complications.

But in the Clogher valley in south Tyrone where he found men and women and made them immortal, the meaning behind the mystery, the secret lost somewhere in chaos, does not seem to me to be of any account. Sheltering there in a cottage doorway from a sudden shower, or talking with men thinning turnips on a hill in Prillisk where he was born, or going up steeply through new-planted trees to the top of Knockmany Hill, one realizes that the present is the past, the people are unchanged.

In the hazel glen behind the house at Springtown where he once lived, the blackbirds sing eternally as he had heard them, through the open window, singing their souls to the rich cool evening. Across the road from the Forth Chapel the girl in the shop talked about the Yankee soldiers who had camped near Aughentain. The stories Carleton had heard in his boyhood had been about Cromwellian soldiers laying siege to the castle of Aughentain.

Leaning on the wall beside the shop the saddler who, fifty years ago, worked in the one-sided town of Clogher, pointed across the little valley to Dunroe and to Richardson's house where the hedge school had been. And it was very easy suddenly to see William Carleton walking those narrow roads, learning a little about books, learning a lot about men and women, his own immortal, imperishable people: leaving us a lot to learn from the story of his days.

In the house at Springtown there was a radio set. Over it the voice of the world came to the quiet valley, mingling with the song of the blackbirds in the hazel glen, with the confused contradictory voices of the previous century. But if you listened carefully you could hear the one voice that mattered most of all, speaking across a hundred years, speaking for the people of that valley, for the people of Ireland, for those who died and for those who still lived, for those who sailed over the sea, even for those who returned to camp where the soldiers of Cromwell once camped in the townland of Aughentain.

III

The road goes down past the Forth Chapel to Ned McKeown's crossroads where most readers of Carleton meet him for the first time in the opening pages of *Traits and Stories of the Irish Peasantry*. It is, possibly, the best place to meet William Carleton. And the best way is, undeniably, through the introductions to Ned and his wife, Nancy. And to Shane Fadh whose wedding would not have been out of place in Homer. And to Jack Magennis of the Routing Burn who came walking down a bog road, saw a black man leaning against a turf-stack, and beside him a dog that smoked a pipe as cool as a Christian. In those pages William is the boy who lived idle days in the valley, who leaped Clogher Karry with the whole world watching him, who tossed the weight over the wooden beam in Clogher Mill and, afterwards, drank sweet poteen with the miller, Frank Farrell. At Ned McKeown's crossroads, too, the boy listened to strong argument about Bonaparte. And he saw on the edge of the crowd the sweet face of Anne Duffy from Augher.

In this unfinished autobiography he recaptures that same note of unspoiled and uncaring innocence. Yet the autobiography brings Carleton out of the valley, annoyed by the carping of relatives who wanted to know when he was going to start working for his living. He went: his mind radiant with the colourful things that had happened to Master Gil Blas when he left his native Santillane to go studying in Salamanca. A very short period of time convinced Carleton that Ireland was not Spain, that the picaresque of Le Sage was by no means the gospel truth that he had taken it for when he borrowed that wonderful book from a travelling packman.

His road from the Clogher valley to Dirty Lane in the slums of Dublin was the road from sunshine and birdsong in idle hazelwoods to a black, terrible world where rotting bodies hung on roadside gallows, where men and women dropped dead with hunger, where bewildered men and women occasionally sold themselves, body and soul, for food or money. Near Killaney in the County

4

Louth he heard the story of the burnings and killings at Wildgoose Lodge, saw the bodies of Paddy Devaun and his fellow-conspirators swinging aloft in pitch-sacks. And the soldiers casually standing guard under the gallows.

Paddy Devaun was hanged beside his own home. And all day long his widowed mother, crossing and recrossing her own threshold, could look up and see, high against heaven, the body of her son. In later years William Carleton, more particularly when he wrote *Rody the Rover,* took it upon himself seriously to advise his countrymen against the horrors of Whiteboyism, and conspiracy, and violence. But no man could have understood more clearly how pitiable all advice would be to something in the Irish people that was symbolised by the mother of Paddy Devaun. For the old woman knew only that in pain she had given her son life, with joy she had watched him teach in the school and clerk for the priest on the altar, that for some reason she could not fathom he had lost the life she gave him on the high gallows in ignominy and pain. She knew and William Carleton knew when he heard her story that it was a sorrowful and foolish land: so sorrowful and foolish that the poets had seen it symbolically as an old bent woman perpetually mourning the death of her sons.

IV

It was also a hungry land. Carleton was born in 1794. He arrived in Dublin about 1818 and fifty years later, in the year that preceded his death, he was writing the beginning of that autobiography that he was never to finish.[2] The terrible years of rebellion and repression did not leave his childhood untouched. Orange yeomanry roamed the country and there was one awful night when his father's house was raided, and his father insulted, and his sister prodded with a bayonet as she lay in her bed.

---

[2] After Carleton's death his unfinished autobiographical manuscript passed to his daughters. O'Donoghue sought them out and brought the script into the public domain by publishing it as volume one of the 1896 edition.

He remembered that incident when, under the influence of Young Ireland, and particularly attracted by the magnetic personality of Thomas Davis, he wrote the sombre story of Valentine McClutchy, agent at Castle Cumber, and of Solomon McSlime, the religious and adulterous attorney. The iniquity of the system of land tenure, the outrages of organised Orangeism, the rabid fervour of the New Reformation making converts whose conversion lasted until the new potatoes came in, were mercilessly analysed by a man who could seldom be cool and rational. But when he really understood his subject he had astounding powers of satirical abuse.

When in the novel, *Valentine McClutchy*, Darby O'Drive, the rascally bailiff, circulated, for the devilment of the thing, the report that the New Reformation Society was ready to receive converts at the rate of five guineas a head, the response among the people of Castle Cumber was almost completely motivated by hunger. Like some fantastic Dance of Death in a medieval nightmare the would-be converts flocked to the house of Mr Phineas Lucre. The hunger that could do such terrible things deepened into terrible famine about the time that William Carleton was meandering his way from the Clogher valley, past Wildgoose Lodge, past Navan, where in a house by a lake he found and read *Castle Rackrent,* past Maynooth where he was reminded of the poor scholar he had failed to be, and reminded of the priest that he had failed to be. Then down the Liffey valley to Dublin city where he found lodgings in a cellar with the people of the streets.

In that cellar in Dirty Lane he saw for the first time the red centre of his country's degraded beggary. And his bred-in-the-bone rural respectability writhed in horror. There had been hungry people and beggars in his native valley, hungry people and beggars on the roads he had tramped on his way to Dublin. Thirty years later, remembering what he had seen in that valley and along those roads, he wrote *The Black Prophet*.

But the beggary that he had seen in country places had been beggary with a difference, almost with a certain dignity, with a link connecting it with a lost way of life in which the wandering poor

6

had a certain mystical significance. There had been the slightly
suspect piety of the voteen, the Shakespearean stature of the fool.
There had been the great figures of Tom Steeple who thought he
was as tall as a towering steeple, and Raymond of the Hats who
added to his monstrous height by wearing three hats one on top
of the other.

For Carleton really saw the two fools, Tom and Raymond, as
tall men, standing high above the legions of urban destitute and
homeless. They were poorer than the poorest, but from the
deepest deeps of misery they stood symbolically erect,
unconsciously speaking wit and wisdom, doing good deeds out
of the warm overflowing of generous hearts, showing the
thousand ways in which that Western Island of beggary could be
as rich as the fabulous East.

Going down the steps to the cellars in Dirty Lane Carleton
must, for a moment, have lost that vision. In shakedowns of straw
with sheets of rag, men and women, in various degrees of drink,
lay asleep. By the light of a red fire he saw the lame, the blind, the
broken and diseased people: and those who, during the day and
for business purposes, had assumed all the infirmities of the flesh.
Crutches, wooden legs, artificial cancers, scrofulous necks, artificial
wens, sore legs, dangled on the dirty walls. Those who were still
awake sang and chatted and shouted slang. And the lad from the
green country felt for the first time the creeping touch of a leprous
obscenity.

V

What all that meant was that William Carleton, the greatest
creative writer who ever, up to that time, set about the
work of interpreting the Irish people, was to know all the horror
of seeing the people that he understood so intimately cut down in
terrible death. When, as a boy, he leaped across the width of the
river at Clogher Karry, admired by the eyes of the whole world,
the only world he then knew, he did not know that the impetus
of the leap would carry him farther than the other side of the water.

He was lazy and he loved idleness. But even more than that, his heart clung to the stability of a life in which a young man had to make no decision, in which everything was as definite as a race and a leap, everything as sweet as stolen apples.

With the instinct of genius he was dreading the long leap out into the world and was holding desperately to delicious days that ever afterwards filled five-sixths of his heart. His instinct was not misleading. He came out of one Irish valley to find the secret of every Irish valley. But he found also a people embittered by divisions, tormented by bigotry, struggling painfully towards freedom and accepting ready-made formulae that made freedom look foolish. He found the people in the cabins living wearily in the shadow of the Big House, the people from the Big House living senselessly over in London.

In that chaos a strong man could have found enough solid footing to keep him standing in one place and looking about him with some consistent steadiness. Daniel O'Connell, in spite of his ultimate failure, was a strong man, even though William Carleton saw his strength as a menace, as a wish for domination and power that would have made him a tyrant if fate had made him a king. But William Carleton was a young man and a poor man, a man with a wife and family, with a growing consciousness of his own literary talent and a need of money.

In the middle of this turbulence he met a man who was stronger than he: stronger in being older, well-read, well-travelled, learned in antiquarian matters, a prose writer of unusual power, and the editor of a magazine called *The Christian Examiner*. He walked the roads of Ireland, talked to the people of Ireland, wrote sketches of his travels which are still of considerable value. But he saw all Ireland under a shadow, the people of Ireland as children of the shadow.

It was not the shadow of landlordism living perilously on a rackrented people. Nor of an an established church squeezing tithes out of the tenants against their conscience. Nor of government made negative by that same landlordism, and by a poisonous sectarianism. Nor of recurring and worsening famine.

And a people living precariously on one vulnerable root-crop.

He saw as many of those things as it did not go against his principles to see. But any evil that he recognised he attributed to the terrible influence of the Church of Rome. His own lean body was racked and feverish with hatred of Catholicism. The division in him between the artist and scholar and the shrieking bigot was intensified by the growing strength of the agitation for Catholic emancipation; by the foaming fanaticism of the New Reformation in which, with many lesser men who were only bigots, and to the intense amusement of Samuel Lover and the wits of Dublin, he played a considerable part. He was a lean proselytiser, so lean that a popular joke about him had it that he sheltered up a gun barrel at Rigby's when the rains came.

When, in his Irish wanderings, Caesar Otway climbed a mountain road and looked down upon Lough Derg, 'he felt no reverence', wrote W.B. Yeats, 'for the grey island consecrated by the verse of Calderon and the feet of twelve centuries of pilgrims'.

To say that he felt no reverence was an understatement. What Otway saw was 'degraded superstition... destined to keep the human understanding in the same dark unproductive state as the moorland waste that lay outstretched around'.

That terrible vision was still in his eyes when he shook hands with William Carleton. And Carleton said that he had read Otway's *Sketches in Ireland*. And that he, as a boy, had made the pilgrimage to Lough Derg. And that he agreed with much of what Otway had written regarding that place.

VI

Here there are two difficulties. William Carleton's father had wanted to see his son a priest. William Carleton had, for a while in his youth, wanted to be a priest. Just as Dennis O'Shaughnessy wanted to go to Maynooth. And most of William Carleton's comical ideas on the true meaning of vocation to the priesthood are satirised delightfully in the humorous, nostalgic story of Dennis O'Shaughnessy, his sesqipedalian words, his sweetheart, who knowing him better than he himself did, advised him to take the kiss and spare the King's English.

William Carleton had also wanted to be a scholar, and his tattered passion for learning gave us forever the glory of Mat Kavanagh, the hedge-schoolmaster, in his subterranean schoolhouse at Findramore. It gave us also the great story of Jemmy McEvoy, the poor scholar, walking, like a prince through a worshipping people, on the road to Munster where the swallows flew in conic sections, where the magpies and turkeys confabbed in Latin, where the bullocks roared in Doric Greek. Carleton himself set out on that road. But when he slept a night at Grehan's Inn in Granard and a furious bull roared at him in his dreams, his heart failed him and he turned for home.

Later on, motivated by a religious fervour not completely above suspicion, he made the pilgrimage to Lough Derg. When he wrote for Caesar Otway's *Christian Examiner* the story of that Lough Derg pilgrimage, he claimed that what he saw there set him moving on a rational course not only away from what he thought of the priesthood but from the faith in which he had been born and bred. It is just here that the first difficulty arises. For nowhere in his works has William Carleton proved that in any period of his life he bothered much to distinguish, on rational grounds, between one religion and another.

Caesar Otway looked at William Carleton and saw the brand snatched from the burning. He listened to the stories he told of the people back in the valley. And suddenly Otway saw the hungry thousands alive and real, living in the cabins, bending the back day after day in the small fields. In the advice he gave to Carleton the second difficulty arises for it was good advice and bad advice. Otway suggested to the young fellow that he should write of the people as he spoke of the people. For a temperament as inchoate and chaotic as that of Carleton seems to have been, that was valuable advice. The inspiration of the precise Miss Edgeworth, that touched the great Sir Walter in Scotland and Turgenev in Russia, might easily have passed over the head of William Carleton in Dublin. Like many young writers he might readily have taken to writing about things as remote from his own experience as dukes and duchesses and captains of dragoons.

Oddly and ironically enough some of his later work descended to that world. But by that time he was, you might say, written-out: his feet had forgotten the touch of the strong earth in the valley that had made him great. Otway's good advice meant that his first great enthusiastic energy set him working in the quarry out of which he himself had been cut.

Otway's bad advice talked of the service Carleton could do to the work of *The Christian Examiner* by holding up to the light the superstitions of the people: the superstitions of pilgrimage and priesthood and prophecies, mass and miracles, sermons and stations and rosaries, voteens and holy wells. Carleton began to see all those things as enemies of the light, enemies of the liberty of the human mind.

Otway offered him money and the hospitality of his home, offered him also the chance to write out of his bones the grudges that a man of talent can collect when he is the poor son of poor people. And Carleton scrambled up on the fence, possibly with the firm intention of becoming a Protestant, but inevitably doomed to end up with a long leg dangling on either side of the rickety division. The one advantage was that, perched on the fence with his heels kicking the air, he could work and eat. Now the fence swayed to one side, now to the other, affected by the fortunes of his own people still walking confusedly on the ground. He had raised himself a little above their poverty. Some shouted at him in bitterness because they thought he had sold them and sold his own past. Some, knowing their own heart in his heart, knowing the ways of men and the unsteadiness of the whole earth, laughed with him when he laughed, were silent when he remembered the sorrow and the lost sunshine.

VII

When Randy O'Rollick, on a visit to the north-east corner of Ireland, commended the Presbyterian Sabbath because it bestowed no privilege of licentiousness and crime, allowed no profane songs after dinner, no gambling, no card-playing, no riotous entertainments, he was very far away from the character intended for him when he was given a name. He was even further away from the true character of his creator.

Randy, in his meditative, unrandyish, unrollicking mood found in the Presbyterian meeting-house 'a higher and more enlightened perception of religious influence, associated more with reason than with feeling'. And in the Catholic chapel 'more impulsive piety'.

Carleton died in 1869 outside the church into which he had been born. The judgment of Randy on things religious was written in 1851. If it is to be taken as Carleton's final decision then he died also outside the church to which, according to his own opinion, he quite obviously belonged. For no man ever used his reason less in matters of religion. He was a million miles of the mind away from the cold wisdom of Aquinas proclaiming that Reason had in man the dominating place. He was a very perplexed pilgrim losing his balance near the beginning of the journey, staggering on in dizzy bewilderment, anxious to please and to pacify as he went, anxious to tell the truth but not always finding it possible, offending all men by the uncertainty of his progress.

He wanted to stand high above all the confusion in some cool rational place. But when he wrote those early tales of which *The Lough Derg Pilgrim* was the only one of real value and submitted them to the editing and interpolating of Caesar Otway, he had taken his place in the terrible procession to the house of Mr Phineas Lucre.

VIII

O' Donoghue catalogued the bulk of the published writings of William Carleton. From that list the search for Carleton can go on through libraries, second-hand bookshops, chimney corners, holes behind the hearth. When Yeats, as a young man, was writing the *Letters to the New Island*, he complained of the scarcity of copies of the greater stories: *The Emigrants of Ahadarra*, *Fardorougha the Miser*, *Valentine McClutchy*, the *Traits and Stories*. Today the situation could still do with improvement, and this volume will certainly help.

A century and a half ago a great Irishman said that the man who had not read William Carleton did not know the Irish people. The words are wisdom now as they were then. Today it would be unnecessary to write a survey of the literary merit of the work he did. That merit is established and permanent.

But this man saw so deeply into our souls, revealed so much in himself of the torture of his time, that we can never afford to neglect him. He heard his father tell stories and his mother sing songs as men and women in Ireland had told stories and sung songs for centuries. Then with the figures that came from the mind of Le Sage dancing like imps down the road before him, he went on the world to find his fortune. He saw the little roads lined with gallows. He saw the black horrors of famine. Around him in the ruin, and within him in his own soul, were the makings of modern Ireland.

Benedict Kiely

Chapter I

Birthplace – McManus's misleading picture – Parentage – The legends
of the elder Carleton – Mrs Carleton's songs – Catholic tolerance –
Removal from Prillisk – Carleton goes to school – The hedge
schoolmaster – State of education.

ALAS! it is a melancholy task which I propose to execute – the
narrative of such a continued and unbroken series of struggle,
difficulty, suffering and sorrow as has seldom fallen to the lot of a
literary man. Indeed, there was something peculiarly calamitous
in my fate, because it was to a disaster, which would have ruined
the hopes and prospects of any other man, that I owe my fame.
This the reader will understand in the due course of time. Goldsmith says that poverty is the nurse of genius – but Goldsmith,
much and enthusiastically as I admire him, has said in this case
what every man of experience feels to be untrue. The metaphor,
indeed, is a poetical one, but he would have come nearer the truth
had he said that poverty is the slave-driver who, with whip in
hand, scourges the slave into the performance of tasks which
otherwise he would never have thought of attempting. I think he
would have spoken more truly had he said that poverty, in
general, is rather the meed or reward than the nurse of genius; he
says as much of poetry. This, however, is a question upon which
men will differ, and on that account I will at once dismiss it. All
I have to say is, that in the events which I am about to detail,
especially those of my later life, the reader may expect nothing
but the strictest and most conscientious truth. This truth, in some
instances, will cause many who are now alive to rest uncomfort-
ably in their beds, and as its expression is the only retribution
which I can now exact for all the unknown distress and sorrow
which their dishonesty has caused me and my family to suffer,
I consider it a solemn duty to literature and literary men not

to conceal it. To do so would be to connive at their guilt. With these introductory observations I commence my narrative.

I was born on Shrove Tuesday, the 20th of February, 1794, in the townland of Prillisk, in the Parish of Clogher, County Tyrone. Prillisk is distant about three quarters of a mile from the town, or as it was formerly termed the City of Clogher. It is only half a town, having but one row of streets, and contains not more I think than from two hundred and fifty to three hundred inhabitants. Small and insignificant-looking, however, as it seems, it is the ecclesiastical metropolis of the diocese to which its gives its name. Before the Union it returned a Member to the Irish Parliament, and one of the last that sat for it was the late Sir Jonah Barrington.[1] It is, or rather was, the residence of the Bishops of Clogher, and the palace, which they occupied for about a month or six weeks every year, is a very fine building, to which a beautiful demesne and an extensive deer-park are attached. The diocese of Clogher is one of those which have been struck out of the list, and very properly, for to my own knowledge its wealthy bishops were always absentees. The people were of opinion that it was worth between thirteen and fourteen thousand a year. The name of Clogher is, I believe, of Druidical origin – the word *Clogh-air* or *or* signifying a 'golden stone'. The tradition is, that in far gone times it was a city of great extent. The cathedral is a plain building, with a large graveyard, as usual, attached to it. In this the bodies of mostly every individual in the parish, no matter of what the sect or creed, are buried. There is, or was, an upright rude-looking stone in it, marked with characters which, it is said, no one has ever yet been able to decipher. Whether they are Ogham or not I cannot say, as I never happened to have seen them. The only other public building it contains is a Quarter Sessions Courthouse, near which is a pair of stocks, an ornament which was not in existence until after I had left the parish.

Prillisk is a small, flat, uninteresting townland with very few

[1] Author of *The Rise and Fall of the Irish Nation, Personal Sketches of his own Times*, etc., who died at Versailles on 8th April, 1834.

16

inhabitants, and all poor. The humble house in which I was born has not had one stone upon another for at least forty years. Notwithstanding this, that clever artist, Henry McManus[1] – who was sent about twenty-five years ago by Messrs Curry and Orr to make sketches of the scenery described in my works – took the liberty of giving, from his own imagination, as vile-looking a hovel as ever sheltered a human being; and this he calls 'Carleton's Birthplace'. Now I trust I am not animated by any unbecoming pride respecting my origin. I have publicly stated that, like that of far greater men, it was beyond doubt humble, but then it was unquestionably respectable. As for Prillisk, I barely recollect our residence in it, but I remember the cottage in which I was born. It was a long, low house with a kitchen as you enter, and two other rooms, one at each side of it. That is all I recall about it, with the exception of a circumstance which will be generally admitted to be a most extraordinary effect of memory. I remember being carried in my mother's arms to a wedding, or a feast of some kind – because the image that remains is a set of tables covered with food placed one after another, at which a large number of men and women, young and old, sat enjoying themselves. I suppose the depth of the impression was occasioned by the novelty of what I saw.

I was the youngest of fourteen children – seven sons and seven daughters – and I was born no less than five years after my next eldest brother, John. Six of my brothers and sisters had died before I ever saw the light. The fact of such an unusual period of time having elapsed between my birth and that of my brother John, gave rise to many odd conjectures. Some said it was a proof that I was destined for something great and extraordinary. Others, on the contrary, shook their heads, and expressed a fear that it might be the other way. They admitted it was very remarkable, certainly, but as Shrove Tuesday was my birthday, and as

[1] Henry McManus, RHA, was one of the illustrators of the 1842 edition of the *Traits and Stories*. He was a Monaghan man, who was afterwards master of the Arts Schools held in Somerset House, London. He died in 1878. A couple of his drawings are in the South Kensington collection.

Shrove Tuesday was the commencement of Lent, a period of penance, fasting, and mortification, they feared that it foreboded a life of suffering and privation; 'or who knows but the boy might become a saint, and instruct them in the application of those severe self-chastisements necessary to subdue sin.' In fact, superstition was at work, and in the spirit of prophecy shadowed forth my future fate. I can add nothing to what I have said of my father and mother, in the autobiographical preface to the large post octavo illustrated edition of *Traits and Stories of the Irish Peasantry*, published by the houses of Curry and Orr about thirty years ago.[1] From that I select the following description of each:

'My father, indeed, was a very humble man, but in consequence of his unaffected piety and stainless integrity of principle, he was held in high esteem by all who knew him, no matter what their rank might be. When the state of education in Ireland during his youth and that of my mother is considered, it will not be a matter of surprise that what education they did receive was very limited. It would be difficult, however, if not impossible, to find two persons in their lowly station so highly and singularly gifted. My father possessed a memory not merely great or surprising, but absolutely astonishing. He would repeat nearly the whole of the Old and New Testaments by heart, and was besides a living index to almost every chapter and verse in them. In all other respects, too, his memory was amazing. My native place was a spot rife with old legends, tales, traditions, customs and superstitions; so that in my early youth, even beyond the walls of my own humble roof, they met me in every direction. It was at home, however, and from my father's lips in particular, that they were perpetually sounding in my ears. In fact, his memory was a perfect storehouse, and a rich one, of all that the social antiquary, the man of letters, the poet, or the musician would consider valuable. As a narrator of old tales, legends, and historical anecdotes he was unrivalled, and his stock of them inexhaustible. He spoke the Irish and English languages with equal fluency. With all

[1] This work appeared in numbers in 1842, was afterwards republished in two volumes in 1843–44, and has been reprinted several times.

kinds of charms, old ranns, or poems, old prophecies, religious superstitions, tales of pilgrims, miracles and pilgrimages, anecdotes of blessed priests and friars, revelations from ghosts and fairies, he was thoroughly acquainted. And so strongly were all these impressed upon my mind by frequent repetition on his part, that I have hardly ever since heard, during a tolerably enlarged intercourse with Irish society, both educated and un-educated – with the antiquary, the scholar, or the humble *seanachie* – any single tradition, legend, or usage, that, so far as I can at present recollect, was perfectly new to me or unheard before in some similar or cognate dress. This is certainly saying much, but I believe I may assert with confidence that I could pro-duce, in attestation of its truth, the names of Petrie, Sir William Betham, Ferguson, and O'Donovan, the most distinguished antiquaries, both of social usages and otherwise, that ever Ireland produced. What rendered this, however, of such peculiar advant-age to me as a literary man was, that I heard them as often, if not oftener, in the Irish language as in the English; a circumstance which enabled me in my writings to transfer the genius, the idiomatic peculiarity and conversational spirit of the one language into the other, precisely as the people themselves do in their dialogues, whenever the heart or imagination happens to be moved by the darker or better passions.

Having thus stated faithfully without either addition or diminution a portion, and a portion only, of what I owe to one parent, I cannot overlook the debt of gratitude which is due to the memory of the other.

My mother, whose maiden name was Kelly – Mary Kelly – possessed the sweetest and most exquisite of human voices. In her early life, I have often been told by those who had heard her sing, that any previous intimation of her presence at a wake, dance, or other festive occasion, was sure to attract crowds of persons, many from a distance of several miles, in order to hear from her lips the touching old airs of the country. No sooner was it known that she would attend any such meeting, than the news spread through the neighbourhood like wildfire, and the people

19

flocked from all parts to hear her, just as the fashionable world do now when the name of some eminent songstress is announced in the papers – with this difference, that upon such occasions, the voice of the one falls only upon the cultivated ear, whilst that of the other falls deeply upon the untutored heart. She was not so well acquainted with the English tongue as my father, although she spoke it with sufficient ease for all the purposes of life; and for this reason among others she generally gave the old Irish versions of the songs in question rather than the English ones. This, however, as I said, was not her sole motive. In the first place, she had several old songs which, at that time – and I believe, too, I may say at this – had never been translated; and I very much fear that some valuable ones, both as to words and airs, have perished with her. Thus it is, that many rich relics of both music and poetry have been lost to us for ever. Her family, however, had all been imbued with a poetical spirit, and some of her immediate ancestors composed in the Irish tongue several fine old songs and airs, just as Carolan did – that is, some in praise of a patron or a friend, and others to celebrate rustic beauties who had been long sleeping in the dust. For this reason, she had many old compositions that were peculiar to her family, which I am afraid could not now be procured at all, and are consequently lost. I think her uncle, and I believe her grandfather, who were long dead before my time, were the authors of several Irish poems and songs, because I know that some of them she sang and others she only recited.

Independently of this, she had a prejudice against singing the Irish airs to English words; an old custom of the country was thereby invaded, and an association disturbed which habit had rendered dear to her. I remember on one occasion when she was asked to sing the English version of that touching melody, 'The Red-haired Man's Wife', she replied, 'I will sing it for you, but the English words and the air are like a man and his wife quarrelling – *the Irish melts into the tune but the English doesn't*' – an expression scarcely less remarkable for its beauty than its truth. She spoke the words in Irish.

This gift of singing, with such sweetness and power, the old sacred songs and airs of Ireland, was not the only one for which she was remarkable. Perhaps there never lived a human being capable of giving the Irish cry or *keen* with such exquisite effect, or of pouring into its wild notes a spirit of such irresistible pathos and sorrow. I have often been present when she has '*raised the keen*' – as it is called – over the corpse of some relative or neighbour, and my readers may judge of the melancholy charm which accompanied this expression of her sympathy, when I assure them, that the general clamour of violent grief was gradually diminished by admiration, until it became ultimately hushed, and no voice was heard but her own wailing, in sorrowful but solitary beauty. This pause, it is true, was never long, for however great might be the admiration which she excited, the hearts of those who heard her soon melted, and mere strangers were forced to confess her influence, by the tears which she caused them to shed for those whose deaths could in no way have affected them. I am the youngest, as I said, of fourteen children, and of course could never have heard her until age and the struggles of life had robbed her voice of its sweetness. I heard enough, however, from her blessed lips to set my heart to an almost painful perception of the spirit that steeps these fine old songs in a tenderness which no other music possesses. Many a time of a winter night when seated at her spinning wheel singing the 'Trougha',[1] or 'Shuil Agra', or some other old 'song of sorrow', have I, then little more than a child, gone over to her, and with a broken voice and eyes charged with tears, whispered: 'Mother dear, don't sing that song – it makes me sorrowful.' She then usually stopped, and sang some other which I liked better, because it affected me less. At this day I am in possession of Irish airs which none of our best antiquaries in Irish music have ever heard, except through me, and of which neither they nor I myself know the names.

Such, gentle reader, were my humble parents, under whose untaught but natural genius, setting all other advantages aside, it is not to be wondered at that my heart should have been so

[1] 'The Green Woods of Truagh' is the name this air is known by.

21

completely moulded into that spirit and those feelings which characterize my country and her children.

I cannot here overlook a circumstance, as I have been told it, connected with my baptism, which is not uncommon in Ireland, and is indicative of a very liberal feeling upon the part of its Catholic population. One of my godmothers was a Miss Jane Barnet, daughter of a respectable Presbyterian farmer, who lived about four or five hundred yards from us. Now, considering the strict notions entertained by members of the Church of Rome, especially respecting exclusive salvation, in which they are of course firm believers,[1] I think it was a great stretch of liberality on the part of my family to allow a non-Catholic female of any class to stand godmother for me. There was a remedy for this, however. Whenever, as in the case of Jane Barnet, such an honour – for such it is considered – as that of standing for a Catholic child is conferred upon a Protestant, whether man or woman, there are always two godmothers or two godfathers, as the case may be – that is, a Catholic and a Protestant – and of course it is the Catholic who is looked upon as the real sponsor. God help us! What liberal-minded man can avoid smiling at this?

How long we had lived in Prillisk before my birth I know not; but I know we did not live long there afterwards. We removed to a small village about a mile beyond, in a southern direction, the name of which is Tonagh, or as it is usually called, Towney. Here we remained for several years, and here, young as I was, I enjoyed much happiness from the striking character of the scenery. Indeed, ever since I remember I was a most enthusiastic admirer of the beauties of landscape, and have made, I might almost say during my childhood, strange little excursions to different parts of the more distant neighbourhood for the purpose of seeing places which I had heard people praise as being pretty. Many an alarm have I inflicted on my family by those dreamy excursions. I may well say dreamy, for they now appear to me like dim and far-off visions, which although full of ideal beauty, not

[1] The belief in exclusive salvation is not peculiar to the Catholic Church, as this passage might imply.

unfrequently bring the tears to my eyes when I am alone – but that is because I was happy then for the first and only time.

It was while we lived in Towney that I was first sent to school. I remember the occasion well. I could not have been more than six or seven years of age, and until that day I had never seen a letter of the alphabet. The reader may judge of the surprise of my family, when they found on my return that I had not only learned the alphabet, both large letters and small, but had actually got as far as b-a-g – *bag*. The master was the celebrated Pat Frayne, a Connaught man who had been a 'poor scholar' in his youth, but who afterwards sat for the picture of the redoubtable Mat Kavanagh in my sketch of 'The Hedge School'. That[1] was my first effort at literature, and my last for some years with Pat. It was *his* first day of opening the school, and also his last in Towney. He had only three scholars, my brother John, a boy named Sam Nelson, and myself; this disheartened him – he left the neighbourhood, and did not reappear for four or five years.

Ireland about this period was in a most sad and pitiful state in consequence of a dearth of schoolmasters. Education was utterly disregarded by the successive administrations of the day; the unfortunate people, consequently, had no schools to which they could send their children. It was this condition of education in the north which occasioned so many poor scholars to be sent to the south, especially to Kerry.

Our neighbourhood was now in a most deplorable state with respect to education, or rather the want of it. In the wealthy and extensive property of Aughentain, and the rich townlands adjoining it on all sides, there were farmers, many, indeed most of them, the descendants of the settlers of James's time, who were worth thousands of pounds. Some of them died with eight, or ten, or twelve safely locked up in their strong boxes, instead of placing them out at interest and allowing them to fructify. These men had daughters, some of them fine young women, yet they never thought of sending them to boarding-schools, or procuring governesses for them, although they could well afford it.

[1] i.e. the spelling lesson.

23

Chapter II

Mrs Dumont's school – Jack Stuart's barn – Carleton falls in love
– Expulsion from school – Findramore – Pat Frayne's academy at
Skelgy – Pat's anecdotes – Sam Nelson's joke – Pat's mode of
correction – How to obtain provisions – The egg trick.

ABOUT a year after Pat Frayne had left Towney, a lady's school
was opened in the next townland to us, called Kark. The mistress
of this school and her daughter Mary Anne were two remarkable
persons. The old lady's name was Dumont, or Mrs Dumow as
she was called – and certainly a true Irish lady she might be
termed. She was a tall, aged woman, always dressed in black;
and a female so dignified and lofty in her manners I have never
since looked upon. In fact, she had the bearing of an empress;
and never did Mrs Siddons, in the queenliest and grandest of her
characters, surpass her in the dignity and stage effect of her
deportment. Not that there was a single syllable or motion or
tone of stage effect either in her voice or manner – both were
natural and peculiar to her birth and education. She had spent a
good deal of her time in France, where she was married to a
distinguished Frenchman named Dumont, who unfortunately
perished in the Revolution, having lost all his property, and leaving his wife and daughter to return to Ireland absolute beggars. A
prouder woman probably never lived, but every one knew that
there was none of that high spirit affected. Nor was this surprising.
One half her blood was that of the Maguire, and the other that
of the O'Neil; a rare amalgamation in Irish veins. Although
proud, she was very popular, and was absolutely worshipped by
the lower classes of the Catholics. Everyone respected her. The
wealthiest Protestant or Presbyterian would most respectfully
raise his hat to her, whilst priest and parson treated her as if she
were the lady of the land.

Here now is what will strike my readers with surprise, especially at the barbarous ignorance and penurious spirit of those wealthy descendants of James the First's planters. To this lady – for a lady she was – the education of their daughters had been entrusted, and though numerous and wealthy, they never once thought of building her a residence or a schoolhouse. So far from that, her only place for giving instruction was a barn, and that only during the summer months – and indeed she was scarcely two seasons in the same barn. She and her daughter went from house to house among her wealthy benefactors, and such was the generous hospitality she received at their hands, that I admit neither of them had much reason to regret a want of residence for their own comfort; still they were unsettled, and often regretted the want of a home. One peculiarity of Mrs Dumont's I must mention – but whether it was compatible with the dignified habits of a lady in those days I cannot say – she was an inveterate snuff-taker. The conversation between herself and her daughter was held in French, except while residing with their friends, in whose presence they were seldom known to speak that language. Her maiden name was Maguire; she was a relation of the celebrated Maguires of Fermanagh.

When Pat Frayne left Towney there was no other male school in the neighbourhood to which I could be sent. In the adjoining townland of Kark, however, in a barn – of which I shall have more to say hereafter – Mrs Dumont kept her school, attended by the young ladies to whom I have already alluded. Their ages ranged from five to eighteen, and some of them were extremely beautiful. Now Mrs Dumont was in the habit of calling during after working-hours at my father's house, and as the reader is already aware, from the character which I have given of him, he was the only man in his station of life capable of holding anything like an interesting conversation with her: on this account she ultimately became a regular evening visitor. I was generally present, and it so happened that whilst my father was entertaining her with some old Irish tale or legend, she began to notice the extraordinary attention with which I listened to their conversation

This directed her attention to me, and after some inquiries about my disposition and intellect, she desired my father to send me to her school, which she then kept in our neighbour Jack Stuart's barn.

I must give a description of that barn, which, as Jack Stuart was an extensive farmer, was a very large one. A road leading up to Aughentain went past it, or rather past the cowhouse or byre as it is there called, and the stables. There was a twist in the road, and a slight fall towards it on the ground out of which the site for the building, which consisted of the office houses, was scooped. In fact, the barn was a loft over the cowhouse and stable, and the door of it on a level with the hay yard, which was about thirty feet above the road that passed. It was one of the largest barns in the parish, if not the very largest. Jack Stuart had two interesting and handsome daughters, of whose dramatic tendencies I shall have something to say by-and-by.

It was considered a great honour that I should be admitted to the ladies' seminary held in this barn. Such in the meantime was the fact. Mrs Dumont, however, received young gentlemen below a certain age as well as young ladies. In this school I was a pupil for about a week, and might have been there much longer had I not fallen in love with Mary Anne, whom, instead of looking to my a-b-ab's, I kept perpetually kissing. She had paid me great attention, and told me by way of kindness and encouragement that I was her own pet scholar, and that she would always teach me herself. In fact I got so fond of her that I had strong notions of marriage, and after having kissed her half a dozen times – the whole school in screams and convulsions of laughter – I openly asked her would she marry me. The very dignity of Mrs Dumont was overcome; she laughed heartily, and taking me by the hand, said,

'So you want Mary Anne to marry you?'

'Yes, ma'am.'

'Well, then, she must marry you – but listen, Billy – go home now – speak to your father and mother, and get their consent.'

I immediately started for home, in the exultant expectation of an immediate marriage, when, induced to look back by the sounds of laughter that I heard behind me, I saw the whole school at the door enjoying the delight with which I looked forward to this visionary but delightful project. I don't think I was six years of age at the time.

Mrs Dumont never corrected any of her pupils. She remonstrated once – twice – a third time – and if her remonstrances failed she immediately sent the delinquents home, and refused to keep them in her school. This was her well-known custom, and it had an excellent result, because it was considered such a disgrace to be turned off, that no corporal punishment could have had so much effect in subduing the impracticable disposition of her pupils. It was making the sense of shame and disgrace the principle of punishment.

I don't recollect what happened for a considerable time after that. I only remember that in the course of the same evening Mrs Dumont called at my father's house, and that there was much laughter, which I have often felt since was at the expense of my anxiety to get married to Mary Anne Dumont.

At some time about this period a conversation took place between my mother and me which clings to my memory. We were in the house by ourselves, and the reason why I put the question which I am about to mention was this: I was taught to say my prayers, and made to say them every night. At first I said them in Irish, but I don't know why I preferred the English version, yet such was the case. I had often heard the name of God mentioned – sometimes as an encouragement to good, sometimes as a word of terror against evil and sin. Young as I was, I had been thinking who God was – and wondered why we could never see Him.

'Mother,' said I to her, 'who is God?'

She looked at me with surprise, and replied, 'He is the Maker of Heaven and Earth.'

'Has anyone seen Him?'

'Oh, no; – nobody sees Him till after they die.'

'Then I hope I'll never see Him. Where does He live?'

'In Heaven.'

'Where is Heaven?'

'Up in the sky.'

'And does God walk in the sky?'

'Yes – He does.'

'And how does it happen that when He walks in the sky He doesn't fall when He has nothing to keep Him up?'

'My dear, you must wait till you get more knowledge.'

In the meantime no schoolmaster came to the neighbourhood, and Mrs Dumont had removed from Jack Stuart's barn to another about three-quarters of a mile farther off – the proprietor of which was also named Stuart – a cousin of Jack's, but a much wealthier man. It was thought both by my father and Mrs Dumont that I might be safely sent to this school, as my marriage mania and my fondness for Mary Anne had long since passed away. I accordingly went – but when asked to say my lessons I refused to do so. I saw that everyone who went was prepared, and had some knowledge of what was expected from them, but I felt conscious of knowing nothing. No force or entreaty could induce me to go up, and after having made several vain attempts to overcome my repugnance, Mrs Dumont was called in to Mr Stuart's dinner. When she had been about an hour absent, a little girl somewhat older than I began to turn me into ridicule about my refusal to learn my lessons – high words ensued between us; from words we proceeded to blows – and in the very middle of our regular stand-up fight, who should enter but the mistress. After inquiring into the cause of the quarrel, and hearing the details, she turned us both off – I first by myself, lest if we were sent away together we might renew the quarrel outside.

This closed my educational course for two years more, or three, when I and my next brother John were sent to Findramore school, then kept by another Connaught man, named O'Beirne, a most excellent teacher, and probably one of the best book-keepers of that day in the north. Several respectable young fellows used to come from long distances to be instructed by him in the art of keeping accounts. At this school my brother and I remained for some time, and well do I remember a challenge that was sent to us by the boys of a neighbouring Protestant school – called the Blue School – in the town of Clogher. The day was Saturday, and each had his little cudgel – big in courage, and prepared for the affray. The masters, however, on each side had got tidings of the projected battle, and prevented it.

I believe my brother and I remained more than a year at this school, and would have remained much longer had not the redoubtable Pat Frayne (Mat Kavanagh) opened another school in the townland of Skelgy, quite convenient to us. A schoolhouse was built for him – a sod house scooped out of the bank on the roadside – and in the course of a month it was filled with upwards of a hundred scholars, most of them males, but a good number females. Pat was a droll fellow, possessed of some low humour, but quite capricious in the administration of punishment. There was also an originality about him in this respect which was certainly very extraordinary. He himself was fond of playing mischievous tricks upon some of the larger scholars, who frequently retaliated upon him, and paid him back with his own coin. Every winter's day each brought two sods of turf for the fire, which was kept burning in the centre of the school: there was a hole in the roof that discharged the functions of a chimney. Around this fire, especially during cold and severe weather, the boys were entitled to sit in a circle by turns. The enjoyment of this right occasioned a great deal of squabbling. The seats about the fire were round stones. I remember we had one scholar, named Sam Nelson, son of a most respectable man who lived within ten yards of our house. Sam was about eighteen years of age, a fine strapping young fellow, possessed of a great deal of dry humour. In consequence of his age and respectability he usually sat at the fire beside the master, who used to indulge in a variety of anecdotes for Sam's entertainment. Sam, on the other hand, returned anecdote for anecdote, or in other words, lie for lie. Now the master had small and extremely well-made feet, and wore the neatest possible shoes, made by the renowned Paddy Mellon. Whilst sitting beside him at the fire, Sam did no literary

29

business whatever, but generally kept fiddling with a short bit of stick with which he seemed to amuse himself, as it were, by beating now the knuckles of one hand and then those of the other. Let us conceive Pat in the act of relating some egregious lie, for he was as great a liar as Sam, when, after a start, and the pause of a moment, he bounces to his feet, and finds a live coal burning in through his shoe and sticking to his very skin. This was Sam's ingenuity, who had laid the coal against his foot during the conversation by the aid of the stick. The trick was well understood by the whole school, who enjoyed it richly; indeed, so much so that screams of laughter burst out in several directions among the scholars. Pat, on looking round to ascertain the persons of those who amused themselves at his expense, found every face solemnly attentive upon the business in hand, and, consequently, though conscious that the matter was enjoyed by the whole school, found it impossible to fix upon any individual for punishment. He sat in a malignant state of meditation for some time, after which he arranged the boys upon their stone seats around the walls of the school, and desired them to remain at their peril without change in that particular position. He then went out, and after some time returned with a large furze-bush in his hand, and, commencing at the right hand side of the door, swept it round against their naked shins until he had completed the circuit, afterwards returning in the contrary direction, ending where he had begun. Thus did he make himself certain that none of those who enjoyed Sam Nelson's practical joke had escaped him.

I need not assure my readers that he contrived to get more butter from his pupils than five families like his could consume. Indeed, it was well known that his wife Nancy sold a great deal of butter in Clogher market, although it was equally well known that they had no cow. I am now painting the state of education and society in the north when I was a boy.

I remember one occasion, in Easter week. The day was that previous to our discharge for the usual holiday. The weather was fine – in fact, it might have been mistaken for summer. Shortly before '*dismiss*' Pat addressed his scholars.

30

'Now, gentlemen,' said he, 'I wish to show you something tomorrow that will astonish you. There are here about one hundred of you; you see that beautiful green field to the left of the door. It belongs to Tom McCrea, an excellent man, whose religious creed can be only guessed at, considering the reply which he gives to those – whether priest, parson or Presbyterian minister – who inquire after it; that reply is well known. In other words, and to render the matter more plain, he politely desires them to go to hell and look for it. It is certainly very decisive, but more than this has never been got out of him. He is entitled to credit, however, for telling truth. Now, tomorrow let each of you bring me an egg – one will be sufficient, but in the meantime I have no objection against two. When you bring them, I will then go to that field, belonging to that pious and religious man, Tom McCrea – who they say is worth ten thousand pounds. I will bring the eggs there, and placing every egg upon a spot of ground which I will consecrate by the repetition of that most charitable of all documents, the Athanasian Creed, I will cause every egg to rise with the lightness of a soap bubble into the air, and it will in this manner disappear for ever.'

The next morning, which, if I may be allowed the blunder, was the eve of the holidays, the number of eggs which appeared was absolutely incredible. Instead of one egg or two, no boy came with less than half a dozen. In fact no egg merchant ever had such a stock. When the eggs were all placed in the field, and the boys all assembled, gaping with expectation and wonder, Pat took up an egg, and after repeating some unintelligible jargon, threw it up into the air, when as a matter of course it fell and was broken to pieces. Pat then declared that one of the stars was out of joint, and that he must defer the completion of the miracle until another day, of which he would give us all due notice. In the meantime, we saw the now famous Ned McKeown waiting with an ass cart upon the road to Kark. Ned at that time, as I have stated in a note upon him in my *Traits and Stories of the Irish Peasantry*, had been reduced to the condition of an egg merchant, The trade was then new – and Ned purchased eggs in Clogher.

Augher, Fivemiletown, Ballygawly, and other neighbouring towns, which he sold for exportation either in Armagh or Newry. No doubt the miracle was completed to Frayne's entire satisfaction as soon as we had disappeared from the field.

Chapter III

Carleton is intended for the priesthood – Popularity of political plays – Catholics and Protestants – Performance of 'The Battle of Aughrim' – A panic – Orangeism – The yeomanry – A nocturnal visit – Removal to Nurchasy – Tulnavert school.

I CANNOT distinctly remember how long I remained with Pat. My brother John made a first-rate arithmetician; but Pat never could succeed in that direction with me. I had no genius for science, nor was I ever able to work out a proposition of Euclid during my life. The terms were perfectly unintelligible to me. The only thing then remarkable about me was my distinction in the spelling lessons. These lessons always closed the business of the school, and all the boys capable of spelling were put into the the class. Each boy put down a pin, which the master placed in the spelling book, and then they all took their places – forming a circle that almost went round the whole school. The head of the class was called King – the second Queen – and the third Prince. In that class I held the first place, nor do I recollect that I was ever dethroned. I went home every day with the coat sleeve of my left arm shining with the signals of my triumph from my shoulder to my wrist.

About this time a classical school was opened in the upper part of Aughentain, and as my father, in accordance with the humble ambition which then prevailed and still prevails among persons of his class, had taken it into his head to make one of his sons a priest, he sent my brother John to that school, with a hope that he might live to see him 'with robes upon him.' John, however, had an aversion to the classics as unconquerable as mine to science. He sulked, and refused to go to school, and by the advice of Pat Frayne my father gave the matter up. I was then pitched upon for the priesthood, but when I was prepared to go, and

33

nicely smoothed up by a new suit of clothes, it was found that the classical master had vanished.

Here, then, was another obstruction to my advance in education. Still, I returned to Pat Frayne, with whom I accomplished little good. I did not at all relish arithmetic, and I consequently made but little progress in it. I was principally engaged in hunting through the neighbours' houses for books of some or any description to read. Sometimes I happened upon an odd volume of a novel, and literally felt entranced by the perusal of it.

At this period, when I was about nine years of age, an extraordinary exhibition of political enthusiasm was made by the Protestant and Catholic young men in this remote district of the north — principally among the Protestants. If I had not been myself an eye-witness of the movement and a participator in it, I really would have imagined that the whole progress of the principle by which the people were actuated was an idle dream. Such, however, it was not, and no man ought to be a better judge of its reality than myself — because, young as I was, I became an active and a prominent character in it. It is unnecessary to say that for some years after the Rebellion of '98 a bitter political resentment subsisted between Protestants and Catholics. Well do I remember it. The party fights at that time were frequent and in many instances fatal. This, indeed, was the period which I selected for my 'Party Fight and Funeral'.[1] In this instance the political rancour became dramatic. The plays of 'The Siege of Londonderry', and 'The Battle of Aughrim'[2] were acted in barns and waste houses night after night, and were attended by multitudes, both Catholic and Protestant. 'The Battle of Aughrim', however, was the favourite, and the acting play. I heard that 'The Siege of Londonderry' had been also acted, but I never saw

[1] In *Traits and Stories*.
[2] The first-named play was written by Colonel John Mitchelburne, governor of Derry during the siege, and was first printed in 1705. The other play was by Robert Ashton, and was first printed in 1756. It was much more popular than Mitchelburne's piece, and is still read by the peasantry.

34

it. This feeling of political enthusiasm directed my attention to the plays, which in their printed shape were school-books at the time. In fact I had 'The Battle of Aughrim' off by heart, from beginning to ending. This came to be known, and the consequence was that, though not more than ten years of age, I became stage director and prompter both to the Catholic and Protestant amateurs. In the mornings and in the evenings such of them – and there were not a few on both sides – as could not read, spent hours with me in attempting to make themselves perfect in their parts. It is astonishing, however, what force and impetus such an enthusiastic desire to learn and recollect bestows upon the memory. I had here an opportunity of witnessing this, for the quickness and accuracy with which they prepared themselves was astonishing.

The play selected for action on this occasion was, of course, 'The Battle of Aughrim', and the theatre the identical barn belonging to Jack Stuart which I have already described. The crowds that flocked to it, both Catholics and Protestants, would, if admitted, have overcrowded the largest theatre in Europe. One element of their great curiosity, independently of the political feeling, was simply the novelty of seeing a play. On the right hand side of the lofted floor which constituted the barn, and under which, as I have said, were the cowhouse and stable, was a range of chairs and forms for the audience to sit upon; on the left was a range of sacks filled with barley, the heaviest grain that grows; on these the other portion of the spectators were placed. It was summer, and the heat was suffocating. I was on the left side, standing behind those who sat upon the sacks, and with my feet upon them. In order to keep myself at ease and steady, I held by a wattle in the roof above me, and in that position enjoyed the play. When it had reached the scene in which the ghost makes its appearance, or rather a little before it, I felt something like a descent of that part of the floor on which the sacks had been stretched. In about a quarter of a minute there was another descent of the sacks, and I shouted out 'the floor is going to fall.' Such, however, was the attention of the audience, that my warning had no effect. The ghost came forward, when a tremendous crash took place, and the last thing I saw was his heels in the air, as he and that portion of the audience with whom I stood, sacks and all, went down together. Fortunately, there was a large beam which ran longitudinally through the barn – by which I mean from end to end. The barn was an old one, and its timbers, as was found afterwards, quite decayed with age. The weight of the sacks, and the crowded audience on the left hand side, was more the the rotten rafters could bear, and the consequence was that one half the barn floor with its weighty burthen was precipitated into the cowhouse and stable. I dropped down upon those who fell, and scrambled over their heads towards those who were on the safe side, by whom I was pulled up without having received any injury.

In this case the force of instinct was exhibited in a remarkable manner. The animals beneath the loft must have heard the sharp jerking noise of the rafters as they gave symptoms of being about to fall, because it was found that they had broken the ropes which held them, and taken shelter under that part of the loft which did not fall. I saw them there with my own eyes, as did every other person, and I need not describe the wonder it occasioned. As it was, scarcely any injury resulted from the descent of the loft, if I except that which was sustained by the ghost, who had his arm broken.

These senseless exhibitions inflamed political feeling very much. In the town of Augher, this stupid play was acted by Catholics and Protestants, each party of course sustaining their own principles. The consequence was, that when they came to the conflict with which the play is made to close, armed as they were on both sides with real swords, political and religious resentment could not be restrained, and they would have hacked each other's souls out had not the audience interfered and prevented them. As it was, some of them were severely if not dangerously wounded.

During the period of which I now write, the country was in a state sufficient, in the mind of every liberal and thinking man, to fling back disgrace and infamy upon the successive administrations which permitted it. This was the period of Protestant, or rather of Orange, ascendancy. There were at that time regular corps of yeomen, who were drilled and exercised on the usual stated occasions. There were also corps of cavalry who were subjected to the same discipline. Now all this was right and proper, and I remember when a review day was looked forward to as we used to look for Christmas or Easter. On those occasions there were thousands of spectators, and it would have been well if matters had ended there. Every yeoman with his red coat on was an Orangeman. Every cavalryman mounted upon his own horse and dressed in blue was an Orangeman; and to do both foot and cavalry justice, I do not think that a finer body of men could be found in Europe. Roman Catholics were not admitted into either service. I think I may say that I knew almost every yeoman in the parish, but I never knew of a Roman Catholic to be admitted into either force, with one exception – his name was William Kelly, a cousin of my own.

Merciful God! In what a frightful condition was the country at that time. I speak now of the North of Ireland. It was then, indeed, the seat of Orange ascendancy and irresponsible power. To find a justice of the peace *not* an Orangeman would have been an impossibility. The grand jury room was little less than an Orange lodge. There was then no law *against* an Orangeman, and no law *for* a Papist. I am now writing not only that which is well known to be historical truth, but that which I have witnessed with my own eyes.

These yeomen were in the habit – especially when primed with whisky, or on their way from an Orange lodge – of putting on their uniform, getting their guns and bayonets, and going out at night to pay domiciliary visits to Catholic families under the pretence of searching for firearms; and it is painful to reflect upon, or even to recollect, the violence and outrage with which these illegal excursions were conducted. Take an instance.

I have mentioned Sam Nelson as one of Pat Frayne's scholars, and of course the schoolfellow of myself and my brother; and I have said, I think, that his father's house was next to ours – in fact it was not ten yards from us; in truth we were in daily intercourse of the most neighbourly and friendly character. We were perpetually in each other's houses, lending and borrowing, and discharging all those duties towards each other which constitute friendly neighbourhood. Sam Nelson was what is termed a humorous or droll kind of good-natured 'slob', and evidently fond of me and my brother. On one occasion he made us a present of a little tin gun or cannon about four or five inches in length, of which we were naturally very proud. Before I proceed farther in this reminiscence I think it necessary to say that my father was one of the quietest and most highly respected men in the parish, considering his position in life. Neither he nor any of his family were ever known to give utterance to an offensive word. They took no part whatsoever in politics, neither did they ever engage in those senseless party or faction fights which were so disgraceful to the country, or give expression to any political opinion that could be construed into offence. Having made these observations, I now proceed with my reminiscence.

One night, about two or three o'clock, in the middle of winter, a violent bellowing took place at our door, and loud voices were heard outside. My father got up, alarmed, and asked who was there.

'Open the door, you rebellious old dog, or we will smash it in.'

'Give me time to get on my clothes,' replied my father.

'Not a minute, you old rebel; you want to hide your arms – open or we smash the door,' and the door was struck violently with the butts of guns. My father, having hurried on his small clothes and lit a candle, opened the door, when in an instant the house was filled with armed yeomen in their uniform.

'Come, you traitorous old scoundrel, deliver up your d—d rebelly gun.'

'My good friends,' replied my father, 'I have no gun.'

'It's a lie, you rebel, it's well known you have a gun. Produce it, or I put the contents of this through you.' And as he spoke the man cocked and deliberately aimed the gun at my father. (I forgot to state that the men appeared with screwed bayonets.) When my mother saw my father covered by the ruffian's gun, she placed herself with a shawl about her between them, and corroborated what my father said, that we had no gun. She was called a liar; it was notorious we had a gun. In the meantime, some others of them began to institute a search. Two of them went into my sister's bedroom, a third man holding the candle.

'Who is this?' said one scoundrel.

'It's my daughter,' replied my mother, trembling and in tears.

'Well,' he returned, 'let her get up until we have a look at her; it's likely she has the gun in the bed; at all events we'll rouse her a bit—' and as he spoke, he put the point of the bayonet to her side, which he pressed until she screamed with pain. At this moment his companion pulled him back with something of indignant violence, exclaiming:

'D——n your soul, you cowardly scoundrel, why do you do that?'

At this moment my mother, with the ready recollection and presence of mind of her sex, exclaimed:

'I think it likely that all this trouble has come from the little tin gun that Sam Nelson gave the children – here it is,' she proceeded – 'here is the only gun that ever was under this roof. If it's treason to keep *that*, we are rebels' – and as she spoke she handed them the gun. They looked at it, and after some ruffianly grumbling they retired. My sister was slightly wounded in the side. My readers will be surprised to learn that one of Sam Nelson's brothers was among this scoundrelly gang, and never once interfered in our behalf. No man knew better than he did that my father had no gun. No man knew better than he that this midnight and drunken visit was a mere pretence, deliberately founded upon the history of the tin gun which his brother Sam had given to me and my brother John. My readers may form an opinion of the state of society, when they hear that there was not an individual present that night in this gross and lawless outrage with whom we were not acquainted, nor a man among them who did not know everyone of us intimately.

Such was the outrageous and licentious conduct of the Orange-men of that day, and of many a day long before and afterwards. As a public writer, guided by a sense of truth and justice, I could not allow such a system as that which Orangeism then was to remain without exposure, and I did not. It is to that midnight visit that they owe 'Valentine McClutchy'. Little they dreamt that there was a boy present, not more than ten years of age, who would live to punish them with a terrible but truthful retaliation.

Soon after this event my father began to think of leaving Towney. A farm of eighteen acres was vacant in a townland called Nurchasy, about two miles towards the south. Hugh Traynor, a very respectable man, although an extensive and notorious private distiller, was the under-landlord, or middleman. From him my father took the farm, and we removed to it without loss of time. I will never forget that removal. All our furniture had been taken to the new place, which I had not yet seen, and every member of our family had gone with it, I alone excepted. In fact my father did not wish me to come until everything should be settled, and I accordingly remained with a married sister of mine, who also lived in Towney, until my father should call in the evening to bring me home. This he did, but not until after night, and many a time since have I thanked God that he did not. The season was summer, and such an exquisitely beautiful night I have never recollected since.

The moon was in the full, and the sky so perfectly clear and cloudless as to present the idea of nothing but that blue void which is so full of poetry and beauty. My father, for what purpose I know not, unless it was to give me a surprise, brought me to the farm by a way quite circuitous, but a way which to me was beautiful beyond the power of language to express. It was the first time I experienced the delight of travelling through new and beautiful scenery by moonlight.

Nurchasy to me was paradise. The view from it of Fardress Glen, so beautifully wooded, and of Fardress grazing-fields, so green and extensive, together with the effect of those small circular groves, peculiar to some portions of the north, absolutely enchanted me. Nothing, in fact, could surpass my happiness. I frequently dreamt of the scenery about me, although I had it before my eyes every day in the week. It was while we were in Nurchasy, which was not more than half a mile from Findramore, that a classical school was opened in the townland of Tulnavert, the property of John Birney, now of Oakley Park, in the county of Down. Like most Irish schools, it also was held in a barn, which belonged to Tom Hall and his brothers, three wealthy old bachelors, who have long disappeared. The man who taught this school was an individual who should have been kept closely confined in a lunatic asylum during his life. He had been one of the earliest students of Maynooth on its first establishment; there he remained until he became insane – a calamity which necessarily caused his removal. The slavish, ill-tempered scoundrel never raised his hand to a Protestant boy, no matter how insolent or provoking his conduct, but if one of his own creed only broke a straw he would chastise him most severely. It was he who sat for the heartless tyrant in 'The Poor Scholar'. By the way, talking of a poor scholar, we had an unfortunate wretch of that description in our school at Tulnavert. Nis name was John Quin, and indeed I may add that he was the scapegoat of the school. It was not he, however, who sat for the character of the poor scholar whom I have made the hero in my tale of that name. There was a man in our Parish called Dominick Donnelly, who was and had been for many years the Mass-server to the successive Catholic clergymen who came to the parish. I believe in my soul the man could not read, but it was not at all extraordinary during my early life to meet persons capable of serving Mass, that is, acting as clerk, who did not know a letter in the alphabet. The memory of some men is perfectly astonishing. When you think, however, of a totally illiterate man giving the Latin responses to the priest during Mass, I will give you leave to entertain some doubts as to the purity of his latinity. This Dominick Donnelly had a son named James, who felt that early ambition to enter the priesthood which is so common to the sons of the peasantry, as well as among their fathers. Poor fellows! Under the peculiar circumstances in which they were placed – trampled upon by a vile and brutal ascendancy, struggling with poverty, and a sense not only of neglect, but of bitter enmity against them – it is not to be wondered at that they should feel anxious to gratify the only ambition left them. Be this as it may, young Donnelly, supported and encouraged in his laudable resolution by his father and family, and aided by a public collection made for him, at what was then termed '*The Three Altars*', by his friends – or in other words, by every Catholic in the parish – was enabled to start for Munster on his pious journey, and from Munster he never returned until he was able, according to the proverbial phrase of all such young missionaries, to make his appearance both as a priest and a gentleman.

Chapter IV

The altars – No chapels – Removal to Springtown – Shoes and stockings not expected – Robbing an orchard – Springs and man-traps – Carleton is caught – A whimsical magistrate – A dangerous exploit.

In order that the reader may understand what is meant by 'The Three Altars', he must know that a Roman Catholic chapel was a rare thing in those days. During the existence of the penal laws, the notion of building such a thing as a chapel for Catholic worship, would have consigned those who could dream of, much less attempt such a project, either to transportation or death. Within my own memory, there was nothing in existence for the Catholics for the worship of God except the mere altar, covered with a little open roof to protect the priest from rain, which it was incapable of doing. The altar was about two feet in depth, and the open shed which covered it not more than three, so that when the wind or rain or snow blew from a particular direction the officiating clergyman had nothing to cover him or to protect him from the elements. In my early life, three such 'altars' were the only substitutes for chapels in my native parish, which is one of the largest in the diocese. There was always a little plot of green sward allowed to be annexed to the altar, on which the congregation could kneel; and as these plots and little altars were always on the roadside, they presented something very strange and enigmatical to such as did not understand their meaning, for the following reason. During the winter months and wet weather in general, those of both sexes who attended worship were obliged to bring with them small trusses of either hay or straw on which to kneel, as neither man nor woman could kneel on a wet sward, through which the moist yellow clay was oozing, without soiling or disfiguring their dress, or catching cold from the damp. Indeed, I must say that during the winter months the worship of God was in one sense a very trying ceremony. These small trusses were always left on the place of worship, lying within a foot of each other, and as I said, presented an unintelligible sight to any person ignorant of the custom. The places of Roman Catholic worship, therefore, were very properly called altars, as it would have been impossible to apply any other term. It was at such altars, of course, that the collections on behalf of poor scholars about to proceed for education to Munster were made. In Dominick Donnelly's son was seen the hero of my 'Poor Scholar'. He paid one visit home as an ordained priest, where he remained for about a month: during this period he gave a detailed but melancholy account of all he had suffered whilst working out his great design. These details his father and brother often mentioned to me, and they harmonize pretty closely with the incidents related in the tale. The Catholic bishop of the diocese in which he had received his education, took him under his protection, and ultimately gave him an appointment as curate. To that curacy he returned, but soon lost his health – from the fact, probably, of having suffered too much in his early struggles. He died within a year, in the odour of sanctity, and passed away with all his virtues, like a beautiful vision rarely seen even amongst those who strive for a noble purpose.

Charles McGoldrick did not remain more than three years in Tulnavert. Whether he was a good scholar is more than I can say. I had only got as far as Ovid's *Metamorphoses*, Justin, and the first chapter of John in the Greek Testament, when all his Protestant scholars left him. A Presbyterian clergyman named Wiley opened a classical school in the town of Augher, not more than a mile from Clogher, and to him they transferred their allegiance. McGoldrick then disappeared, and I heard no more of him.

In the meantime, my father, who did not seem gifted with what phrenologists term inhabitiveness, took a dislike to Nurchasy, but I must admit in his justification, for a very excellent reason. He paid his rent punctually to the middleman and poteen distiller, but the latter did not at all pay *his* rent punctually to the head landlord. One of my brothers discovered accidentally, and as a friendly scout, that the head landlord was about to come down upon the property for the rent. My father, therefore, having heard that there was a farm of twenty-two acres to be let in a townland called Springtown, took it. McGoldrick, although I have dismissed him, was still teaching in Tulnavert at that time. The proprietor of Springtown was also a middleman, and lived a couple of miles up beside a river that was one of the contributories to the northern Blackwater. He lived on the very edge of the Slebeen Mountains, which divide the counties of Monaghan and Tyrone. He had an illicit stillhouse near a little stream that ran to it from the river, and this he let at a rent to such as required a structure of the kind, and indeed I must say he was seldom without a tenant. I never liked Springtown much. With one exception the scenery was dull and common-place. The exception I speak of was a wild but pretty glen which stretched behind our house, and through which ran a mountain stream that was known about a mile further inland as the Mullin Burn.

Our departure from Nurchasy pressed very heavily on my heart. I was drowned in tears during the whole day of the flitting. This, however, was little compared to what I felt subsequently, because on the day of our departure from Nurchasy I had not seen Springtown nor had an opportunity to contrast it and Nurchasy with each other. The contrast indeed was fearfully against Springtown. The latter place removed me from the classical school of Tulnavert, not more than a mile and a quarter from Nurchasy, to a distance of four miles from it. I had altogether a journey of eight miles to perform on my way to and from school.

How strange and primitive were the habits of those days, and how amazingly have they changed for the better since! During the summer months, for instance, scarcely a boy at the school ever wore shoes and stockings. The sons of men who were worth thousands used to go barefooted and barelegged, and after the winter had passed away and the warmth of spring returned, our anxiety to throw off the shoes and stockings was incredible. We coursed in mad gambols through the green fields in a wild exultation of spirits which nothing could surpass.

When about fifteen, I began to be famous for activity, speed of foot, and intrepidity. I felt an ambition for performing difficult and dangerous enterprises. When I lived in Towney, and was about nine years of age, half a dozen lads considerably older than myself had set their hearts on robbing Jack Stuart's orchard. This orchard was not enclosed – a very rare thing – but stood in a field behind his house and close to his garden. These young cowards, influenced by a report that he had spring-guns and man-traps about the foot of every tree, were afraid to venture on the robbery themselves. After attempting to procure some thought-less boy to effect their object, they succeeded in prevailing upon me to make the attempt. Though little more than a child, I was celebrated throughout the neighbourhood for climbing trees, walls, and other elevations. Indeed I have often wondered since that I did not break my neck or some of my limbs. Fortunately, however, no accident of the kind ever occurred, a circumstance which only increased my foolish and adventurous courage. These lads procured the coat of a full grown man, in which they encased me, and after the proper directions I went to execute their pur-pose. They told me to go round the garden, and then by turning to the left, I would come among the trees of the orchard. This I did, with the tail of the coat trailing after me, and succeeded not only in climbing the most promising tree, but in the course of a few minutes had the large pockets of the coat filled. At this moment Jack Stuart walked past the end of his dwelling-house; by this movement, had he looked towards the orchard, I must necessarily have been discovered. Without a moment's hesitation, I immediately sprang from the tree, and on alighting, felt some-thing sharp cut the big toe of my right foot between the ball that adjoins it and the toe itself. The alarm and terror prevented me from feeling the pain which I otherwise would have felt, but when I got to Towney and gave the lads the apples, the blood was pouring very copiously out of the wound, and the pain became excessive. This accident was so serious that it produced an investigation into the matter by several of the neighbours. I was forced to describe the circumstances just as they had happened between the lads and me; and the consequence was that they were caught and brought into Jimmy McCrea's stable, where McCrea himself horse-whipped every one of them within an inch of his life. The affair, however, soon began to assume a graver and more alarming character. I allude, not to my wound, which, however, kept me for upwards of a fortnight in the house – but to the conduct of Jack Stuart, which, upon investigation, was such as deserved little less than transportation for life. His paltry orchard consisted only of about half a dozen apple-trees. On that very evening – nay, in less than an hour, eight or ten of the neighbours, among whom was my father, proceeded to the orchard in question, and upon examining the locality, they discovered upwards of two dozen pieces of sheet iron, sharp and polished like lancets, set in the ground, each one of them calculated to penetrate the sole of a shoe if the weight of the body came upon it. It is true they were neither man-traps nor spring-guns, but a very dangerous sort of instrument notwithstanding. They were known by the name of 'snakes'. Every person possessed of orchards or fruit-trees of any kind was at liberty to use them upon the very necessary and reasonable condition that he should keep up due advertisements in order that the public might be aware of the danger. The indignation against Jack was both excessive and general. He never overcame the breaking down of his barn, or the shame of the transaction I have just related. He sold his property and went to America within a year afterwards, to join his brother, who had been there during the preceding quarter of a century, and where, it was said, he became immensely rich.

Whether 'snakes' were generally used in the north I cannot say, but I certainly know that man-traps and spring-guns were resorted to in my native parish. Painted advertisements upon boards, where the letters were as large and legible as those on a common signpost, were placed on the boundary of the forbidden premises, so that in this instance due notice was given, and the public placed upon their guard. These man-traps and spring-guns were put up by the late Sir William Richardson, of Augher Castle, one of the most popular men ever known in the county.

If he was popular, however, he was equally whimsical, indeed so much so that his ludicrous whims contributed very much to his popularity. If two men, for instance, had a quarrel, and that one of them summoned the other before him as a magistrate, if he saw that they were well matched in age, personal strength, and vigour, his method of administering justice was to furnish each of them with a cudgel, conduct them to the backyard of the Castle, and propose to them at once to decide the quarrel between them. This, to fighting people such as the Irish are, made them worship him. If two neighbours had a dispute one of them would say to the other:

'Come, you scoundrel, are you willing to go before Sir William?'

'Never say it again,' was generally the reply.[1]

This original method of distributing justice, however, was so generally resorted to, that by degrees the private disputes became so numerous that they demanded ten times more time than Sir William could bestow upon them, especially as he was then growing old. He accordingly had it announced that in future he would cease to act as a magistrate. In fact, there was such laxity in moral law, and every other kind of law, at the time of which I write, that many circumstances took place which, although strictly true, will not be entitled to credibility; this I presume is one of them.

I must now return to the man-traps. Sir William had taken it into his head that the cattle of the neighbouring farmers were in the habit of trespassing upon his property – whereas, if the truth must be told, the offence was the other way. The result proved this. One morning a cow of his own was found to have broken her foreleg by a man-trap, while passing through a gap in a ditch, which divided the property of his friend and next neighbour, the priest of the parish, from his own. This occurrence abolished the spring-guns and man-traps, and indeed it was time it should.

Soon after our family removed to Springtown, I began to feel the uncomfortable length of road I had to traverse on my way to

---

[1] Carleton has introduced the character of this magistrate, and some of the scenes in which he took part, into 'Valentine McClutchy'.

school and home again; so did a schoolfellow of mine named James Nealy, and one or two others who lived near me. By keeping to the open road the distance was, as I have said, and as I thought then, not less than four miles; but on the last visit I paid my native parish, I went over the ground again, from mere curiosity, and I am now of opinion that the distance cannot be less than five. During the short winter months I was obliged to start at day-break, and it was generally quite dark when I reached home. Accordingly we began to calculate on the advantage of making a short cut across the country, which would have saved us a mile and a half or two miles. The only objection to this was a river – one of the tributaries to the Blackwater – which we had to cross, and as there was then no bridge (there is an excellent one now), we could not cross it during flood or wet weather in general. In summer we passed over a weir that changed a portion of the current of the river into the 'race' which supplied Clogher Mills. In summer, then, we went along this weir, when the water was low, with as much ease and safety as we walked on the common road; but in winter, and especially when the river was in flood, the weir was impassable.

I remember – and good cause I have to do so, for to this day I can never think of my madness without a shudder – I say I remember one Saturday (in July, I think), when we were detained in school upwards of an hour and a half by an incessant down-pouring of rain. On Saturday, which was our repetition day, we always got leave at one o'clock. At all events, when it ceased raining we started for home. There were about ten of us going the same way – never reflecting that, after such a deluge, the river must be a deep and powerful current whilst following its obstructed course over the weir. Judge of our consternation, then, when we found that it was up in high flood, and the torrent furious across the weir. This weir, like every other, was backed by about five yards of large stones, packed together to a depth of at least three yards; its length across was about twelve or thirteen. The stones that broke the current of the river and drove a portion of its water into the artificial mill-race, were built with a slope until they came down on a level with the natural bed of the river itself. This description can be understood, I fear, only by those who know what a weir is, and why it is constructed.

At all events, when we arrived there, the river was foaming and roaring in its white rage over the weir and down its side into its natural and original channel, from which the weir had forced a portion of it into the mill-race. There we stood, sadly disappointed by this terrific obstruction. To attempt to cross the weir would seem to be not only madness, but death. Our only resource, apparently, was to retrace our path for a considerable distance; when a thought struck me for which I have never since been able to account. I resolved to cross the weir; and as soon as the resolution was made, I deliberately entered the stream that went over it, grasping the edge of it, which was of firm square stone, and began to work myself across by moving my fingers along slowly, inch by inch. Had I raised a hand from the ledge, or lost hold of it, I was lost – dashed to pieces on the rough upstanding stones, against which I would have been beaten into a shapeless mass. My progress, of course, was slow, for the rushing water was nearly up to my mouth, and the reader is to recollect that my motion was sideways, and that I was lying against the current of the river and the stones of the weir. At that time, and at that school, we wore satchels, as a soldier wears his knapsack. I was not many minutes at this frightful and most perilous attempt, when I found the water that rushed over the weir much deeper and stronger than I had imagined. My clothes and satchel, and my very body, were all under the violent and rushing stream, and, in fact, I was told afterwards that there was no part of me visible but my head. In this way I sidled slowly across, until I reached the middle of the weir, the torrent up within an inch of my mouth. At this place there was a slight depression of about a yard in length, and here indeed was the *locus periculi* – the hopeless place of danger. What I felt at this spot, as the water was rising gradually to my very mouth, I cannot now recollect, although I have often tried. It was more like a dream than a reality. I had no distinct thought of anything, not even of danger. When in the very midst and lowest part of this depression, I felt that the waters were up to my under-lip; and had they risen an inch higher, I must have been carried off and smashed to pieces. Presently, I found that my under-lip was more than an inch above the current. This fact at once gave me courage and strength. I moved across somewhat more quickly, and found as I advanced that the waters were shallower and their impetuosity was less. In the course of ten or twelve minutes I found myself upon dry land, dripping with water. On looking at my schoolfellows, I perceived that some of them had been called up to a cottage upon the face of an elevation about a couple of hundred yards above them, inhabited by a man named Tom Booth. During my performance of this insane act there was no one within the cottage but his wife Molly and a little girl. Poor Mrs Booth was unable to bear what she conceived to be the certainty of my death – the certain result, as she imagined, of such an unaccountable attempt. When I was in the very centre of the depression – in the moment of greatest danger, my body invisible, and, as she supposed, at last swept away by the flood – she fell into a deep swoon, and the little girl, alarmed at her condition, called up the boys to her assistance. This accounted for the presence of some of them at the cabin; but of what had happened there at that time I knew nothing.

At all events I was now safe, and the cheers and acclamations of my affectionate schoolfellows were loud and long. After bidding them good-bye, I immediately swam across the mill-race which was formed by the weir; the water, though deep, was slow and therefore safe.

On my way home I began to reflect upon the folly of which I had been guilty, and consider the account I should give of my condition to the family at home. To tell them the risk I so wantonly and madly ran, would, I knew, get me, what I well deserved, a good scourging. I accordingly told them a lie; that I fell into Clogher Karry – the name of the river at that place – and was nearly drowned. The last portion of the statement consoled me, because I felt that it was very near the truth.

Chapter V

Fondness for nature – Another love affair – Blighted affection – Anne Duffy marries – A brutal master – Retaliation – The superstitions of the elder Carleton – His death.

I WAS certainly a strange boy, with a good deal, I take it, of natural poetry in me. There was a beautiful hazel glen, as I have said, behind our house in Springtown. This glen was alive with blackbirds and thrushes, and upon a fine, calm summer evening was vocal in a hundred places with their melody. There was one beautiful thorn-tree, at the foot of a steep piece of ground which stretched from the back of our house to the edge of the glen; on this a particular blackbird sat and sang as regularly as the evening comes. With the music of this bird I was so intensely delighted, that I used to go to bed every fine evening two hours before my usual time, for the express purpose of listening to the music. There was a back window in the bedroom where I slept; this I opened, and there I lay until I fell asleep with the melody in my ears.

At this time I fell in love with a bouncing young wench, the daughter of a tailor called Cormick McElroy – father to one of my favourite tailors, Billy Cormick. Although anything but alluring, she made advances, which I could not understand, I suppose because they were utterly unintelligible to anyone. She was three or four years older than I was, but I am bound in truth to say – although I suppose I should blush to admit it – that she never made an advance that did not occasion her a good drubbing at the hands of the young swain she loved. They say that there are some animals who love you better the more you beat them, and I am of opinion that this young virago was one of them. I never saw anything in the shape of woman whom I detested so much.

This reminiscence is a prelude to the greatest love event

of my life. I was still going to school at Tulnavert, advancing in the classics, and had got as far as Ovid's *Metamorphoses*, which charmed me more than any book I had then ever read; in fact, I cannot describe the extraordinary delight with which I perused it. The sense of task work was lost, because I did it *con amore*. I had often read of love, but I never, for a moment, dreamt of what it meant. 'Tis true, when I was at school with Mrs Dumont, I felt that I would prefer one little girl to all the rest, but that was not love, only a mere childish predilection.

The time was now approaching, however, when I was to feel the exquisite charm of 'first love' in all its power. The 'festivals' were then expected and enjoyed with spirit and zest which have long passed away. Preparations were then made for Christmas and Easter of which we now know little or nothing. Easter was within ten days of us, and I felt the more anxious for its arrival because I had got a full suit of new clothes, by far the most respectable I had ever worn. I felt that I was quite a young gentleman; and as I was then fifteen years of age, I began to have vague notions of something that I did not well understand. In the 'Forth',[1] which was our place of worship, I felt somehow exceedingly anxious to show myself off on the next Sunday, which was Easter Day. The 'Forth', in which there was one of the 'altars' that I have already described, was a circular green about one hundred yards in diameter. It was surrounded by a grassy ditch, apparently as ancient as the 'Forth' itself. On this ditch were verdant seats; and upon these seats, to the right hand as you turned up towards the altar, sat the young men, opposite to whom on the other sat the young women. They were thus separated, and never, under any circumstances, joined or spoke to each other until after they had left the 'Forth'. Notwithstanding this devotional sense of decorum, I am bound to say that the eyes on each side were not idle, and that many a long and loving look passed between the youngsters of both sexes.

At length, the Easter Sunday came, and a glorious one it was.

---

[1] 'Forth' is properly *fort* – that is, a *rath*, or earthen rampart.

I went abroad in my new suit for the first time in public, and certainly, if the spectators did not entertain a favourable opinion of my whole appearance, I know one who did. Until the priest came, the men chatted to each other, and so did the women; but the moment he entered the 'Forth', all the congregation assumed the best places they could, and dropped on their knees, prepared to join the devotions of the day.

There was at that time a vocal choir of young men and women in the parish, who, in virtue of their office, were obliged to kneel around the altar, where they sang some very beautiful music. Among the females was one tall, elegant, and lady-like girl, whose voice was perfectly entrancing. Her name was Anne Duffy, daughter of George Duffy, the miller of Augher Mill. She knelt that Sunday, and, in fact, every Sunday, on the left hand side of the priest, next the altar; while I, more by accident than anything else, placed myself in the same position on the other side, so that we were right opposite to each other. Whether it was the opportunity of having her before me, or her beauty, I cannot decide – probably it was both together – but I said no prayers that day. My eyes were never off her – they were riveted on her. I felt a new sensation, one of the most novel and overwhelming delight. After Mass I followed her as far as the cross-roads at Ned McKeown's. Ned's was a corner house, with two doors of entrance – one to the kitchen, and the other into a small grocery shop, kept by a man named Billy Fulton. It was a great convenience to the neighbourhood, especially to those who lived in the mountain districts, or what was termed the 'Mountain Bar'. Before Mass, a great number of both sexes, but principally men, lingered about these cross-roads, engaged in chat upon the usual topics of the day: the most important, and that in which they felt the deepest interest, was the progress of the Peninsular War. Bonaparte was their favourite, and their hopes were not only that he would subdue England, but ultimately become monarch of Ireland. From what source they derived the incredible variety of personal anecdotes respecting him it is impossible to conjecture. One of the most remarkable, and which was narrated and heard with the most sincere belief in its truth was the fact of his being invulnerable. It mattered nothing whether he went into the thickest part of the battle or not, the bullets hopped harmlessly off him like hailstones from a window.

Now Anne Duffy's father was a great politician, and sometimes spent half an hour at the cross-roads, both before and after Mass, and Anne herself occasionally stopped a short time there, but very rarely. At all events I saw her there again, and our looks met. She appeared to be amused by my attention, which she seemed to receive agreeably, and with pleasure. Well, I went home a changed man – of fifteen years of age – wrapped up from the world and all external nature; the general powers of my mind concentrated into one thought, and fixed upon one image, Anne Duffy.

There has been much controversy upon the subject of love at first sight. I, however, am a proof of its truth. The appearance of the sun in the firmament is not more true. I went home, elated, entranced – like a man who had discovered a rich but hidden treasure. My existence became important. I had an interest in life – I was no longer a cipher. I had something to live for. I felt myself a portion of society and the world. How I spent the remainder of the day I scarcely remember, especially as to association with my companions on this festive occasion. All I know is, that Anne Duffy was never for a single moment out of my head, and when I was asleep that night she appeared as distinctly before me as she did during the day; but with this difference, that her beauty was more exquisitely angelic and ideal, and seemed to bear a diviner stamp.

For nearly five years after this my passion for her increased with my age, although I thought when I first fell in love with her that nothing could have added a deeper power to it. For upwards of four years I knelt opposite her at the altar; for upwards of four years my eyes were never off her, and for upwards of four years I never once, while at Mass, offered up a single prayer to heaven.

As I grew up, she seemed to feel a deeper interest in me. The language of her eyes could not be misunderstood. Through the medium of that language, I felt that our hearts were intimately acquainted, precisely as if they had held many a loving and ecstatic communion. During the period of this extraordinary passion, I indulged in solitude a thousand times in order, to brood over the image of her whom I loved. On returning home from Mass of a summer Sunday, I uniformly withdrew to the bottom of the glen behind our house and there, surrendered myself to the entrancing influence of what I felt. There in the solitude of that glen I felt a charm added to my existence which cannot be described. I knew – I felt – that she loved me. This habit of mine was so well known by my family that, when dinner was ready and they found that I was absent, they knew perfectly well where to call for me. After the first six months I could not rest satisfied with parting from her at the 'Forth'; so, for three years and a half, I walked after her, and never turned back until I left her at the town of Augher, at the turn which led by a side street to her father's mill; and this during the severity of winter and the heat of summer.

Now this I am describing was my silent – my inner life; but the reader is not to imagine that it prevented me from entering into the sports and diversions of the day. I devoted myself to athletic exercises until I was without a rival – until, in fact, I had a local fame which spread far beyond the limits of my native parish. I was resolved to make myself talked of – to be distinguished by my excellence in these feats – and the ambition which I then felt owed its origin to my love for Anne Duffy. I remember well that when nineteen years of age, my appearance in fair or market caused crowds to follow the young fellow who stood unrivalled at every athletic sport which could be named. This fact is well known and remembered by some of the oldest inhabitants of my native parish to the present day.

The reader will consider it strange that during this long period of devoted and enthusiastic attachment, I never spoke to Anne or declared my passion. It is, however, a fact, that during the period I allude to, a single syllable of spoken language never passed between us. This, however, is easily accounted for. My father died in the early course of my passion, and the family began to feel with some bitterness the consequences of decline. Had I spoken to Anne, and gained her consent to marry me, I had no means of supporting her, and I could not bear the terrible idea of bringing her to distress and poverty, both of which she must have endured had she become my wife.

I was sitting before our kitchen fire one evening (in autumn, I think), thinking of her as usual, when my eldest brother came in, and after having taken a seat, communicated the following intelligence.

'Did you hear the news?' said he.

'No,' replied my mother, 'what is it?'

'Why, that the miller's daughter' (by this appellation she was generally known, and not by her Christian name) 'the miller's daughter was married this morning to M. M., of Ballyscally.'

The sensation I felt was as if something had paralysed my brain or my heart. I was instantly seized with a violent dizziness, and an utter prostration of bodily strength; an indescribable confusion seized upon me – thought for a moment abandoned me – and I laboured under the impression that some terrible calamity had befallen me. So long as she remained unmarried, I still entertained a vague and almost hopeless hope that some event might occur which, by one of the extraordinary turnings of life, might put it in our power to marry. Even this faint hope was gone – my doom was irrevocably sealed, and the drapery of death hung between her and me. I rose from my chair with difficulty – I staggered out, and went into the barn, where I wept bitterly. My life had now lost its charm, and nothing but a cold cheerless gloom lay upon it and my hopes. During three or four months this miserable state of feeling lasted. I was, however, in the heyday of youth – just in that period of existence when sorrow seldom lasts long. The sensation gradually wore away, and after a lengthened interval I recovered my usual spirits. A short but interesting anecdote will now close this extraordinary history of my first love. I think it was in the year 1847 that I resolved to pay a visit to my native place. When I left it, many years before, it was with a fixed resolution never to write a letter home, or to return to my friends, unless I had achieved some distinction which might reflect honour upon my name. Fortunately I was able to accomplish this strange determination; and what is, after all, not strange, I do assure my readers that Anne Duffy, though the wife of another, was a strong stimulus to my pursuit of fame, and in the early period of my literary life a powerful element in my ambition. She would hear of the distinction I had acquired, she would probably even read of the honourable position I had reached, by universal consent, in the literature of my country.

On paying this visit to the City of the Stone of Gold, I went first to Lisburn, where my friend John Birney, the solicitor, resided. With him I stayed for a few days, when we started for Clogher, his native town; and it was rather singular that the very inn we stopped at had been during my boyhood the residence of his father, who was a most respectable magistrate, and a man deservedly loved by the people of all creeds and classes. It was to John Birney that I dedicated the first series of my *Traits and Stories of the Irish Peasantry*. He had a good property about Clogher, and on this occasion, as he was going there to collect his rents, we went together. I stayed at the inn, which had formerly been his father's house, and so did he. One day after, I had been about a week there, I received an invitation to breakfast with a gentleman who lived in a pretty, secluded spot, formerly called 'The Grange', but changed by its present proprietor into 'Ashfield', if I remember correctly. After breakfast, he proposed – or I proposed, I forget which – to take a walk up to what was once Ballyscally, but which was now a scene of perfect desolation. Out of seventy or eighty comfortable cottages the gentleman in question had not left one standing. Every unfortunate tenant had been evicted, driven out, to find a shelter for himself where he could. Ballyscally had, I think, been the property of the See of Clogher, but how it came into this person's possession I know not. Upon second thoughts, it must have been I who proposed the walk in that direction, and for this reason: there was but one house left standing in Ballyscally – certainly the best that ever was in the town – but that house, as I knew for many a long year, was the residence of the husband of Anne Duffy.[1] We went up by Ballyscally, which had consisted of houses scattered over the top and side of an elevated hill, that commanded a distant view of a beautiful country to an extent of not less than fifty miles. The long depression of the land before you to the west and north under the hill constitutes that portion of the county known in ancient Irish history as the 'Valley of the Black Pig'. My companion brought me up to see an obelisk which he was building, on the top of a much higher hill than Ballyscally. It was nearly finished, but we reached the top with some difficulty, and after all saw very little more than we could see from its base. Like many other similar and useless structures it was called 'B—'s Folly'.

As we returned, I proposed that we should pay a visit to *her* husband's house, then, as I said, the only one in all Ballyscally. Up to this moment, she and I had never exchanged a word. What she might have expressed, had she known I was on my way to visit her, I do not know, but, notwithstanding every attempt to keep cool, I felt my heart palpitate as it had not done for years. We shook hands, and had some commonplace conversation, when after a few minutes her husband came in; and as he and I had known each other long before his marriage, we also shook hands as old acquaintances. After a little I looked at her, and then turning to him,

'Michael,' said I, 'there stands the only woman I ever loved beyond the power of language to express. She had my first affection, and I loved her beyond any woman that ever breathed, and strange to say, until this occasion we never exchanged a syllable.'

'Well,' she replied, 'I can say on my part – and I am not ashamed to say it – that I never loved man as I loved you; but there was one thing clear, that it wasn't our fate ever to become man and wife. Had you married me it's not likely the world

[1] It was old style in the North of Ireland to speak of the house as the man's only.

would have ever heard of you. As it is, I am very happily married, and lead a happy life with as good and as kind a husband as ever lived.'

Michael laughed, and appeared rather pleased and gratified than otherwise. We then shook hands again, I took my leave, and that was my first and last interview with her whose image made the pleasure of my whole youth for nearly five years.

While we were in Springtown, McGoldrick, the classical teacher, left the country. Wiley, the Presbyterian clergyman, was a Trinity College man, I think, and had the reputation of being an excellent scholar. He was a dwarf, and I was told by one of his scholars, John Trimble, who had been an old schoolfellow of my own with McGoldrick, and afterwards resided as Doctor Trimble at Castle Bellingham, that in or out of hell he was matchless for the most savage brutality. His instrument of punishment was a cudgel, with which he belaboured the boys, when deficient in their lessons, so inhumanly that he often knocked them down, and not unfrequently cut them to the skull. Trimble was one of the bravest and most courageous boys I ever met, and, besides, the most generous and honourable. He was at this time about nineteen, and I know not where a finer or handsomer young fellow of his age could be found. Upon one occasion Wiley struck him a severe blow with his cudgel, a fact which gratified the recipient of the blow very much. It was the first time he had dared to strike him, for Trimble was of a highly respectable and wealthy family. John, however, having received the degrading blow, caught the cudgel, twisted it out of the wretch's hand, and immediately began the praiseworthy act of retributive justice. I said that Wiley was a dwarf, but he was one of the most powerful dwarfs I ever saw in my life. He had a head the size of a mess-pot, and a neck like a bull, while his arms were powerful and of an immense length. Altogether, the eye could not rest on a more scowling and ferocious-looking animal. On this misshapen carcase did generous John Trimble set to work, and with such spirit and vigour, that Master Wiley was the subject of a sick bed for more than a fortnight afterwards. When he got up, he threatened a

60

prosecution; but his case was too bad for that. Every scholar he had withdrew from him, and he also left the neighbourhood, after a residence of only a few months. I think it was my father's intention to have sent me to him, had he not been deterred by the reputation of his unnatural cruelty.

I was once more without a classical school to go to. Education seemed to fly from me. I was extremely anxious to acquire classical knowledge, and what to do with me my father and family knew not. It was at this period that my father caught the malady of which he died. He went to dine with our sister Mary, whose husband lived in the next townland to us – that of Kilrudden. The day was Christmas Day, and they had a fine turkey. My father met my sister and her husband at the 'Forth' already described, and went home with them to dinner. I remember the day well. The early part of it was dry and rather agreeable; at all events it gave no presage of the severity that followed. The most awful downpouring of rain I ever witnessed set in when they were about half way; they were drenched to the very skin, and my father was obliged to sit the whole day in his wet clothes. My brother-in-law pressed him to take some spirits, but he had made a vow upwards of thirty years before against every kind of drink, except at a wedding or christening, and consequently refused to take that which might have saved his life. In many things he was a strange man. In matters of religion I never knew any individual who resembled him, or I should rather say who approached him, in what I must term a senseless and superstitious kind of piety. That he was a man of the most stainless and inoffensive life – of the sweetest temper and the strongest and tenderest affec- tions – were facts known to the whole parish. He was perpetually praying; in fact his beads were scarcely ever out of his hands, either by night or day. He prayed, with his head in his hands, even on his way to Mass on Sunday, when one would imagine he could have got enough of it; he prayed on his way home again. He prayed on his way to fair or market, and he prayed on his way home again also. His charity, too, was far beyond his means, for he had the kindest and most generous of hearts; indeed

61

no man ever sympathized in a more Christian spirit with human misery. His fear of ghosts was ludicrous; and many a time my honest mother, who was utterly insensible to any feeling of the kind, used to laugh at him for his absurd weakness.

I will give one illustration of his fear of ghosts. He was in the habit of going during the winter nights – indeed during every night in the year, whether winter or summer – up to the parlour to pray. This was not common prayer; it was penance of the severest kind got from certain specimens from Butler's *Lives of the Saints*, a favourite book of his. When going to pray he always brought a round rod, about as thick as the upper end of a horsewhip, on which he knelt, perhaps for a couple of hours, repeating rosaries and prayers to no end. One winter's night he was so engaged, when I noticed a fox-terrier we had, called Trig, go into the room where he was engaged in prayer. Trig returned almost immediately, and soon after him my father, beads in hand, and with a pale face.

'Mary,' said he to my mother, 'I have something strange to tell you.'

'What is it?' asked my mother.

'Why,' said he, 'while I was at my prayers this moment, I felt a cold and deathlike hand laid upon mine; what could it mean?'

'How can I tell?' replied my mother.

'It was as cold as ice,' he proceeded, 'and just touched the hand I had the beads in – isn't it very strange?'

'Why, it is rather strange,' returned my mother; 'I can make nothing of it.'

'I know what it means now,' replied my simple father, 'it was a temptation to turn my mind from the prayers I was saying. I think it was an evil spirit. Get me the jug that has the holy water in it, and I will go and commence my prayers again.'

He accordingly got the holy water, and went once more into the dark room, and resumed his devotions. He had not been three minutes there, however, when Trig, the dog, urged by what motive I know not, went into the room after him, and almost immediately returned again, instantly followed by my father, now in a state of terror which language could scarcely describe.

'I declare to my God,' said he, 'the evil spirit touched my hand again.'

'Why,' said my mother, 'hadn't you the holy water?'

'I had,' he replied, 'and sprinkled it all about the room, and especially the spot I was kneeling on; but in spite of all, a hand as cold as death or ice touched mine.'

'Go back,' said my mother, 'and take a candle with you.'

This he did, and in a few minutes the dog once more followed him, and placed his nose upon his hand as before. This development of the mystery satisfied him and set all right; but, had he not thus discovered it, he would have laboured under the impression that there had been something supernatural in the matter.

On returning home that night from my sister's, my father complained of being unwell, and the next day was only able to go about a little. On the second day he was worse, and on the third took to his bed, from which he never rose. He was ill for six weeks, and died after a long series of terrible sufferings – but as a Christian. The priest who administered to him those rites of the Church peculiar to the hour of death declared that during the whole course of his long life, he never witnessed so edifying a deathbed. His remains were attended to the graveyard in Clogher by the largest funeral concourse remembered in the parish.

Chapter VI

A candidate for the priesthood – Pat McArdle's scheme – Carleton
takes the road as a poor scholar – His adventures – Curious dream –
Its result – Pat Frayne's departure – Studying the classics.

As for me, who was my father's favourite, I was in a state of
indescribable sorrow for months. The marriage of Anne Duffy
and his death were the two bitterest calamities of my early life.

As they say in the country, my father seemed to take the good
luck of the family with him. We were soon on the decline, and I
felt exceedingly anxious to acquire classical knowledge in order
to prepare myself for life. The prospect before me was dark and
dismal. After much reflection upon my ultimate fate in the world,
and feeling how incapable I was from want of education to discharge any respectable duty in it, I proposed to my family that
I should go to Munster as a poor scholar. In fact, with respect to
education, there was no other opening for me. I was the more
inclined to this as a nephew of our own parish priest, the Rev.
Edward McArdle, had come to the same resolution. Mr McArdle
had two nephews, one of them a namesake of his own (Edward),
who had attended McGoldrick's school at Tulnavert so long as it
was there. That nephew was then a student at Maynooth. His
brother now assured his uncle that he was resolved to enter the
Church, but as his (the priest's) housekeeper, his sister-in-law,
a Mrs Buckley, would not suffer his uncle to keep him in his
house, he said he was resolved to go to Munster to prepare
himself, as so many others did. The name of this candidate for
church honours was Pat McArdle, and if Mrs Buckley, who was
the most incarnate devil that ever existed in the shape of woman,
had never done anything worse than keeping this drunken
scoundrel out of the priest's house, she would have had very little
to answer for. As it was, he got a sum of fifty pounds from his

64

reverend but unsuspecting uncle to enable him to work out his object, with a promise of still further support whenever he should require it. It was now the month of May, and my relatives were preparing my humble and unpretending outfit. I got a new suit of clothes and four shirts, with as many classical books as could be procured. Pat McArdle and I were to go together, and all my family, with the exception of one brother, were delighted that a lad so young and utterly inexperienced as I was should have the advantage of his society on the journey. I know that I myself was delighted, and derived great courage from the anticipation. My brother James, however, did not at all relish this notion of having Master Pat as my companion on the way; because he was better acquainted with his character than we were. The truth is, he was a scheming scoundrel, seldom sober, and, as my brother supposed very correctly (as the event proved), had not the slightest notion of going to Munster as a poor scholar.

'The thing is ridiculous,' said my brother; 'a fellow past thirty years of age, better dressed in his suit of black than his uncle the priest himself, to think of going up to Munster as a poor scholar! He has no more notion of it than I have.'

At all events he called at our house the evening before we were to start, in order to arrange that I should meet him, the next morning, in the town of Aughnacloy, at a friend's place, whose address he gave us. He brought me a Latin testimonial of character, written by his uncle, who had given my brother an English one before. This, however, he said was more authentic, and a certain evidence that it could not be written by anyone but a priest. He was a very smooth gentleman, extremely plausible in his manners, easy and insinuating and, altogether well qualified to get through the world. He asked me if we had any other testimonials to my character than those of his uncle, to which my brother replied that I had a letter from the Rev. James Garland, the Catholic curate of the adjoining parish of Errigle Truagh, to a young man then closing his studies as a poor scholar in Munster, with whose address he was acquainted. This young man's relations, who were rather wealthy, lived a little off the mail-coach northern road that ran between Aughnacloy and Emyvale. Their name was Murray. Master Pat seemed very much satisfied with this, and expressed his hope that we might yet live to see each other bishops.

'What money do you intend to give him?' said he, addressing my brother. 'You ought not to stint him in that respect.'

'That's a subject we have not made up our minds on,' replied my brother, 'but we'll think of it. You know,' said he, 'we are not rich.'

'Well,' replied Pat, 'place whatever sum you intend to allow him in my hands. I am able to manage it better than the poor inexperienced boy is. I'll be his banker, and pay it out to him as long as it lasts, seeing in the meantime that he is not imposed on.'

'You are very kind,' replied my brother, 'and when we are able to see how much we can afford him, we'll have more talk about it.'

'But then we start tomorrow, you know,' said the other.

'Well,' replied my brother, 'but you know that I go with him as far as Aughnacloy, where we are to meet, and then we can settle it.'

Master Pat, however, did *not* go to Munster, because he had no such intention. His object was to get fifty pounds from his pious but simple uncle, and having accomplished this, he disappeared, and left me to pursue my journey alone. Had my brother been fool enough to allow him to become my banker, there is no earthly doubt that my bank would have failed. I never saw him afterwards.

In my tale of 'The Poor Scholar' I have represented my father as a living man, whereas he had been dead for about a year before. The love I bore him was a rare affection even from a son to a father. I was his idol, not merely the child of his affection, but of his worship. The evening McArdle left us was, as the reader knows, the last I was to spend at home until my return from Munster. What I am now about to relate is very singular, but quite true. On that night all my sorrow – all my grief rather – for my father revived with as much vehemence and power as I first felt on the occasion of his death. I got his clothes – I pressed them to my heart, I kissed them, and lapsed altogether into such a state of distraction, as revived the grief which all those around me had felt at his death. At length I was overcome by the excess of what I felt, and when urged to go to bed I did so, when I fell fast asleep. The scene, however, where I have described my mother as gently kissing me while I was asleep, and crying over me in a low voice, is perfectly true, as I learned afterwards from my sister.

When morning came we had an early breakfast, of which I could partake but slightly, and that after having been forced to it by my mother. Before I awoke in the morning they had, by my brother James's advice, sewed five pound notes in the cuff of the left sleeve of my coat, and placed thirty shillings in silver in one of the pockets of my trousers, for immediate use as I proceeded on my journey. They also gave me a needle and thread, and a penknife, that I might be able to rip my sleeve when I wanted a pound, and sew it up again without the knowledge of anyone.

I have described the separation, exactly as it happened, in the tale of 'The Poor Scholar' itself, leaving my father out, so that it would be impossible to give it here without repeating myself. I have also described the journey as far as the town of Granard, together with my accidental meeting with Lenehan, the benevolent farmer, and the motherly kindness of his equally Christian and benevolent wife. My outfit was simple enough, but a portion of it very significant of the object of my journey. My satchel consisted of a piece of greybeard linen, made after the manner of a soldier's knapsack, and worn in the same fashion. At a first glance, everyone could see that it was filled principally with books, whose shapes were quite visible through it, and the consequence was that my object as a young traveller was known at a glance. I never stayed in the towns as I went along, but always at the small roadside inns, where I was treated with kindness to which I really could scarcely render justice by description.

I need not say that during this journey I had a heavy heart and a sorrowful one. I was leaving all those who were dear to me,

67

probably never to see them again. I was going to a strange country, to mingle with a people among whom I had not a single friend. In fact, I was very much to be pitied, and the only thing which sustained me and checked my grief was the novelty of the scenery as I went along. Many a jaunt I got in empty post-chaises as I advanced – and many a time was my satchel carried for me by some kind fellow traveller who happened to be going my way.

At length I reached the town of Granard, where I stopped at a small inn kept by a man named Grehan. Here I was treated with the usual kindness. Indeed, during this youthful pilgrimage such was the respect held for those who appeared to be anxious to acquire education, that, with one exception alone, I was not permitted to pay a farthing for either bed or board in the roadside houses of entertainment where I stopped. Two of these were kept by Protestants, who were equally generous. The one man made me pay was a Catholic, and so far as I could see was what is called a *voteen*,[1] because while I was at my supper he advised me very seriously not to go to bed without saying my prayers. He also asked me several questions about my family, and whether I went regularly to confession; but notwithstanding the interest he felt in my soul, I had to pay thirteen pence after breakfast in the morning; that was three pence for my bed, five pence for my supper of excellent flummery and new milk the preceding night, and five more for my breakfast that morning. God knows it was cheap enough, but still he was the only man who charged me anything.

In Grehan's little inn I slept very soundly, but still I had a dream that sent me back to my family. I dreamt that I was pursued by a mad bull, and overtaken. The bull was about to gore me, when I awoke in a perspiration of terror. In the morning I dressed myself, breakfasted with the family, assumed my equipments for the resumption of my journey, as they thought; but the moment I got outside the door, I turned to the right-about, and started for home with a great heart. The dream of the mad

[1] *Voteen* means devotee, but is usually applied only to foolish or hypocritical devotees.

68

bull, aided by other motives still more natural and strong, accomplished the fact of my restoration to my family.

This turned out to be a most agreeable event to all parties. During my short absence from home, my mother and the other members of my family were nearly in despair, and charged themselves with a very deep degree of guilt and heartlessness for having allowed me, then so young and ignorant of the world, to undertake such a journey. In fact, the house was a scene of grief and weeping; my mother was nearly distracted, and there was an intention of sending one of my brothers after me for the purpose of tracing me out and bringing me home. At first, it is true, the notion of going to Munster originated with myself. My ambition to acquire learning, however, was not so strong as my domestic affection. On the morning of my return I felt as if I could tread upon air, especially as I diminished the distance between me and Springtown. My object was to give them a surprise at home, because, to say the truth, I suspected the remorse they felt. Most fortunately, no one saw me until I entered the house – when my dear mother uttered an exclamation which it would be difficult to describe, and rushing to me with a tottering step, fainted in my arms. The tumult which ensued in the family was one of delight and joy. That day was indeed a happy day. The neighbours, having heard of my return, were equally delighted; many of them had spoken in very severe terms to my relations for having allowed me to go at such an age. This return home, under different circumstances, to be sure, is described at the close of 'The Poor Scholar'.

Here was I again for upwards of two years left without the means of acquiring classical knowledge. My old friend Pat Frayne, however, had been permitted by kind-hearted Andy Morrow, who was our neighbour, to open a school in the house in which he himself and all his ancestors had been born. Pat was charged no rent, but got a cow's grass, and ground for as many potatoes as he could plant free. This was by way of compensation for keeping the house inhabited; it would otherwise have fallen into ruin. I now returned to enjoy Pat's instructions, but I had no relish for arithmetic or science in any shape. I spent an unpleasant time with him, and felt myself degraded when sitting among a parcel of bare-legged monkeys whom I looked upon with contempt. Still I forced myself to my business, and got a tolerably good notion of Gough's *Arithmetic*. Even here, however, Pat was attended by his usual luck, as well as myself. I thought it would be no harm if I learned book-keeping to qualify myself for a clerk in some shopkeeper's or merchant's office. I was consequently about to procure a copy of Jackson's *Book-keeping*, had not a law case between Andy Morrow's niece, Miss Kitty, and our next neighbour, Robin Young, a wealthy and substantial farmer, intervened. Miss Kitty was entitled by her grandfather's will, or her father's (I am not certain which), to one half of the townland of Kilrudden, which Andy Morrow at the time, and for some years before, had held as an occupier, but in trust for her. Young proposed for her, was accepted and went to reside in the house then occupied by Pat Frayne, who on that occasion finally left the country, and returned to his native Connaught, where, it seems, he had a wealthy but childless brother who invited him and his family home.

Again I was without means of acquiring that knowledge on which my heart was set – knowledge of the classics. I had gone before this beyond the Fourth Book of Virgil, and if ever a schoolboy was affected almost to tears, I was by the death of Dido. Even when a schoolboy, I did not read the classics as they are usually read by learners. I read them as novels – I looked to the story – the narrative – not to the grammatical or other difficulties.[1] The field was new to me, and consequently possessed a singular charm for me. The truth is, I read the classics through the influence of my imagination, rather than of my judgment.

[1] In this, Carleton resembled Pope.

Chapter VII

Tom Jones – Amoranda – Keenan's classical school – The 'infare' at Cargah – The Ribbonmen – Carleton made a Ribbonman – Extent of the organization – The oath of the society – The grip.

WHILE at Tulnavert School, I formed one of those schoolboy friendships, which are so common among lads such as we were, for a young class-fellow called William Short. He asked me to go home and spend a few nights with him, an invitation which I gladly accepted. His father lived in a wild mountainous district and possessed a large tract of rough mountain ground. When I went there I felt astonished at the undoubted evidences of his wealth. While on this visit I saw for the first time an odd volume of *Tom Jones*; but I have not the slightest intention of describing the wonder and the feeling with which I read it. No pen could do justice to that. It was the second volume; of course the story was incomplete, and, as a natural consequence, I felt something amounting to agony at the disappointment – not knowing what the *dénouement* was.

It was a little before this that I met first the thing in the shape of a novel that ever came into my hands. It was published as a pamphlet, but how I came by it I don't recollect. The name was *Amoranda, or the Reformed Coquette*. She, Amoranda, was a young lady of great fortune and surpassing beauty, and better still for herself, she was the sole mistress of that fortune, responsible to none. Of course, she was surrounded by hundreds of admirers, all suitors for the hand of a lady at once so beautiful and so wealthy. She acted the thorough coquette – encouraged them all, but accepted none. At length one lover made his appearance, a gentleman very superior to her other worshippers, and to him she seemed to give something like a preference; but when he made his proposals she told him that if she were capable of deciding for herself it would be in his favour. In the meantime she preferred her present life; it was better, she thought, to have many worshippers than one. Life with a husband must be an insipid thing, and besides, she preferred being admired to being loved. The disappointed gallant took his farewell, and left her to enjoy the admiration which was so grateful to her vanity. Still she could not banish the image of the last visitor from her memory, and she began to feel something like regret that she did not give him at least a longer trial; however, it was now too late. It seemed that he was so deeply affected by her rejection of his suit, that he went to the Continent with the intention of spending the remainder of his life there. This information she had in a letter from himself, and she was deeply affected by it. In the course of a few months afterwards, during the season of autumn, a carriage was passing the public road, which was quite convenient to her magnificent residence; the horses, it seems, took fright at something, the carriage was overturned, and an old gentleman of a very dignified and venerable appearance was so severely injured, that it was found necessary to ask Amoranda if she could give him shelter during the illness which was occasioned by the injuries he had received. Amoranda, coquette as she was, possessed a generous and humane heart. She sent her own carriage for him, and he was received by her with a most hospitable welcome. The story then goes on to their conversation during her guest's recovery, and after he became able to walk with her through the beautiful grounds attached to the castle. The venerable sage gained her confidence; she was not at heart a coquette, but she despised men, and took delight in encouraging them in order to secure their punishment by afterwards rejecting them. She said it was her great property that brought the majority of them about her – that she never loved but one, who unfortunately had gone to the Continent, and she was never likely to see him again. A few days afterwards his wig became disarranged, by some accident, in her presence, and an artificial nose displaced, and there he stood before her – the only man whom she had ever loved!

We were drowning flax the day I read this, the first novel that had ever come into my hands, and I was lying among the green beets as they were tumbled out of the slide car on which they were drawn to the flax-pond. Such was the delight with which I read, and such my disappointment that there was no more of it, that I actually shed tears.

I now began to look out for books of fiction and entertainment. It is true I had read all those cheap amusing little works which were at that time the only reading books in the common schools, from *The Arabian Nights* downwards. Need I say with what an enthusiastic delight I read them – but they only stimulated the taste for fiction by which I was then absorbed. I had now little on my hands to do as a student, but so anxious was I for this sort of amusement, that I went throughout the greater part of the parish hunting for books of entertainment.

Although the state of education was, at the period of which I write, very low, and knowledge scanty among the people, yet it is surprising what a number of books, pamphlets and odd volumes, many of these works of fiction, I found among them. If you examined the number of Catholic families in the parish, you would find that one half of them could not read; yet several of these utterly illiterate persons had many of the works I have alluded to, most carefully laid up, under the hope that some young relation might be able to read them. I remember two, by which I was much struck – *The Life of Edward, Lord Herbert,* and Defoe's *History of the Devil.*

After having ransacked almost all the old cupboards and boxes in the parish, I accidentally heard of a relative of mine who, I was told, was curate of a place called Glennon, in the parish of Donagh, county Monaghan. What was most agreeable to me, and least expected, was that he kept a classical school. On making further inquiry among my family, and having consulted my uncle – brother to my father – I discovered that Mr Keenan (for such was his name) and I were second cousins. This information afforded me great satisfaction. I accordingly went to a family named McCarron, who held a fine farm in the townland of

73

Derrygola, in the adjoining parish of Truagh. The wife of Patrick McCarron was my mother's niece. Here I stayed for a few days, and then proceeded to the house of a man named Traynor, with whom I understood my cousin Keenan lodged. Traynor's house was immediately beside the chapel, and a comfortable one it was. Fortunately I found my reverend cousin at home, and on making myself known to him I was very kindly received. His family and ours lived at least thirty miles from each other, so that except in blood relationship we were utter strangers. I gave him a history of my past life and education, and mentioned the declining circumstances of the family, expressing deep regret that I had not had an opportunity of completing my classical education. The man saw at once the object of my visit, and asked me could I not attend his school.

'If I had a house of my own,' said he, 'I could with pleasure afford you a place of residence, but as it is I am only a lodger here.'

I told him that I had relations in the neighbouring parish of Truagh, about five miles distant, with whom I could live.

'Well, in that case,' he replied, 'the sooner you come the better; whatever I can do for you I will feel very happy in doing. I only hope,' he added, smiling 'that you are not a better scholar than myself. Before you go, you must take a drop of dram,' and in a couple of minutes I got a bumper of as good poteen as ever ran through the eye of a still, as the phrase is. I went to Keenan in the year 1814 and remained with him until the year 1816. I lived at Derrygola for some time with my relations the McCarrons, who were wealthy people, and most affectionate to me. My residence with them was the most delightful period of my youth. Keenan, as I said, was only the curate of the parish of Donagh. Glasslough was the next town to his residence, that is to say, about three-quarters of a mile from it. The parish priest of Donagh was the Rev. Mr McMullan. The parish was not a large one, and Keenan's salary was so small that he was unable to live without the assistance he derived from the profits of his school. He collected oats besides from the parishioners, both Catholic and Protestant, and indeed I may affirm with truth that he was treated with more liberality by the latter class than by the former. The Protestants, however, could well afford to be liberal, as they were by far the more wealthy.

While I was with Keenan a brother of his returned from the Peninsular War, accompanied by a Portuguese wife. I remember bringing a common low-wheeled car for them, covered with a feather bed and quilt, to the 'Westenra Arms' in Monaghan, where they stopped the night before. Paddy Traynor, with whom Keenan lodged, contrived to make room for them in his house. Here, however, they did not remain long. Keenan's brother had either saved money in the army or got it with his wife: be this as it may, he was able to open the largest grocery and liquor establishment that ever was seen in Glasslough.

There were then at Keenan's school three individuals whom I will mention. Two of these were full-grown young men. One of them was Mr Peter McPhillips, who afterwards kept the 'Westenra Arms' Hotel in Monaghan for many years; the others were Frank McGough and John McNally. When Keenan's brother opened the grocery establishment in Glasslough, his brother the priest went to reside with him, and honest Peter McPhillips, one of the full-grown pupils just mentioned, and than whom a man of more sterling integrity never lived, gave up all notions of the priesthood, and went to conduct the peninsular hero's establishment as a grocer. In the meantime I had removed during the winter from McCarron's of Derrygola to Traynor's, with whom Keenan had lodged. From Traynor's I went for some months to the house of a man named Moynagh, whose residence was in Donagh, that being the name of the town from which the parish itself is named.

Of course it must not be supposed that I neglected to visit my mother and family during this period of absence. So far from that, I went home, I think, at least once a month, if not oftener. These visits sometimes lasted three or four days, and I not unfrequently went to Clogher market on these occasions – feeling naturally anxious to see and meet many of my young friends, who were

75

also as anxious to see me. I may add here for once that there never was in that part of the country a young fellow more popular or better loved by persons of all creeds and classes – by the Protestants as well as by the Catholics. On such occasions, however, my associates were generally of my own religion. During those reunions I was struck with one fact, for which I could not by any means account. These young fellows, and others, frequently looked with a very mysterious kind of inquiry into my face, and occasionally asked me what age I was. I generally replied, 'I'm in my nineteenth year,' upon which the expression of their faces became lengthened and indicative of disappointment. This puzzled me very much: I could not by any train of reasoning understand it. I now return to a particular visit I made to see my mother and other relations at Springtown. The day was Saturday, and the month either June or July, when, having started for home from Glasslough, a distance of at least sixteen miles across the country, which to me was nothing, I had arrived at the townland next to Springtown, named Cargah, immediately above which was a very pretty smooth eminence ending in a flat greensward. On this table-land I found there was a dance, in which was engaged a number of young men and women, with nearly every one of whom I was acquainted. It was not, I soon found, an ordinary dance, but what they call in the north an *infare*, or the haling home of a newly-married bride to the house of her husband, of which she is to be the future mistress. At these *infares*, there was generally such a dance as I found on the table on Cargah Hill, animated to a greater sense of enjoyment by plenty of excellent poteen whisky. Here I danced with the bride, whom I looked upon for the first time, and several other girls with whom I was intimately acquainted. Even at this time I was celebrated as a dancer. After my last dance was concluded, I stood to observe the progress of the general amusement, when I observed the young fellows getting together into knots and looking at me as if I had been the subject of their conversation. Before this period the bridegroom had forced me to take two glasses of the poteen, which, as I was not in the habit of drinking

76

anything in the shape of spirits, had got a very little into my head. They offered me a third glass, which I refused, lest my mother might observe the signs of drink upon me. After some time, about half a dozen of them were led behind a dry green ditch by a red-haired fellow named Hugh Roe McCahy, who lived in the townland of Cloghleim, not half a mile distant. He was one of those important individuals who make themselves active and prominent among their fellows, attend dances and wakes, are seldom absent in fair or market from a fight, and, I may add, lose no opportunity of giving rise to one when everything else fails them.'

'William,' said he, 'aren't you ashamed to be ignorant of what is going on about you over the whole country?' He had a prayer-book, or what is called a *manual*, a book of Roman Catholic devotion, in his hand as he spoke – a fact which greatly puzzled me, as I was perfectly aware that he could not read. I had once before this, while book-hunting throughout the neighbourhood, called upon him and found in his house an odd volume of Catholic theology in Latin. The fellow was rapid in his language as well as in his personal motions.

'Why,' said I, 'what is going on in the country?'

'I will tell you,' he replied; 'but first take this *manual* in your hand, and repeat after me what I will say.'

He then went over the oath of Ribbonism, which he had got by heart, until he concluded it; after this he made me kiss the book.

'Now,' said he, 'you're *up* – you're a Ribbonman; all you want is the words and signs – and here they are.'

He then communicated them to me, and, although but a schoolboy, I went home a Ribbonman.

Here was a new view of life opened to me, and that with such dexterous rapidity, that I found myself made a member of a secret and illegal society by this adroit scoundrel, before I had time to pause or reflect upon the consequences. In like manner were hundreds, nay thousands, of unreflecting youths seduced into this senseless but most mischievous system.

I now discovered that the whole Catholic population, with the exception of the aged heads of families, was affiliated to Ribbonism. In fact it was not only almost impossible, but dangerous, to avoid being involved in the system. If a young man happened to possess the sense and spirit to resist the Ribbonmen's importunities to join them, he would probably be waylaid and beaten by persons of whom he knew nothing.

The following is the Ribbon oath, a curiosity in its way:

'I A. B., with the sign of the Cross do declare and promise, in the name and through the assistance of the Blessed Trinity, that I will keep inviolate all secrets of this Fraternal Society from all but those whom I know to be regular members of the same, and bound by the same solemn oath and fraternal ties:

'1st. I declare and profess, without any compulsion, allegiance to his present Majesty, George the Third, King of Great Britain and Ireland.

'2nd. That I will be true to the principles of this Society, dedicated to St Patrick, the Holy Patron of Ireland, in all things lawful and not otherwise.

'3rd. That I will duly and regularly attend on the shortest possible notice, at any hour, whether by night or by day, to perform, *without fail or inquiry*, such commands as my superior or superiors may lay upon me, under whatever penalty he or they may inflict for neglecting the same.

'4th. I will not deliberately or willingly provoke, challenge or strike any of my brothers, knowing him to be such. If he or they should be ill spoken of, ill-used, or otherwise treated unjustly, I will, according to circumstances and the best of my judgment, espouse his cause, give him the earliest information, and aid him with my friendship when in distress as a Ribbonman.

'5th. I also declare and promise that, I will not admit or propose a Protestant or heretic of any description as a member of our Fraternal Society, knowing him to be such.

'6th. That, whether in fair or market, in town or country, I will always give the preference in dealing to those who are attached to our national cause, and that I will not deal with a Protestant or heretic – but above all with an Orangeman – so long as I can deal with one of my own faith upon equal terms.

'7th. That I will not withdraw myself from this Society without stating my reasons for the same, and giving due notice to my superior or superiors; and that I will not without permission join any other society of different principles or denominations, under penalty of God's judgment, and whatever penalty may be inflicted on me – not including in these the Masonic Institution, Trade Societies, or the profession of soldier or sailor.

'8th. That I will always aid a brother in distress or danger by my person, purse, and counsel so far as in me lies; and that I will not refuse to subscribe money, according to my means, for the general or particular purposes of this our Fraternal Society.

'9th. That I will not, under the penalty inflicted by my superiors, give evidence in any Court of Law or Justice against a brother, when prosecuted by an Orangeman or heretic; and that I will aid him in his defence by any means in my power.

'10th. That when forced to take refuge from the law in the house of a brother or of any person friendly to our national cause, I will not have any improper intercourse or foul freedom with his sister, daughter, wife or cousin, and thus give cause of scandal to our Society.

'Having made the above solemn declaration and promise of my own free will and accord, I swear true and real allegiance to the cause of Ireland only, and no longer to be true as a subject nor to bear allegiance to George the Third, King of Britain and Ireland; and I now pray that God may assist me in my endeavours to fulfil the same; that He may protect me and prosper our Society, and grant us to live and die in a state of grace! – Amen.'

I may as well give what were then the 'Words' and the 'Grip', as I am on this subject. The words were as follows: – '*What age are we in?*' Answer. '*The end of the fifth.*' '*What's the hour?*' Answer. '*Very near the right one.*' '*Isn't it come yet?*' Answer. '*The hour is come, but not the man.*' '*When will he come?*' Answer. '*He is within sight.*'

The grip was, when shaking hands, to press the point of the

thumb on the second joint of the forefinger, and if the person with whom you shook hands was a brother, he was to press upon the middle joint of your little finger. Such were the words and grip of Ribbonism about the year 1814.

The reader will observe that there was a vagueness and a want of object in this ridiculous oath which gave conclusive evidence that it must have proceeded from a very ignorant source. I subsequently made inquiries into its origin, but could never ascertain the name of any man possessed of the slightest claim to respectability in connection with it. It originated with, and was confined to, the very lowest dregs of the people. That some scheming vagabonds must have been at the head of it, or the bottom of it is evident enough. Money was subscribed for fictitious objects, but where it went to no one could tell. In the county Louth it was set going by an Orangeman called Gubby (evidently an assumed name), and I think it was afterwards discovered that he was a native of Middleton, in that part of the county Tyrone which projects into the county of Armagh. This discovery, however, was made too late – for he had left the country.

I am not a friend to any of these secret societies, because they were nothing but curses to the country. The Orange system is a curse to the country, and will be so as long as it exists. It is now comparatively harmless, but at the period of which I write it was in the very height of its ascendancy, and seemed to live only as if its great object were to trample upon 'Popery'. The truth, however, is, if there can be an apology for Ribbonism, that it was nothing more nor less than a reactive principle against Orangeism, of whose outrages it was the result. In my works I have depicted both systems to the marrow, without either favour or affection, as the phrase has it. I never entertained any ill feeling against the people on either side; it is their accursed systems which I detest.[1]

---

[1] Carleton has described Orangeism in his *Valentine McClutchy*, and Ribbonism in *Rody the Rover*.

Chapter VIII

The party fight – Orange and Ribbon funerals – Athletic sports –
Runaway marriages – Lough Derg – The pilgrimage – Walking on
water – Change of religion – The female pilgrims – Nell McCallum.

HAVING shown the reader how I was made a Ribbonman, and
stated that it was actually impossible to live safely in the country
without joining the society, I must add a few words more upon
the subject before I dismiss it for the present. I have said that the
evening on which I had the honour of being admitted as a member of the society was that of Saturday, and as I made my visit
home on this occasion but a short one, I resolved to be present
in my class on the following Monday morning. I accordingly
made my appearance there at the proper hour. On that day I
made a discovery which surprised me not a little. Frank McGough
and John McNally – both have been dead for more than half a
century – and myself were walking in the chapel yard, while
Keenan had gone to meet some person on business at his lodgings
immediately at hand. I don't recollect what the topic of our
discourse was, but I remember that McGough, looking me
severely in the face, said:

'William, are you a good historian?'

'The worst in the world,' I replied, 'I never read a line of
history in my life.'

'You don't know, then, what age we are in?'

'Oh, yes I do,' I returned, 'in the end of the fifth.'

'Well, as to time – what's the hour?'

'Very near the right one.'

'Isn't it come yet?'

'The hour is come, but not the man.'

'When will he come?'

'He is within sight.'

We then shook hands and gave the grip, and McNally, who was also a member, joined us. The reader may thus judge of the hold which Ribbonism had upon the lower classes of society, when it wrought its way into the schools. This, however, he will not wonder at, when he is told that there was scarcely a Lodge schoolmaster in Ireland who did not 'hold articles', or in other words, who was not master of a Ribbon Lodge.

Keenan's brother was soon after this period attacked with a liver complaint, and in the course of a few months died, leaving whatever property he possessed to his Portuguese widow, a sweet, lively little woman, who soon afterwards became the wife of Peter McPhillips, with whom she removed to Monaghan, where, as I have said, he kept the 'Westenra Arms'. It is due to Peter to say that he never was connected with Ribbonism. He possessed too much sense and judgment to associate himself with a system so vague, unintelligible and nonsensical; not that he was acquainted with its absurdity, or the mischiefs and murders to which in many cases it ultimately led.

Now that I am on this subject, I cannot forbear to mention an event connected with, and resulting from, the combined influence of these two accursed systems – Orangeism and Ribbonism. In point of time, it occurred at least four or five years previous to the occasion on which I was seduced into Ribbonism. There is in my *Traits and Stories of the Irish Peasantry*, a full and historical detail of it, under the name of 'The Party Fight and Funeral'. In other words, it was the greatest battle that ever took place in the North of Ireland between the two parties. The reader need not expect me to describe it here, because I have done it at full length elsewhere. It occurred in the Lammas fair of Clogher, and never since that terrible day was the town of Clogher crowded with such vast numbers of people.

Such a fight, or I should rather say battle – for so in fact it was – did not take place in a state of civil society – if I can say so – within the last century in this country. The preparations for it were being made secretly for two or three months previous to its occurrence, and however it came to light, it so happened that each party became cognizant of the designs of the other. This conflict, of which I was an eye-witness – on my way home from school, being then about fourteen years of age – was such as never had a parallel. The reader may form an idea of the bitterness and ferocity with which it was fought on both sides, when he is informed that the Orangemen on the one side, and the Ribbonmen on the other, had called in aid from the surrounding counties of Monaghan, Cavan, Fermanagh and Derry, and if I mistake not, also from Louth. In numbers the belligerents could not have been less than from three to four thousand men. The fair day on which it occurred is known simply as 'The Day of the Great Fight'.

There was a man named 'Jerry Boccagh',[1] or 'Hop and Go Constant', for he was frequently called both, who fell the first victim to this violent feeling of party spirit. He had got arms on seeing his friends, the Orangemen, likely to be defeated, and had the hardihood to follow with charged bayonet a few Ribbonmen, whom he attempted to intercept as they fled from a large number of their enemies, who had got them separated from their comrades. Boccagh ran across a field adjoining the town in order to get before them on the road, and was in the act of climbing a ditch, when one of them, who carried a spade shaft, struck him a blow on the head which put an end to his existence.

The person who killed this man escaped to America, where he got himself naturalized, and when the British Government claimed him, he pleaded his privilege as an American citizen, and was not given up. Boccagh was a very violent Orangeman and a most offensive one.

On the part of the Ribbonmen, a man named Hacket or McGaughy, who lived not half a mile from our house, performed a very extraordinary exploit on that remarkable day. He got his skull broken by a blow inflicted with the butt of a gun, and yet he walked home afterwards, a distance of two miles – but the next morning I saw him in bed as insensible as a log. Sir William Richardson and other magistrates were at his house, accompanied

[1] *Boccagh* means a cripple, and is mostly used in reference to impostors or malingerers.

by a Surgeon Shone, who trepanned his head with very equivocal success, for although he recovered so far as to be able to walk about, he never got beyond idiocy, and died in about three months afterwards. He sat for the picture of Dennis Kelly in 'The Party Fight and Funeral'.

In those days there were such things as Ribbon funerals and Orange funerals. For instance, it sometimes happened that when a Ribbonman was murdered – Hacket's case was considered a murder – the Ribbonmen attended his funeral in a body, every man wearing a red silk ribbon indicative of the murder that had been committed. This, however, occurred only occasionally, and in cases where party spirit ran high and bitter. I do no think there has been an instance in my native parish within the last thirty-five or forty years.

I now return to my own position. So far as education was concerned, it seemed to fly from me. Keenan closed his school at Glasslough, and opened one upon a much larger scale at Dundalk. He now ceased to act officially as a priest, and disencumbered himself of all parochial duties, even as a curate. As a classical teacher he possessed one good habit which cannot be too often imitated. He made Latin the language of the school, with those boys, at least, who were sufficiently advanced for that purpose. He also made us write extensively in Latin, and kept us constantly translating passages from the best English authors into the old Roman. In fact, when I left school, I could have spoken or written Latin as fluently as English. His advanced pupils in their conversation with each other, whether in school or out of school, generally spoke in Latin. Of course, when he removed to Dundalk, I returned home to my family, although I thought Keenan would have brought me to Dundalk along with him. He was, however, at this time in straitened circumstances. His brother, if he had money, left him none; all his property went to the widow, who, however, was childless until after her second marriage. Peter McPhillips married her, or rather she married Peter, who received with her all the property her husband had left her.

Here was I once more at large – without a single object or

prospect in life. My brother John had married and left us; so that the family was reduced to four – viz. my mother, my brother James, my sister Sarah, and myself. My sister had proposals for marriage from two young men, who were each extremely anxious to be successful. Beyond the respect due to their characters, she entertained scarcely any other feeling, with the exception of a slight predilection for one of them. She and I differed in our opinion of them, but not much. I made one of them my choice, and she ultimately married him, with the consent of us all. He immediately took her home, so that we were reduced to three – or rather four – my mother, my brother, myself, and a servant maid.

At this time I indulged in the practice of every athletic exercise that could be named; yet at this time, strange as it may appear to the reader, I devoted at least six hours out of the twenty-four to self-instruction. In fact my time was regularly divided between study and amusement. Writing Latin was a great amusement of mine. I imitated the flowing and redundant style of lines as well, at all events, as I could; but that which baffled me most, and tried my powers of imitation severely, was my attempt to imitate the curt, condensed style of Sallust. After several efforts at imitating the Latin historian, I ultimately gave him up.

Nothwithstanding this habit of study, no wake missed me, no dance missed me. I was perpetually leaping, and throwing the stone and the sledge. No football match was without me. I have gone five miles to wakes and dances. We had not only what were known as common dances in those days, but we had what were politely called balls. The difference between a ball and a common dance was this. At the ball we had whisky: every gentleman subscribed a tenpenny bit, and when a sufficient sum was obtained, the whisky was purchased, and the subscribers each brought his sweetheart, his sister, or some female friend or relative. It is unnecessary to say that the ladies paid nothing. There was then, indeed, great simplicity of manners, and a number of those old, hereditary virtues which had their origin in the purity and want of guile which consecrated domestic life. During all my association with these pastimes and harmless amusements, I never knew a single instance of a female coming to shame or loss of character. That many runaway marriages resulted from them, is a well-known fact; but, at the period of which I write, more than one half the marriages of the parish were runaway marriages. There was neither scandal nor impropriety connected with them. All this is very easily explained. Let the readers suppose a young man and a young woman to have conducted a love affair, or as it is called in the country, a 'courting match'. Perhaps they have been so engaged for a year – perhaps for two – perhaps for four, and perhaps for seven; I have known several whose duration went to seven. Perhaps – and it is usually the case when the term of courtship is prolonged – the state of their circumstances does not justify them in undertaking the serious responsibilities of domestic life; but be this as it may, it not unfrequently happens that courtships last seven years and more in the case of cautious and prudent persons, who have the sense to look before them, and to apply to their own circumstances what the result of an improvident marriage must be. These, however, are exceptions; in good truth the general rule is a hundred to one the other way. There is not a country in Europe where so many rash and unreflecting marriages are made as in Ireland; the habit has been the curse of the country. The youngsters manage their 'runaways' in the following manner; they first determine upon 'running away', which is only another phrase for getting married: the lover selects the house of some relation or friend of his own, and after having given notice to that friend or relation of his intention, and having gained his assent, he informs the friend of the night when he and his sweetheart will come to their house as a 'running away couple'; and in order that they may not be without the means of celebrating the event with a due convivial spirit, he generally places a gallon of unchristened whisky in their hands. The night of their arrival at the house of that friend or relation is of course a jolly one. On the next morning the friend or relation goes to their respective families and discusses the fact of their 'runaway'. The girl is then brought home to her family and remains there until the marriage takes place.

Now I have two observations to make on this, or rather two facts to state in connection with it; the one is, that no human being ever heard of a runaway taking place except at night; the other is, that if the families of the young couple cannot, or will not, come to terms – as in the case of social factions sometimes happens – and that the marriage is absolutely broken off, no Irishman living would ever think of marrying the girl afterwards. This fact to her is a verdict of celibacy for life, and yet she is received in society like any other young female of her class. The reader may ask why this is so, especially if 'runaways' are not considered improper; the reply consists in the following fact: it sometimes happens – but I am proud to say very rarely indeed – that in cases where, *after the 'runaway'*, the match has been hopelessly set aside, the lapse of time has brought a fact to light which accounts for the single blessedness to which the female in a 'runaway', where the parties are at enmity and refuse their consent, is uniformly doomed. I have explained all these national usages at full length in my tale of 'Shane Fadh's Wedding'.[1]

During this time, between my studies and amusements I had a very pleasant life, with the exception of some uncomfortable glances at the future. I now bethought me of opening a classical school, but upon looking closely through the neighbourhood, or rather the whole parish, I could find only three pupils upon whom I could reckon as certain to attend. I consequently gave all hopes of a school to the winds. I took a fancy for strolling through the country in quest of adventures, and on these occasions I uniformly assumed a studious aspect – always had some classical or other book in my hand, and walked with a mock heroic gait, which, had the people been gifted with common sense, would have made me ridiculous. I was, however, excessively fond of histrionics, and strutted about uttering such sesquipedalian and stilted nonsense as was never heard. This, especially among the females, made me very popular. The fact of my entering into conversation

[1] See also Carleton's *Alley Sheridan, or the Runaway Marriage, and other Stories*, republished in 1857 by Philip Dixon Hardy, from *The National Magazine* of 1830.

with them was considered an honour, of which they felt duly proud, and of which they did not fail to boast in a spirit of triumph. I was at this time dressed in black, and looked upon by the public as the young priest, for such is the term bestowed upon every candidate for the office. This character I sustained with a lofty dignity which would have thrown a penetrating man of common sense into convulsions of laughter. My style was as fine a specimen of the preposterous and pedantic as ever was spoken. I gave the girls pompous specimens of my wonderful and profound learning, by repeating for their edification quotations from Greek and Latin, which I translated for them into wrong meanings, indicating a slight but rather significant appreciation on my part of their comeliness and beauty. During this queer and comic period of my life, I was considered one of the finest and best made young men in the parish. I was then in the very bloom of youth – six feet high – with, it was said, a rather handsome and intelligent set of features – my early fame at all athletic exercises was still unrivalled, and, in fact, I was looked upon as a kind of local phenomenon in my way. Those who have read the sketch of 'Denis O'Shaughnessey going to Maynooth' will understand this. To me it was a pleasant time, and would have been much more so, were it not for the shadows of the future.

I have already mentioned the extraordinary piety of my father. During my early youth he has frequently, during the winter evenings, amused me and the other members of our family by superstitious anecdotes connected with the far-famed purgatory of St Patrick called Lough Derg, or the Red Lake, situated in the county of Donegal, within three miles of the next little town of Pettigo.[1] Midsummer had set in, and now that I had nothing to do, and as it was that season of the year when the lower classes of the Irish make their stations to Lough Derg, I bethought me of the miraculous anecdotes which I had so frequently heard from my

---

[1] Calderon, the Spanish dramatist, wrote a play on the legends of this place, entitled *El Purgatorio de San Patricio*, which has been admirably translated by Denis Florence McCarthy. The traditions concerning Lough Derg were known all over Europe in medieval times.

father. A warm imagination inflamed my curiosity so powerfully, that I resolved to make a station to that far-famed scene of penitential devotion. I expressed my intention of doing this to my mother and brother; they were delighted at the pious spirit which had promoted such a holy resolution. I accordingly prepared to go – but in consequence of a suggestion from my mother, I laid aside my best clothes, and put on a black suit, which I had cast off, indeed without much necessity, for at this time I was as proud of my person as a peacock, and paid great attention to my dress and appearance.

Nothing but Lough Derg was now in my head, and my resolution was fixed upon this pious journey. A circumstance mentioned by my father had fastened strongly on my mind; this was a historical fact which had occurred not many years before the period of which I write. Lough Derg is in the centre of a lake in the wild and gloomy mountains of Donegal, and can only be approached by a boat. The property in which it lies belongs to the Leslies of Glasslough. They had leased the ferry of the island to certain persons, who had contracted to pay them two hundred a year. I think it was in the year 1796, that a boat filled with 'pilgrims', as they are called, was lost, on its way across to the lake, owing to the drunkenness of the boatmen. My father's anecdote, or rather legend, went on to state that there was a holy priest in the boat who, when it sank with its freight, deliberately walked over on the waters of the lake until he reached the island in perfect safety. I recollect observing to my father when he told me this legend:

'It is strange that if he had the power of walking upon the water, he had not the power of saving the boat and all that were in it.'

He paused and looked at me, but said nothing.

The account of my visit to this purgatory under the title of 'The Lough Derg Pilgrim' constituted my *début* in Irish literature.[1]

[1] This sketch was the first composition of Carleton's printed, in *The Christian Examiner*. It is included in some editions of the 'Traits and Stories', and was somewhat modified by Carleton at a later time.

I had in my early life a strong disinclination to enter a boat, and on this occasion my reluctance was increased by the recollection of the disaster on the lake. I will now quote a passage from the original account of my pilgrimage, which will exhibit the state of mind in which I made it.

'I very well remember that the first sly attempt I ever made at a miracle was in reference to Lough Derg; I tried it by way of preparing for my pilgrimage. I had heard that a boat had been lost there about the year 1796,[1] and that a certain holy priest who was in her as a passenger had walked very calmly across the lake to the island after the boat and the rest of the passengers in her had all gone to the bottom. Now I had from my childhood a particular prejudice against sailing in a boat, although Dick Davery, a satirical and heathenish old bachelor who never went to Mass, used often to tell me with a grin (which I was never able rightly to understand) that I might have no prejudice against sailing, "because", he would say, "you may take my word for it you'll never die by drowning." At all events, I thought that should any such untoward event occur to me, it would be pleasant to imitate the priest; but that it would be infinitely more agreeable to make the first experiment in a marl-pit on my father's farm than on the lake. Accordingly, after three days' fasting, and praying for the power of not sinking in water, I slipped very quietly down to the pit, and after reconnoitring the premises, to be sure that there was no looker-on, I approached the brink. At this moment my heart beat high with emotion; my soul was wrought up to an enthusiastic pitch of faith, and my whole spirit absorbed in feelings where hope, doubt, gleams of uncertainty, visions of future eminence, twitches of fear, reflections on my expertness in swimming, on the success of the water-walking priest aforementioned, and on the depth of the pond, had each insisted on an equal share of attention. At the edge of the pit grew large water-lilies, with their leaves spread over the surface; it is singular to reflect upon what slight and ridiculous circum-

---

[1] This accident occurred in 1795.

stances the mind will seize when wound up in this manner to a pitch of superstitious absurdity. I am really ashamed even while writing this, of the confidence I put for a moment in a treacherous water-lily, as its leaf lay spread so smoothly and broadly over the surface of the pond, as if to lure my foot to the experiment. However, after having stimulated myself by a fresh *pater* and *ave*, I advanced – my eyes turned up enthusiastically to heaven, my hands resolutely clenched, my teeth locked together, my nerves set, and my whole soul strong in confidence – I advanced, I say, and lest I might give myself time to cool from this divine glow, I made a tremendous stride, planting my right foot exactly in the middle of the treacherous water-lily leaf, and the next moment was up to my neck in water. Here was devotion cooled. Happily I was able to bottom the pool, or could swim right well, if necessary, so I had not much difficulty in getting out. So soon as I found myself on the bank, I waited not to make reflections, but, with a rueful face, set off full speed for my own home, which was not far distant; the water all the while whizzing out of my clothes by the rapidity of the motion, as it does from a water-spaniel after a swim. It is strange to think what influence vanity has over our principles and passions in the weakest and strongest moments of both. I was not remarkable for secrecy at that open, ingenuous period of my life; yet did I not now take especial care to invest either this attempt at the miraculous or its concomitant failure with anything like narrative. My act of devotion had a bad effect on my lungs, for it gave me a cough that was intolerable, and I never felt the infirmities of humanity more than in this ludicrous attempt to get beyond them. This happened a month before I started for Lough Derg.'[1]

My 'Lough Derg Pilgrim' is probably one of the most extraordinary productions that ever appeared in any literature. It resembles a coloured photograph more than anything else. There is not a fact or incident, or a single penal step of duty – and God knows there is many a penal step to be taken there – which is

[1] This differs slightly from the original or earliest version of the pilgrimage.

not detailed with the minuteness of the strictest truth and authenticity. There is not even an exaggeration of any kind in my account of it. The course of duty during the three days which constitute the term of each individual pilgrimage is such as no man, with flesh and blood capable of suffering, and gifted with a good memory, could readily forget. The Hon. Charles Gavan Duffy, now in Australia, made a pilgrimage there, long subsequent to mine, and he assured me that the truth and extraordinary accuracy of my description of it surprised him more than anything he had ever read.

It was that pilgrimage and the reflections occasioned by it, added to a riper knowledge and a maturer judgment, that detached me from the Roman Catholic Church, many of whose doctrines, when I became a thinking man, I could not force my judgment to believe. Still, although I conscientiously left the church, neither my heart nor my affections were ever estranged from the Catholic people, or even from their priesthood. One of the warmest friends and most enthusiastic admirers I ever had was the late Dr McNally, the Catholic bishop of my native diocese of Clogher. So is the present Catholic bishop of Kerry, a man for whom I entertain the most sincere and affectionate esteem. Dr Murray, professor of divinity in Maynooth College – probably the first theologian of his day and in his church, and author of the far-famed standard work *De Ecclesia Christi*,[1] I have the honour also to number among my Catholic friends and admirers. With these I could mention many others, all of whom, like those already named, know that I was educated for the Catholic priesthood.

The day at length arrived when I was to start on my pilgrimage to Lough Derg. It was not any conviction of penitence for sins that I had committed, nor even from any strong impression of religious duty – for of religion at that early period of my life I knew nothing – it was not, in fact, from any one motive which a pious Christian could urge – nor from any penance imposed

[1] Dr Patrick A. Murray, the Maynooth professor, was a Monaghan man, and was born in 1811. Beside his great theological works, which are held in high esteem, he wrote admirable criticism and poetry. He died in 1882.

92

on me by the priest at confession for any sins I may have committed – that I undertook this pilgrimage. Not at all. The feeling which urged me was a strong poetical sense of novelty. My father's narratives and legends in connection with Lough Derg would have had comparatively little effect, or at least but a commonplace one, upon a commonplace mind; but, as I have said, the poetry of my youth, excited by a strong curiosity, or rather exciting a strong curiosity, absolutely forced me to see this remarkable place famous in the history of the Irish Catholic Church for so many centuries.

I started early in the morning, and set out on my way without a single thought of anything but my anxiety to look upon the far-famed Lough Derg, and to understand in my own person, and by my own experience, what the performance of a station then meant. This piece of knowledge I certainly acquired to my cost – I performed the station most exactly and literally, and I solemnly protest that the punishment of the treadmill would be mere amusement compared to it.

As I have already remarked, owing to a suggestion of my mother, I had not my best clothes on. The whole affair, from beginning to ending, was to be penitential. I did not wear even my best shoes, nor any stockings. In former times this station had to be performed without shoe or stocking, but, I suppose in consequence of a subsequent relaxation of discipline, the wearing of shoes was now allowed. After having advanced ten or twelve miles, I overtook two women, whose description I will quote from my original sketch in 'The Lough Derg Pilgrim'.

'The first that I suspected to be fellow-pilgrims were two women whom I overtook upon my way. They were dressed in grey cloaks, striped red and blue petticoats, drugget or linsey-wolsey gowns that came within about three inches of their ankles. Each had a small white bag slung at her back, which contained the scanty provisions for the journey, and the oaten cakes, crisped and hard-baked, for the pilgrimage at the lake. The hoods of these cloaks fell down their backs, and each dame had a spotted kerchief pinned round her dowd cap at the chin, whilst the remainder of it fell down the shoulders over the cloak. Each had also a staff in her hand, which she held in a manner peculiar to a travelling woman, that is – with her hand round the upper end of it – her right thumb extended across its head, and her arm, from the elbow down, parallel with the horizon. The form of each, owing to the want of that spinal strength and vigour which characterizes the erect gait of man, was bent a little forward, and this, joined to the idea produced by the nature of their journey, gave to them something of an ardent and devout character, such as the mind and eye would seek for in a pilgrim. I saw them at some distance before me, and knew by the staves and white bags behind them that they were bound for Lough Derg. I accordingly stretched out a little that I might overtake them; for in consequence of the absorbing nature of my own reflections, my journey had so far been a solitary one, and I felt that society would relieve me. I was not a little surprised, however, on finding that as soon as I topped one height of the road, I was sure to find my two old ladies a competent distance before me in the hollow – most of the northern roads are of this nature – and that when I got to the bottom, I was as sure to perceive their heads topping the next hill, and then gradually sinking out of my sight. I was surprised at this, and perhaps a little nettled, that a fresh active young fellow should not have sufficient mettle readily to overtake two old women. I *did* stretch out, therefore, with some vigour, yet it was not till after a chase of two miles that I found myself abreast of them.'

This journey excited in me a strange and rapid variety of sensations. One of the females, who was spokeswoman, on ascertaining that I was for the 'Island', and seeing that I was dressed in black, supposed or rather pretended to suppose, that I was a priest – a mistake in which my vanity allowed her to persist. As we advanced, we either overtook, or were overtaken by, others whom we recognized at once by their garb and outfit as destined for Lough Derg.

As we approached Pettigo there was actually a little crowd of us. The lodgings in which the general class of pilgrims stop go by the name of 'Dry Lodgings' – that is to say, lodgings in which the proprietors do not keep or sell liquors. It is not my intention to dwell here upon the penitential character of this station. It is enough to say that I performed it to my cost – not in purse, but in suffering. Two slight meals of oaten bread and lukewarm water, or, as they call it, 'wine', is the liberal allowance for three days; that is to say, you have two single meals for two days, or one meal each day, and are obliged to abstain altogether from food during the third.

While I was there, my two female fellow-travellers kept their eyes upon me closely. They and I left the island in the same boat, for they appeared to feel that as we had come to it together, it was right that we should go home together, so far as our several destinations permitted. On reaching Pettigo, where I was resolved to take a sound sleep, the spokeswoman proposed that we should proceed about eight or ten miles further, to a very respectable lodging-house where we could find every comfort and convenience. I permitted myself to be guided by her, and when we arrived there it was late in the evening. For the first and last time during my life, I experienced the fierce and united attacks of hunger and sleep. At all events, after a hasty meal I went to bed, and certainly never during my life did I sleep so soundly. I forgot to inform the reader that during the journey to the island, and not long after our first meeting each other, there came on a shower, and to my surprise the elder of the two women pulled out of her pocket a hare-skin cap, and clapped it upon her head to protect it from the rain. I observed before that she also had on a man's frieze jacket under her cloak, a fact for which I could not account. I now give a short quotation concerning this woman, for she was a notorious character, and as I learned afterwards, remarkable for frequently changing her dress, in order to prevent herself, as much as possible, from being known as one of the most thievish shulers that ever appeared in the north of Ireland. As an author, I took a fancy for describing her, and she figures in more than one of my works. On her appearance in my sketch of 'The Lough Derg Pilgrim', she was at once recognized by the whole

95

northern public. I now quote an account of our separation:
'I did not wake the next morning till ten o'clock, when I found the sun shining full into the room. I accordingly dressed myself partially – I say partially, for I was rather surprised to find an unexpected chasm in my wardrobe; neither my hat, coat, nor waistcoat being forthcoming. But I immediately made myself easy by supposing that my kind companion had brought them down to be brushed; yet I relapsed into something more than surprise, when I saw my fellow-traveller's redoubtable jacket lying on a chair, and her hare-skin cap on the top of it. My misgivings were now anything but weak; nor was I at all improved either in my religion or philosophy when, on calling up the landlady, I heard that my two companions had set out that morning at four o'clock. I then inquired about my clothes, but all to no purpose; the poor landlady knew nothing about them, but she told me that the old one brushed them before she went away, saying that they were ready for me to put on whenever I wanted them. The landlady desired me to try if I had my purse, and I found that the kind creature had certainly spared *it*, but showed little mercy to what it contained, which was one pound in paper and a few shillings in silver; the latter alone she left me.'

Now I appeal to my readers whether this does not look very like fiction, and I daresay it will be considered as such. There is not, however, one syllable of fiction in it. I was, at the time I made this pilgrimage, one of the most easily imposed on and most credulous young fellows that ever existed. This woman was notorious throughout most of Ulster. Her name was Nell McCallum, and as I discovered afterwards, she had been one of those well-known characters who were engaged in carrying illegitimate children up to the Foundling Hospital in Dublin. Along with the peculiar accomplishments for which it seems she was remarkable, she had the reputation of being a perfect female Proteus. I heard afterwards, that at the time she sent me home shorn, she lived with a daughter of hers near Armagh. She was subsequently prosecuted for robbing a carman, and transported.

Chapter IX

Break up of the family – A trial of strength – The miller of Clogher – His death – Michael Carleton advises his brother to work – A great leap – Carleton apprenticed to a stone-cutter – Buckramback the dancing master – Mickey McRory the fiddler – Stone-cutting abandoned – Happens on *Gil Blas* – Its effect.

HAVING thus paid the due penalty of all my transgressions in a double sense, I was once more engaged in study and the enjoyment of athletic exercises. The circumstances of our family were now rapidly on the decline. My brother James became an invalid, and took to drinking horseradish tea. Indeed, for some years past, he never imagined himself well, and persisted in drinking an extraordinary variety of herbal drugs, all of his own decoction. The poor fellow was the most confirmed hypochondriac I ever met. Without assistance he was unable to manage the farm, and the consequence was that we were obliged to give it up; this we did, having surrendered the furniture of the house to the landlord. All we took out of it was one cow and that year's crop of oats; this was simply what we could justly claim after having settled with our landlord.

Here now was the family dissolved for ever. My mother, my brother and I went to reside with my sister Sarah. We did not, however, go empty-handed. We had twelve sacks of oats, which we brought to Clogher Mill, where we got it kiln-dried and ground, and upon that occasion I performed one of those athletic feats for which I was then famous, not only throughout my own, but the adjoining parishes. This will be the last feat but one which I shall be under the necessity of mentioning. Let not the reader blame me or tax me with vanity. I am recording the humble events of my early life, and I can truthfully assert that I derive more gratification from the limited fame which I enjoyed in consequence of my local celebrity for those youthful exploits than ever I did from that won by my success in literature. This I think every rational reader will understand. The name of the miller of Clogher, with whom I was acquainted since my boyhood – not a very long period at the moment I am writing of – was Frank Farrell. He was, without exception, not only the most powerful, but the most powerful-looking, man I ever saw walk upon two feet. If he had possessed courage and spirit equal to his size and strength, no man could have had any chance with him in a pugilistic contest. The largest man and the most powerful pugilist I ever saw was the English champion, Ben Caunt, whom I went expressly to see when in London during the year 1850. Compared, however, with Frank Farrell, he was a man of almost commonplace size. It was well known that Farrell was not a man of courage; the tremendous strength he possessed slept in him. He was kind, good-natured, heavy, quiet, placid, inert and sluggish; and would as soon have thought of throwing himself from the steeple of Clogher Cathedral – where, by the way, he came by his death – as of entering into a quarrel, or fighting with any man. He was, however, remarkable for one solitary exploit which no other individual in the parish could perform. The old mill of Clogher, that of which I am writing – a new one has been erected since – was an aged building, white with mealy cobwebs, and absolutely, if one were to judge from the symptoms of its decay, tottering to its fall. It was found necessary to put a large beam, fastened in some manner to the shaking side walls across it, in order to keep them in their position. With this beam Frank Farrell's solitary but as yet unrivalled feat was connected.

My brother James and I were one day in the mill while our corn, which we had taken with us from Springtown farm, was in process of being ground. Frank and about a dozen others were talking while we were attending to the sacks, which were receiving the meal as it came out of the millage. At length Frank entered into conversation with us, and began to compliment me upon my athletic exploits. My brother and I looked at each other, for we felt conscious of what was coming. There was a smile of triumph

98

on Frank's good-humoured face, as he looked at the beam in question – which I could have wished anywhere else.

'Come here,' said he. 'Do you see that beam?'

'I do,' I replied.

'Well,' he proceeded, 'I'm told that nobody has any chance with you in throwing the shoulder-stone. Do you think now that you could throw a half hundredweight over that beam?'

'No,' I replied, 'but I am told that you can; yet I can scarcely believe it.'

'Will you try it?' said he.

'Not,' I returned, 'till you set me the example. I will not believe it till I see it.'

He got the half hundredweight, stripped off his coat, stood in the proper position, and heaved the half hundredweight up to the beam. It lit on the beam, where it appeared for a few seconds uncertain whether it would fall back or tumble to the other side. It did tumble to the other side, and he seemed satisfied. I protested this was a failure, and so did everyone present. Frank was more successful at the next attempt, the half hundredweight went over without touching the beam, but had very little to spare. The feat, however, was accomplished.

'Now,' said he, 'follow my example.'

I felt my blood rise – a combative and energetic spirit surged upon me. I haven't been beaten, thought I, during either this season or the last; and if I am beaten now I can afford it. Those present felt a kind, gratifying sympathy for me, and in that spirit kindly dissuaded me from the attempt. So far as I was concerned, this only made matters worse; pointing out difficulties was never the way to deter me from them; and I at once expressed my intention of making the attempt. My brother also did everything to dissuade me, but while discussing the matter I observed that the mill was becoming filled with people, who flocked in to witness the result. When I expressed my intention to make the trial, a young man named Dickey communicated my resolution to the inhabitants of the village, not ten yards off, and they made their appearance in numbers to witness what was about to take place.

I need not disguise the fact; I was fond of that kind of fame, as who that is successful at athletic sports is not? The presence of those people gratified me, and gave me both courage and resolution – I almost think I may add strength. I stripped; I seized the half hundredweight, I swung it before me with both hands, and then letting it come down with its own impetus until it raised itself behind me, I took it on the back swing as it rose towards my shoulder, and by this piece of skill I hurled it to the beam at least fifteen or twenty pounds less than its actual weight. This was a discovery of my own, of which I had been in possession for more than a year, and it should be explained by action rather than by description. In the twinkling of an eye, the feat was accomplished – the weight went clearly over the beam without touching it, and from that moment Frank Farrell's pride in the performance of his remarkable feat was brought low. Except myself, no other man in the parish was ever able to accomplish it, although hundreds made the attempt. Old Bill Dickey, who kept the public-house in Miltown, and of whom I shall have something to say again, brought Frank Farrell, my brother and myself to his establishment, and treated us to some of as good poteen as ever was drunk. In the course of a couple of days my exploit was known to the whole parish, and added largely to my fame.

Poor Frank's end was a melancholy one, as I have stated, I think, in 'The Battle of the Factions'. In my day most millers were carpenters; Frank was no exception to this rule, and had the reputation of being an excellent artisan. In the cathedral of Clogher there is a set of bells, one, the largest, being, it is said, a ton in weight. Frank was engaged in his capacity of carpenter to adjust something in connection either with the bells or the belfry. While so engaged, he took it into his head to try whether he could lift the great bell, and made due preparation for this tremendous effort by placing a thick board across the mouth of the bell, under which he stood and actually raised it about six inches. The result was fatal to him; he had severely injured his spine, and in the course of three months the bell was rung over his coffin.

I now led a very desultory life. I had no fixed residence, no abiding shelter – no home. I passed from one relative to another, and was often asked by my wealthy neighbours to go and spend a week or a month with them. Many of them expected me to read and translate Latin or Greek for them, but this anxiety to hear the learned languages was almost uniformly confined to those who themselves could not read, and were of course totally illiterate. Such is human nature; we always value that which we don't possess more than do those who possess it. In this way I paid many a pleasant visit to friends and acquaintances throughout the parish – if those visits could be called pleasant which were paid by a homeless young man, who had not an object in life towards which he could look with the least hope.

I was now in my twenty-first year, one, I think, the greatest and most remarkable for youthful exploits. My eldest brother Michael lived in a townland named Aughenclash, not five minutes' walk from the residence of my sister Sarah, or Sally as we always called her. This eldest brother of mine and I never could, and never did, pull well together. He was perpetually abusing me for my idleness, which he attributed to me as a crime, although he knew right well – no man better – that it was the result of circumstances over which I had no control, and besides, he knew that I read the classics several hours a day. So far as I was concerned, the tongue of Timon of Athens was eulogy compared to his; there was a low, gnawing, bitter, sneering spirit in it which was never laid so long as I was in his house. I had been living with him, much to my vexation, for a couple of months.

'Why don't you go and learn a trade?' said he to me one evening after he had come in from his work in the fields. 'Look at Lanty Doain,[1] the stone-cutter, see how comfortable and wealthy he is. It wasn't spending his time on going about the country, attending wakes and fairs and dances, throwing the stone and leaping; sure I'm told you are going to leap Clogher Karry – no less. I believe you got one wet jacket there already, and that

[1] Duane?

ought to be enough for you; but I suppose you wish to get another.'

Now this requires the following explanation. The river at which the scene of my crossing the weir occurred is there called the Karry; and the reason why I thought of leaping it is easily told. About a quarter of a mile above that spot was a portion of the same river which ran through the meadows of a man called David Aikins. The reader recollects my mention of a young fellow named Edward McArdle – nephew to our parish priest of the same name. This McArdle, a small, tight, active little fellow, beautifully and symmetrically made, was one of the most celebrated leapers ever known in that part of the country until my appearance. He had leaped a celebrated leap across that portion of the river which ran through Aikins' meadows. This leap a son of Old David Aikins', named Charley, had shown me a few days before. I need scarcely say that I cleared it with the greatest ease. Charley then told me that McArdle had expressed an intention of leaping the Karry, but added that on looking at it he had given up the notion – stating as his opinion that the Karry could not be done by any man. He and I then went to the Karry and looked at it.

'He was right,' said Charley; 'no man could do that.'

I looked at it again – and again – and again. It was a dead level, there was not the difference of an inch, I think, between the height of the banks on either side. Well, I looked and paused – and calculated – went to the brink – walked back to take a view of it from the starting point of the run which I would have taken, and then said:

'Charley, I will leap it; if I fail I can only get a wet coat as I got at the weir, but the weir was no failure, and neither will this, or I am much mistaken.'

'I would not recommend you to try it,' said he. 'I don't think any man could do it. If anyone could, though, it would surely be yourself. Well,' he added, with a smile, 'if you had failed in cross-ing the weir you'd have been dashed to pieces – but if you come short here, all you can get will be a wet jacket.'

'Well, Charley,' said I, 'tell the boys of the neighbourhood that on Friday evening next I will try it at all events – and if I fail it will only be, as you say, a wet jacket.'

It was with reference to this intention that my eldest brother spoke, when he alluded with such a bitter sneer to my intention of trying to leap, for it was now very well known throughout the neighbourhood. This dialogue between Charley Aikins and me occurred upon Wednesday, and on the following day a circumstance took place which was very near settling me in obscurity for the remainder of my life. I was then living, as I said, with my eldest brother, who certainly made my life miserable. Not that the poor fellow was devoid of brotherly affection towards me – on the contrary, not one of my relations entertained higher or more sanguine hopes of my success. These hopes, however, were in his view altogether disappointed, and he saw nothing for me except a trade or to till the earth as a common labourer. Indeed, to tell the truth, I was much of the same opinion. Lanty Doain, the celebrated stone-cutter, I knew intimately, and I felt that it would be an agreeable thing to learn that trade from a man who was not only my friend, but a warm admirer. I accordingly went to his house the next day, without consulting anyone, and he agreed, but with great reluctance, that I should go to him as an apprentice. He would not have consented to this arrangement had I not assured him, that if he declined it, I would enlist before twenty-four hours. Lanty knew a little of classics, and was very proud of what he knew. On that occasion he got down a Justin and translated a portion, of which I only recollect the words because I thought I had discovered the Latin term for Lord Lieutenant for the first time – *præfectus ipsius* – the Lord Lieutenant – *propositus mediis* – over the Medes; and so on. This bit of Latin told in his favour, and placed him out of the category of common stone-cutters. I accordingly went home with a fixed but somewhat desperate resolution to learn his trade. This was the day before the leap, but I said nothing about having apprenticed myself to Lanty Doain, even to my brother. After I had left Lanty, I felt as if I had accomplished my own ruin and utterly destroyed my hopes for life. For the first time a new and indignant feeling took possession of me – a feeling that burned bitterly and hotly into my heart. I became misanthropical. I detested the world. Everything went against me and my family. The latter, among whom, of course, I was forced to include myself, were almost beggars, and nothing for me, in the shape of any opening in the future, offered itself except the hard shapeless granite – the chisel and the mallet. I could almost have pitched myself down a precipice.

At length Friday evening came, and accompanied by Charley Aikins and about a dozen others, I went to Clogher Karry, the scene of the approaching feat – or failure. Judge of my surprise, when, on our arrival there, we found about sixty or seventy persons awaiting us. The reader must perceive that the resolution I had come to with Lanty Doain the day before, and the depressing train of thought – if not absolute despair – under which I laboured, were badly qualified to raise my spirits or prepare me for the exploit I came to perform. After again looking at the leap, with anything but that enthusiastic confidence which I ought to have felt, I appeared cast down, indifferent, and in low spirits. This was observed, and spoken of in side whispers, and I heard one of them saying, 'He's hovering.' I felt at the moment that the last speaker uttered the truth. My heart was down, and never in my life did such an unaccountable sense of depression sink me. There I stood before them, a fine well-dressed young fellow, in my twenty-first year; an individual from whom great things were expected – yet what would I be in a week? A working-man, no better than one of themselves, with a paper cap on my head and a coarse apron before me. The persons assembled, seeing that there was something wrong with me and that my whole bearing evinced marks of hesitation, asked me would I try the leap. I immediately stripped off my coat and waistcoat, my shirt and stockings, and went to the spot from which I had intended to take my run. This was a little blackthorn bush, not two feet high – that blackthorn bush is there to this day. At the moment I felt in my soul that the spirit of cowardice was upon me and within me. With this impression I took my run from the little blackthorn,

towards the part of the bank from which I was to spring. I ran –
and as I approached the edge my pace became gradually slow,
and I concluded the run with a walk that would have done credit
to a philosopher. This I repeated half a dozen times under such a
sense of shame as I need not attempt to describe.

It fortunately happened that Billy Dickey, who kept the
public-house down at Miltown, was one of the spectators; in
fact, the ground we stood on was his own.

'Billy,' said I, 'I am in low spirits; run down – you won't be
ten minutes – and bring me up a naggin of whisky.'

'I will,' replied honest Billy, 'and lose no time about it.'

Billy returned in about twenty minutes with half a pint, instead
of a naggin. I took the bottle and went up to Tom Booth's,
already mentioned, whose cottage was not more than a hundred
yards above us, on the side of the elevation. I took the bottle –
Molly supplied me with a teacup, and a drinking-glass without a
bottom. Into this cup I poured a glass of the whisky, to which
I added the proper quantity of water. I drank it, and sat awhile;
after this I took another, and sat about ten minutes more. I felt
the reaction begin – it proceeded – my spirits became light and
were rising rapidly to elevation. I joined the crowd below, I ran
about, I gambolled, and in fact seemed almost frantic.

'Now,' said I, 'stand aside – I feel that I shall do it;' and in
order to leave nothing calculated to assist me undone, I tied my
pocket handkerchief about my waist. I went again to the little
blackthorn – I felt as if I could tread on air – I took my run – I
flew to it and in the twinkling of an eye was on the other side
safely and triumphantly. I then went down the river until I came
to the steps that were in the mill-race, below the weir. These I
crossed, came up along the weir, and joined the spectators.

The cheers were loud and long, and the honest compliments
paid to me most gratifying. I had achieved my greatest feat – I had
done that which has never been done from that day to this,
although many persons, confident in their own success at leaping,
came to the place with an intention of following my example, but
after looking at it they shook their heads, and very calmly

105

returned home. This I have been told many times. It is called *'Carleton's Leap'* until this day.

I suppose the reader will not regret that the account of this last exploit closes my exhibition in those youthful exercises during my residence in the north, and, I may add, for ever.

I was to have commenced my apprenticeship at the stone-cutting business on the week but one following. I thought, however, that I would pay a visit to an uncle of mine who lived in a townland called Skelgy; he was my father's brother, and an affectionate man he was. His family consisted of four sons and two daughters. The sons were not of large stature, but were regular dandies in dress. They were engaged in the linen trade, and used to produce the best specimens of linen cloth that ever went to Fintona market – for Fintona was the great linen market town of Tyrone. Their sisters were lively, handsome girls, and equally fond of dress. We had not seen each other for at least a year, and they consequently felt very glad of my visit.

At that time there was a dancing school in the townland of Kilnahushogue, quite beside them. It was attended only in the evening, a regulation which was a great convenience to the young folks in the country, who could not afford to give midday attendance. The pupils were numerous, and it fortunately happened that the school was kept in a large empty house, otherwise there would not have been half room for such a crowd of pupils. My cousins, both male and female, all attended this school, at which every one was obliged to appear in their best dress. My cousins insisted that I should accompany them every evening and take lessons. Now as to jigs, reels, and hornpipes, I could have beaten the master himself all to nothing. I described the man, his school and some of his scholars, many years ago in Gunn and Cameron's *Irish Penny Journal*,[1] but the description has appeared since in a volume of my short sketches called *Tales and Stories of the Irish*

---

[1] Gunn and Cameron's was a Scotch firm which started *The Irish Penny Journal* in 1840. They also published other periodicals, and will be referred to more specifically in the second volume of this work. The *Tales and Stories* appeared in 1845.

Peasantry – not *Traits and Stories of the Irish Peasantry*, which is a different work altogether – in fact, my greatest. As the man's character was an extraordinary one, even to notoriety, I will give it here as I wrote it upwards of thirty years ago.

'Buckramback was a dapper, tight little fellow with a rich Tipperary brogue, crossed by a lofty strain of illegitimate English which he picked up whilst abroad in the army. His habiliments sat as tight upon him as he could readily wear them, and were all of the shabby genteel class. His crimped black coat was a closely worn second-hand, and his crimped face quite as much of the second-hand as his coat. I think I see his little pumps – little white stockings – his coaxed drab breeches – his hat, smart in its cock, but brushed to a polish and standing upon three hairs, together with his tight, questionably coloured gloves – all before me. Certainly he was the jauntiest little cock living – quite a blood, too, ready to fight any man, and a great defender of the fair sex, whom he never addressed except in that high-flown, bombastic style so agreeable to most of them, called by their flatterers the complimentary, and by their friends the fulsome. He was, in fact, a public man and alive to everything. You met him at every fair, where he had only time to give you a wink as he passed, being just then engaged in a very particular affair; but he would tell you again.

'At cock-fights he was a very busy personage, and an angry better from half a crown downwards. At races he was a knowing fellow; always shook hands with the winning jockey, and then looked pompously about, that folks might see he was hand and glove with people of importance.'

Buckramback had been a drummer in the army for some time, but it appears he possessed no relish whatever for a military life, as his abandonment of it, without even the usual form of a discharge or furlough, together with a back that had become cartilaginous from frequent flogging, could abundantly testify. It was as well known that he had been a rebel in 'Ninety-Eight', as that he had been flogged so often that in the end he became insensible to the infliction. It was also said that on the last occasion of his punishment, which, if report were correct, was the twelfth time, he requested to be brought to Lord Cornwallis, before whom, it is added, he danced a hornpipe in contempt of all efforts to subdue him. Lord Cornwallis, said rumour, was on this occasion so much amused by the drollery of the exhibition and the indomitable spirit of the little fellow, that he gave him a letter of approbation, and on asking what name he was to insert, the answer, given with a heroic sense of triumph, was, 'Buckramback'. 'Buckramback' was, considering everything, a good dancing master; he taught quadrilles, waltzes, and other fashionable dances, unknown among the peasantry until his day.

Mickey McRory on this occasion was his fiddler – quite as extraordinary a man as the other, if not more so. Mickey was blind, but one of the richest humorists that ever lived; he was also the best country performer on the violin I ever heard, and possessed of the greatest variety of Irish music. 'Shane Fadg's Wedding' in *The Traits and Stories* was suggested by the wedding of my brother John, which was the largest I ever witnessed. Mickey McRory was the fiddler, and in consequence of my intimate knowledge of him, ever almost since my childhood, I rescued him from obscurity in Gunn and Cameron's admirable *Journal* where there is a very truthful and graphic account of him, under his real name, 'Mickey McRory, the Irish fiddler'. He was the best representative of his class that ever lived. About six months ago, I was much surprised by reading an account of his death in a northern newspaper. The notice was headed, 'Death of a Public Character'. It appears he had retired many years ago to a farm which was managed by his brother; and there he enjoyed the close of a long and harmless life in comfort and independence. My sketch of him made his fortune. After its appearance, he was unable to attend to one-tenth of the claims that were made upon him. He was a strictly sober man, though surrounded during his life with almost irresistible temptations. The article on his death alluded to the fact of my having selected him as the model of his class. He died aged about ninety, and, it is said, had an immense funeral.

I have already mentioned the arrangement between Lanty Doain and me, and given the reader to understand the pain and the distracted state of feeling which it cost me. I mentioned this arrangement to my uncle's family; they received it with indignation and scorn, and never ceased until they actually shamed me out of it. I consequently broke my engagement with honest Lanty, a fact which gratified him, as his consent had been only gained by my threatening otherwise to enlist.

When I left my uncle's, I knew not where to go. My eldest brother happened to meet Lanty Doain at mass, who informed him of my apprenticeship. I was to live and board with Lanty and to remove to his place on the following Monday, or in other words, the very next day. The very next day came – week after week came – but the 'prentice lad did not make his appearance. The 'prentice lad, in fact, was practising quadrilles and waltzes under little 'Buckramback', who felt very proud of him as a pupil.

When the visit to my uncle's was concluded, I returned very reluctantly to my brother's, conscious of the reception I was to meet. It was brief, but decisive. He kindly suggested to me to open a dancing school and earn money – he saw nothing else for me – but as to making his house a home whenever it suited my own convenience, he thanked God there was an end to that – a meal of his food I should never eat, nor ever sleep a night under his roof.

I was prepared for this, and I walked about for some time with a hope of being able to think upon something – some plan or project with which I could associate even the slightest hope. At length I went down to my brother-in-law, Roger Hacket's, a walk of only four or five minutes. He was at this time building a new house, and was indeed altogether in good circumstances. I found no one at home but my sister – and I knew the full extent of her affection for me – of that brother of whom she was so proud.

'Sally,' said I, 'I know not what to do – nor where to go. I have now no home – no friend – I am a burthen upon everyone.'

I was overcome by the contemplation of my situation, and

for a long time I wept bitterly. She also was deeply affected, as was evident by the tears she shed over the melancholy circumstances of the case, but she had little in her power to offer by way of consolation. Still, she attempted to soothe me as well as she could. With her I remained about a month, but during that time I could perceive without difficulty that her husband felt my residence in his house a grievance. This was the man to whom I had induced my sister to give the preference as a suitor for her affections, and, of course, he owed to me his success in obtaining her as his wife, a fact with which the ungrateful scoundrel was well acquainted.

Upon what incidents apparently of little moment do some of the most important events of our lives turn! It was while residing here that I accidentally got a perusal of a work which filled me with a charm it would be hopeless to do justice to by description. The work I allude to was *Gil Blas*. I did not then even know that it was fiction, but took it for granted that all the adventures were true. The effect it had on me in my unsettled and uncertain position in life – to fill my imagination with such a romantic love of adventure, as made me wish myself a thousand times the hero of some that might resemble those. I got the perusal of the book from a pedlar, who carried books about for sale, with a variety of other goods. I had finished it only a few days before the occurrence of the event which I am now about to relate.

Chapter X

Leaves his family at last – Father McArdle – Wildgoose Lodge – Fate of Paddy Devaun – The wayside gibbets – Journeyings in Louth – Becomes a private tutor – Sir Harcourt Lees' dogs – Carleton makes verse – Gaynor and Talbot the pipers – The dance.

I HAD been residing with my brother-in-law for about a month, when I strolled out one day to the house he had built. The thatcher was on the roof, for the house was nearly finished, and when I joined honest Roger, we had a few words of conversation upon some trifle or other, when he said – adopting the style of language of my own brother:

'Do you not feel ashamed to lead the idle life you do? Do you not feel ashamed to be a burthen in this manner upon your friends? You've now come to the age of a full-grown man, and how can you expect to lead such an idle life at the expense of others; and why don't you take a spade and work? Many a better young fellow than you has a spade in his hand.'

Now I knew that Roger had a good deal of money at this time; I knew, too, that he always carried notes about him, for such was his habit; he would not, in fact trust them out of his own pocket.

The indignation I felt was so deep, and, I may add, so just, that I could scarcely prevent myself from trampling the ungrateful rascal under my feet – and I often regretted since that I had not done it. I restrained myself, however, and simply said:

'Roger, will you give me a pound, and I will be no longer a burthen upon *you* or anyone else in *this* parish. Give me a pound.'

'No,' he replied, 'nor a shilling – nor a penny.'

At this moment I had not a coin in my pocket – but I looked at him and said, 'You may hear from me yet.'

From that spot I started with a bitter and indignant heart, without one moment's preparation, friendless, moneyless and alone – but not without hope, for I had read *Gil Blas*. The hour of my departure was about eleven o'clock, and I never slackened my pace till I had gone a distance of more than twenty-five miles – some miles, indeed, beyond the town of Castleblayney. The purport of that day's journey, however, was not absolutely a vague one. On the road, somewhere near Castleblayney, a widow from the townland next to my sister's, called Lisbarry, kept, I had heard, a carman's inn for many years. I had also been told that there was a distant relationship between our family and hers. I knew, besides, that a niece of hers, with whom I was well acquainted, had been for a couple of years residing with her, and I resolved to call and make myself known to her aunt through this young woman. I did so – and nothing could be more affectionate or hospitable than their reception. Every attention was paid to me, and the kindest inquiries were made after all my relations and her own. I communicated all the information I could on these subjects, and the night passed very agreeably until the hour of rest arrived.

'Now,' said she to me, 'you don't know the honour I am about to do you – you are not to sleep in this house tonight, in the first place.'

I thought that was rather a strange way of doing me honour.

'Where then am I to sleep?' I asked.

'Quite at hand,' she replied. 'Did you not observe the pretty building in what appears to be our garden – indeed, what was our garden?'

I said I had observed it, and felt rather surprised at what it could be.

'Well,' said she, 'that's Lord Blayney's shooting lodge, and you'll have the honour of sleeping in his bed this night,' and so I had, and right soundly I slept in it.

The next morning, when breakfast was over, she asked me after a short pause where I was going; I replied 'that I did not know.'

'You don't know!' she exclaimed. 'My good young man, what do you mean?'

'Why,' replied I, 'that I am going upon the world.'

'Upon the world!' she exclaimed again. 'But why leave your family?'

'I have no family,' I replied.

'Oh, don't say that,' she replied, 'you have brothers and sisters, who will keep you until something turns up. Indeed, my poor boy, you must go back to them.'

'Nothing on the face of God's earth will induce me to go back to them. I have no right to expect that they should support an idler like me – besides, if I did, they would not do it. No, let what may happen, I won't go back. I'll try what the world's made of.'

'The world! – and how can you meet a strange world that knows nothing about you? Did they give you any money when you were leaving them?'

'No,' I replied: 'I asked my brother-in-law and he refused.'

'And have you no money?'

'Not a penny.'

'God be about us!' she exclaimed; 'I don't understand this – but at all events I can't let you out of my hands with empty pockets.'

She proceeded at once to a mahogany chest of drawers, which she opened, and taking out twenty-four tenpenny bits – as they were called – amounting to one pound, she bade me put them in one of my pockets. I obeyed her readily.

I now considered my journey of the day before as one of favourable omen, indicative of my future success in life; and with a light heart I resumed my travels. The reader knows something of my old schoolfellow, Edward McArdle. He was now the priest of the parish of Killaney, in the county of Louth, and lodged in a farmer's house at a distance of about three miles from the town of Carrickmacross, and about two or one and a half from the celebrated Wildgoose Lodge, the scene of the dreadful tragedy which had occurred the preceding year. Of this tragedy I had never heard a syllable, although the account of it in the papers must have gone over all the dominions of George the Third – in whose reign it took place – if not over Europe itself. This ignorance of mine is not at all surprising, when I inform the reader that during my whole life, until the moment of my arrival at McArdle's lodgings, I had never *seen* but three newspapers in my native parish, nor ever as much as had one of them in my hand. The priest received me kindly – but as he was out at 'station' every day in the week except Saturday, I boarded with the family.

I had now nothing to do; the poor priest had not a book in his possession, with the exception of the missal – so that I had nothing even to read; I accordingly strolled out every day – it was autumn and the weather glorious – and amused myself by traversing the country, which was pretty well intersected by excellent roads. One day I went on, guided by the turnings of the way, until I reached a cross-road in a small village, where I perceived a number of soldiers, standing and chatting to each other, and passing their time as best they could. I looked on before me when I had reached this queer little place, and perceived something like a tar sack dangling from a high beam of wood, or rather from the arm which projected from it. There was a slight but agreeable breeze, the sack kept gently swinging backward and forward in obedience to the wind, and I could perceive long ropes of slime shining in the light, and dangling from the bottom.

I was very much astonished, and could form no conjecture as to the nature of this spectacle; so, with a view of ascertaining what it was, I applied to the soldiers who were near me.

'Pray,' said I, 'what is the nature or meaning of that object which I see up the road there?'

'Why,' said one of them, the sergeant, 'is it possible you don't know?'

'I certainly do not,' I replied, 'nor can I guess what it means.'

'Well, sir,' said he, 'that object is a gibbet – and what you see swinging from it in the pitched sack is the body of a murderer named Devaun; Paddy Devaun swings there – and it's just where he ought to swing.'

He then gave me for the first time a brief outline of the inhuman and hellish tragedy of Wildgoose Lodge. The effect upon me was the most painful I ever felt from any narrative. It clung to me until I went to bed that night – it clung to me through my sleep with such vivid horror that sleep was anything but a relief to me. When Mr McArdle came home that evening, he gave me, in reply to my inquiry an account of the whole tragedy, and pointed out Wildgoose Lodge, which was visible from the garden of the house in which he lodged. Little either he or I dreamt at that period that I should, at no very distant day, make that frightful tragedy the subject of one of the most powerful descriptions that ever came from my pen.[1] I was so completely absorbed by the interest it excited, that I went to the very low elevation on which the house stood, and observed the scenery about it. The house had been rebuilt and was inhabited by a decent and very civil family, named Cassidy, if my memory does not fail me. As those who may read this autobiography may not have read my tale of 'Wildgoose Lodge', if tale it can be called, I will give them a short sketch of the facts with which I was made perfectly acquainted during my residence in the parish of Killaney, where the awful tragedy was enacted. Like many another black national crime, this one resulted from Ribbonism. The members of that accursed Ribbon Society, instead of confining themselves to those objects for which it seems to have been originally designed – a union of Irishmen against their Protestant enemies, and the penal enactments which oppressed them at the time – departed from their original object, and employed its murderous machinery not against its open and common enemy, but in the following up of private and personal feuds, and enmities amongst themselves. The name of the family who lived in Wildgoose Lodge before the midnight burning was Lynch. They were a very moral and pious family, peaceful and industrious. Ribbonism was prevalent at that time, but they deliberately and firmly kept themselves aloof from it. They were frequently solicited to join, but declined. At length, they received a nocturnal visit; their door was smashed in, and the house was filled with ruffians, who beat and maltreated

---

[1] The episode of 'Wildgoose Lodge' in the *Traits and Stories* is certainly one of the most terrible narratives ever penned by Carleton.

115

them with such brutality, that one of them recovered from the injuries he had received with great difficulty.

At length, when the Lynches recovered, they took proceedings against the leaders in this inhuman act of violence, whom they knew perfectly well. They prosecuted these men at the Dundalk Assizes, and had two of them transported. Revenge among the Ribbonmen was now the predominant feeling. I have said in several parts of my illustrations of Irish life, that the hedge schoolmasters were almost always what is called 'article bearers' – in other words, that each of them was the master of a Ribbon Lodge. In this case it was so; the man named Devaun, who projected and conducted this slaughter, was the parish schoolmaster, and the parish clerk, who taught his school in the very chapel itself. He was the man who served mass every Sunday in the year, and was the last individual on whom suspicion could be supposed to rest.

While I resided in the county of Louth, so near the scene of the outrage, I had an opportunity of learning, as every man had, that the incidents connected with it were as well known to the public as if that public had been present at them. There were many assembled upon that fatal night who knew not the object of the meeting until they arrived at the very spot. Afterwards, when the trials took place, and the Government prosecutions had closed, and when there was no apprehension of legal proceedings against any others than those who had been convicted, several whom Devaun had summoned without disclosing to them the frightful object in view, actually admitted that they had been present, and had no hesitation in giving full details of the deeds which were done. To this fact, added to another which I will mention, I owe the accuracy with which I have detailed the proceedings. These were, however, known through the public papers which reported the trial. A copy of these papers I got afterwards from the Rev. Dr Stuart, rector of Lough Swilly.

The meeting on that woeful night was summoned by Devaun, who made the chapel – the House of God – the scene in which the blind and wretched dupes were sworn to execute, without

116

hesitation or inquiry, that which *at a proper time* should be made known to them. Whisky had been subscribed for, and the greater number of them had been primed with it. On the very altar of God, every preparation for the projected crime was made; on the very altar of God, the ignorant dupes were sworn to perpetrate what, with the exception of those who were in the secret, they knew nothing of.

I said that while I resided with the Rev. Edward McArdle I amused myself by walking about during the day – sometimes a distance of ten, twelve, or sixteen miles from McArdle's lodgings. On these occasions, I found that the greater part of the county of Louth was studded with gibbets. Sometimes two bodies, or rather two tar sacks, might be seen hanging after the manner of Devaun. On more than one occasion I have seen four. The gibbets were set up near the residences of those who had been convicted of the crime. During that autumn, fruit in the county of Louth was avoided, as something which could not be eaten. This I knew to be a fact, because I was an eye-witness of it. There were in all twenty-four dead bodies swinging from gibbets in different directions throughout the county of Louth. The autumn was an unusually hot one; the flesh of the suspended felons became putrid, and fell down in decomposed masses to the bottom of the sacks; the pitch which covered the sacks was melted by the strong heat of the sun, and the morbid mass which fell to the bottom of the sacks oozed out, and fell, as I have stated in Devaun's case, in slimy ropes, at the sight of which I was told, many women fainted. Every sack was literally covered with flies, which having enjoyed their feast, passed away in millions upon millions throughout the country. Devaun, in accordance with the general principle which prevailed in this distribution of justice, the object of which was to make the consequences of the crime fall with a deeper impression on the public, as a warning and example to others – Devaun, we say, was gibbeted within a couple of hundred yards of his own mother's door; and such was the view she took of the fate which fell upon her son, that on going out of her own door, which commanded a view of the gibbet, she uniformly exclaimed, 'God be merciful to the soul of my poor marthyr.' It was quite clear that the affection of the mother prevented her from assenting to the belief that her son could be guilty of such a crime.

Whilst on this visit to my friend McArdle, I took journeys of considerable length throughout the county of Louth. It is not a county remarkable for beauty of scenery – although there are some striking exceptions to this observation. During these explorations of the country, the reader will be amused to hear that I was also in quest of employment. For instance, on passing the house of a gentleman, I made it a point to inquire his name, whether he was married or not, and if married, what family he had; were his children young or old, boys or girls; were the boys at school, or had they a private tutor, to conduct their education at home. I was perpetually thinking of *Gil Blas*, but hitherto I met with no adventure likely to be beneficial to my hopes or prospects. I got into an anxious mood, and felt deeply dejected because I knew that I could not abuse the hospitality of my friend, or reside much longer with him.

One day I went out as usual to traverse the county. I had thoughts of going towards Corcreagh, the village where Paddy Devaun's body was hanging. I had, however, been there several times before, and now resolved to take some other course. I accordingly followed a road which led right on before me – a road that was new to me – and I had proceeded about half a mile, when I came to a field of wheat, where there were half a dozen men reaping. I looked about me, and noticed a respectable-looking house, on the other side of a flow bog, about a quarter of a mile distant. The reapers were at the very edge of the road, with nothing between us but a low, dry, grassy ditch, over which I stepped, and entered into conversation with them.

'Who lives,' I asked, 'in that house with the back of it towards us?'

'Mr Pierce Murphy,' replied a fine young fellow.

'What family has he?' I inquired

'Sir,' said the other, 'he has a small family of children, but his wife is very anxious about their schooling. They had a tutoress teaching them, but it seems she and the mistress couldn't agree, so she left them, and they now want someone to teach the young folk. If you're a tutor, sir, they'd be likely to engage you. I think you had better try.'

He pointed out a patch that went through the flow bog, and I accordingly directed my steps to Lowtown, the residence of Mr Pierce Murphy. On reaching the house and knocking, I was told that the master was in Dundalk market, and that the mistress was out in the field with the men who were reaping. I asked to be shown to the field, and a servant-maid brought me to the gate which led into it, where she left me. On presenting myself, I told Mrs Murphy that I had just learned she wanted a tutor for her children. She said she did, and asked me what education had I received – I told her I had received a classical education. Had I ever discharged the duties of private tutor before? No, I never had. Was I a native of that part of the country? No, I was from Clogher, in the county Tyrone. Had I testimonials? No, I had no testimonials. Under these circumstances it was unnecessary to say more about it; she could not think of engaging a stranger without testimonials. Where did I reside? I told her I was on a visit to Mr McArdle, the parish priest, whose guest I then was. She brightened at once and told me she would write to Mr McArdle, who of course would recommend me, as I was his friend. I was to call the next day but one, and she would give me an answer.

We then separated upon very good terms, and after traversing the country for miles, I returned home, anxious to communicate the good tidings to my old schoolfellow. In short, I removed to Lowtown on the Saturday evening following, and on the next Monday morning sat down in a private room, set apart for the purpose, to instruct the children of Mr Pierce Murphy. On seeing my charge assembled, I felt anything but an accession to my importance. My pupils, with one exception, were female children, the eldest not eleven – her sister about nine, and a brother about seven. A very strong disposition to laugh seized me, and were it not for the generous liberality of my salary, which was twelve guineas a year, I should scarcely have known how to act.

My relative Keenan was now the master of a large school at Dundalk, and I thought it better to remain where I was for a while, until I should consider what was best to be done – for to continue there for any length of time was out of the question. Murphy's house, though a two-storey one, was inconveniently small. It consisted of a small parlour, which also discharged the duty of a drawing-room, and behind it was a small closet, containing a bed only for a single man. In this bed Murphy slept; his wife, having the charge of the younger children, lay near them upstairs. Mrs Murphy was rather a fine woman, with a face which would have been a good one, were it not for the ludicrous expression of lofty and pompous consequence which was stamped upon it. She was, however, of a respectable, though I believe reduced family, and was educated in a nunnery in Drogheda. Her face when in a state of anger was anything but prepossessing. Still she was what they call 'a fine animal'. As for her worthy husband Pierce, though not exactly a vulgar man in his speech – that is to say, he had no 'brogue' – yet was he the most overbearing and most brutally tempered man I ever met – in fact, a low-minded, ignorant ruffian. From morning till night his voice was never heard about the place or in the fields, except in a loud tone of abuse, directed to someone or other, and occasioned by nobody knew what or whom. There was a thatched house attached to the slated one, and a long passage passed from the parlour to the kitchen, which was large, and, if I may use the expression, wealthy. There were three female servants, independently of a young lady, a niece of Mrs Murphy's, who lived with her and superintended the washing. 'God help her!' I often ejaculated – for the business she went through was nothing short of slavery – and most inhuman slavery.

Murphy was a very large farmer – the yard attached to his house was one of the largest I ever saw connected with any farmer's establishment; his hog yard, too, was upon a tremendous scale; the number and size of his stock gave indications of immense wealth. In fact, it was his farm and stock which I described

120

as belonging to Bodagh Buie O'Brien in 'The Miser'; but beyond this, there is no resemblance between either the men or their residences. Murphy was a ruddy-faced, stout man, dressed in a loose black coat; but still in such trim, with his soiled shoes and crumpled hat, that nobody could ever mistake the hard-working farmer, any more than from his loud, impetuous voice, they could the vulgar, overbearing ruffian. He was detested by the poor and labouring classes of the surrounding neighbourhood – but as he gave much employment, they took care not to exhibit this sentiment in their conduct. I led a melancholy life here, without any society, without a single book to read – in fact, without any earthly object on which I could fix my attention. I did not sleep in the dwelling-house, but in a small hut or room in a long line of similar ones, containing but one bed and one chair, adjoining the kitchen, and opening into the yard. There was no fire or fireplace, and all I can say is that the bed was a good one. The number of barn-door fowl and poultry about the yard surpassed anything I ever witnessed. No day ever passed, so long as I was there, that we had not a goose, turkey, pair of ducks, or a couple of fat fowl for dinner.

Murphy became almost insane if any trespass was committed upon his property. He seemed like a madman during these paroxysms. If a strange dog, for instance, came into his farmyard, led there by instinct peculiar on certain occasions to those animals, he would deliberately take down his gun and shoot him on the spot, even when he knew him to belong to some neighbour. This made him exceedingly unpopular, as it was but natural it should.

I will now mention an anecdote in connection with this unfeeling habit of shooting his neighbours' dogs, which I feel certain will not be disagreeable to the reader. One of his next neighbours was the late well-known Sir Harcourt Lees,[1] who was the Protestant

[1] The Rev. Sir Harcourt Lees was one of the most notable opponents of 'Popery' in Ireland during the early years of the century. He published many lucubrations on the subject, and was the cause of a host of polemical writings. The student of Macaulay may remember his allusions to him.

rector of the parish, and lived in a very fine rectory house, together with the glebe lands attached to it, known as Essexford. Sir Harcourt was one of the greatest sportsmen of the day, and kept a pack of hounds, with whom I have often seen him. He also kept pointers, setters, spaniels, retrievers, and every other variety of sporting dog which a wealthy man, devoted to the sports of the field, might be supposed to keep. One rather dim moonlight night, about half an hour after dark, there came into Murphy's farmyard a beautiful setter belonging to Sir Harcourt Lees; there happened to be there one of his own dogs, a very fine pointer, also. Murphy had two or three fowling-pieces, and always kept one of them charged for safety of the house and premises; it was discharged and recharged every night. I was standing in the yard, at the door of my own comfortable dormitory, when Pierce came out, and having discovered that the dog was Sir Harcourt's, ran into the house and bringing out the gun, stood at a distance of about twenty yards and fired. One of the poor animals fell, and Murphy addressing me, said:

'Go and bring over that dog. I will have him buried.'

'I will do no such thing,' I replied; 'I shall have nothing to do with your dogs or any man's dogs.'

'Won't you?' said he; 'well, never mind – I won't forget this.'

'I don't care whether you do or not,' I replied.

'Here, Toal Harte,' he shouted to one of his servantmen, 'come here.'

'What is it, sir?' inquired Toal.

'Go over there,' said he, 'and bring me that setter of Sir Harcourt Lees'. You and Tom Reynolds must bury him.'

Honest Toal – and an honest fellow he was – went across the yard, and returned bearing the offender between his two hands. Murphy looked closely at him, and starting with an oath, exclaimed:

'Why G—d— your soul, you scoundrel, this is not Sir Harcourt's dog – but my own.'

'And G—d— your own soul,' replied Toal, with spirit, 'whose

122

fault was that? And why do you swear at me for your own mistake?'

'Go and bury her,' said his master, recharging his gun. 'Go and bury her.'

'I'll be d—d if I do,' replied Toal – who was probably one of the most powerful young men in the whole county of Louth, and a terrific opponent either with fist or cudgel – 'It wasn't to bury your dogs I hired with you – and you ought to be ashamed of yourself for attempting to shoot the dog of any respectable gentleman – especially as you know you were fined for it once before.'

Murphy, having recharged his gun, went over with a stealthy step, with a hope of getting another shot at Sir Harcourt's setter, but returned disappointed – the dog had disappeared.

'Now,' said Toal to me, after Murphy had gone in, 'by all that's beautiful, I'm as glad of this as a pound note in my pocket. You don't know how this overbearing scoundrel makes himself offensive to the respectable gentlemen of the neighbourhood. Neither sick nor poor likes a bone in his body, and it is because he knows this that he strives to offend them in every way he can.'

As winter came in, I found the long evenings hang very heavily on my hands. I accordingly went up pretty frequently to the cross-roads of Corcreagh, where there was a respectable public-house or tavern kept by a bachelor named Peter Byrne and his three brothers. They were wealthy and respectable, and very well educated. Peter himself had a really great natural talent for painting. Some of his water-colour productions were astonishing. He was altogether a very intellectual man, had read much and possessed a surprising memory. Many a conversation we had together, and he was perhaps the first man who ever made a guess at my future fame. I had amused myself by writing poetry during my leisure hours while at Murphy's, and I ventured to show him from time to time specimens of it which surprised him beyond belief.

Here I met a very rare character, who usually spent a month in this hospitable establishment. He was a blind piper, whose name was Gaynor, and his pipes, to look at them, did not appear to be worth half a crown – they were so small and contemptible-looking. When he began to play, however, every sound ceased, every tongue was hushed, every ear open, and every spirit rapt and borne away by the incredible and unparalleled charm of his melody. He reminds me of what I have since read of Carolan; his habits were not at all those of a common piper. He was perfectly conscious of his own genius, and would under no condition play for a common dance. He went about with his pipes, as Carolan did with his harp, not to perform for the vulgar sports of the common people, but for the respectable classes, from the lower gentry down to the wealthy gentleman farmer, with whom he resided a week, a fortnight, or perhaps a month, and so sincerely was he respected and so highly was his music appreciated, that a visit from him was considered an honour.

Many a long year afterwards, I gave him and another piper named Talbot a place in Gunn and Cameron's *Journal*.[1] Talbot was a prodigy, not merely as a performer, but as a mechanic. He, too, was blind, but no gentleman dressed better. He played upon what were called 'the grand pipes', and such was his mechanical skill that he made his own pipes; these for elegance and gorgeousness of ornamentation surpassed anything of the kind on which the eye could rest. He was also an organ-tuner, and made an exquisite harp, for which he got a large price. He had also the honour of performing before royalty.

Murphy's children were amiable little creatures, and by no means deficient in intellect. Their mother's pride, however, was strongly offensive to any young fellow of feeling. Although educated, as she said she was, in a nunnery, she was as deficient in all the results of education as any woman I had ever met.[2] She could talk upon no subject but the nunnery, the everlasting nunnery, and all the anecdotes connected with it and its internal

[1] This sketch is reprinted in *Tales and Stories*, 1845.

[2] Usually, Carleton's treatment of women is very chivalrous. It is one of the best features of his works. The portrait of Mrs Murphy bears some resemblance to Mrs Burke in *The Emigrants of Ahadarra*.

machinery. To anyone of mind or intellect, her conversation, apeing the polish of a high-born lady, was an insufferable exhibition. I dreaded to meet her; the more so as she looked upon it as a high gratification to make me the recipient of her egregious vanity. In consequence of this, I spent most of my evenings out, amusing myself as best I could. Murphy was a sober man. He took one tumbler of punch after dinner every day; but although I sat at the same table with him, from the first day I entered his house until that on which I left it, he never once asked me to join him in his festivities.

He had a great many cottages upon his property, in which those who worked on his immense farm resided. In one of these cottages lived a man named Cassidy, a labourer. His brother being a professional piper, was engaged at almost all the dances in that and the neighbouring parishes. He played very well, had the use of his sight, and was a droll but civil fellow. It was Toal Harte who mentioned him, and as he knew that time during these winter evenings was rather a burden to me, he asked me to go over and hear Cassidy play whenever he happened to be at home. It was not every evening, he said, that he was to be found at home, but whenever he was, the youngsters of the neighbourhood flocked to the house, where they had a dance. Lonely as I was, this was a relief to me. I accordingly went there, accompanied by Toal, and the humble little family felt highly honoured by my presence. I know not how it happened, but a very favourable and popular character of me went abroad. It was said that I was of a high old family, that my predecessors had been very great people, and that neither Pierce Murphy nor his proud piece of a wife were fit to wipe my shoes, that there was no end to my learning – it was very well known that I knew the seven languages – and that a Protestant lady, with a great estate, had fallen in love with me, and offered to marry me if I would only change my religion and take up hers, which I refused to do. Such is the Celtic imagination.

I was very glad to go to hear the bagpipes along with honest Toal Harte. Several evenings I went and sat looking at the young folks dancing, with a good deal of dignified gravity, that is to say, the gravity of a young gentleman whose high blood and descent had raised him far above the amusement of the lower class. In the meantime, notwithstanding all this dignified dissimulation, I was dying for an opportunity of showing them what I could do under the influence of the pipes, and for this reason: I knew that if there was any one exercise more than another for which in my native parish I was celebrated, it was that of dancing. In fact my friend, the late Dr Petrie, who was appointed editor of a work upon the social antiquities of Ireland, engaged me to describe the incredible variety of dances peculiar to the country. I gave him a history of them, but the work failed for want of funds.[1] In real jig or horn-pipe I was unapproachable. At length, conscious as I was of my powers, and urged forward by an unequivocal impulse of vanity, I could restrain myself no longer. I arose, looked around me, and asked one of the handsomest girls present to dance with me. She accepted the invitation as an honour, and as we stood up, I, in accordance with the usual form, asked her what tune she preferred, to which the accustomed reply was:

'Sir, your will is my pleasure.'

I then asked the piper to play up 'Jig Polthogue', one of the liveliest and most popular of Irish jigs. Need I say that they were thunderstruck – 'the young gentleman,' 'master of the seven languages!' 'well – well – isn't he a wondher?' I heard whispered quite distinctly. I was determined, however, not to stop there. I had danced my jig – I was now resolved to dance my reel – and I accordingly took out the same proud and blushing girl, and after the accustomed forms we danced 'Miss McLeod's Reel'. More wonder – more amazement – and what I felt most agreeable of all, more admiration – of the young gentleman who was master of the seven languages. Now, I thought to myself, I will give them a surprise for which they are scarcely prepared – I will dance a hornpipe in a style which they have seldom seen. I accordingly expressed my intention of doing so. Everyone knows it is a *single*

---

[1] This must refer to Petrie's work on *Ancient Irish Music*, of which one volume and a portion of a second were published by the Society for the Publication of the Ancient Melodies of Ireland.

dance, in other words, it is danced without a partner. After having stated my intention, the piper asked me:

'What will I play, sir?'

'The College Hornpipe,' I replied, and I accordingly set to work; and I may observe here, that when a mere youth, I was in the habit of practising hornpipes in our own barn, and that during the course of this practice I invented several hornpipe steps which I never saw surpassed, and which of course were peculiar to myself.

These three performances were crowned by what followed. I had about me in silver the price of a quart of whisky, and as I knew from Toal Harte that there was a small shebeen house not a quarter of a mile off I sent for a bottle, and the night ended very agreeably. As a mark of respect to me, upwards of a dozen of the young men present accompanied Toal Harte and me home, although the distance was not more than a quarter of a mile.

Chapter XI

The *Edinburgh Review* on Carleton – Throws up tutorship – A ride in a hearse – Dundalk – Drogheda – A shirt as security – Unexpected wealth – Ardee – The mathematics.

THE reader sees – and must have long seen – that there never was any man of letters who had an opportunity of knowing and describing the manners of the Irish people so thoroughly as I had. I was one of themselves, and mingled in all those sports and pastimes in which their characters are most clearly developed. Talking simply of the peasantry, there is scarcely a phase of their life with which I was not intimate. That, however, is not so much in itself, because many have had the same advantages, but not only a cultivated intellect, but strong imagination, and extraordinary powers of what I may term *unconscious* observation, existed in my case. I take no pride from these, because they were the gifts of God. My memory, too, although generally good, was then in its greatest power; it was always a memory of association. For instance, in writing a description of Irish manners, or of anything else connected with my own past experience, if I were able to remember any one particular fact or place, everything connected with it or calculated to place it distinctly before me, rushed from a thousand sources upon my memory. With the natural habits of my life, arising as they did from my position, accompanied as they were by the gifts which God had bestowed upon me, is it surprising that I have painted the Irish people with such truthfulness? In my early life I was unconsciously learning the important lesson which experience with all its various advantages taught me. I could no more forget it than I could forget my own name. The *Edinburgh Review* felt and expressed this so far back as October 1852. In that number, it utters the following verdict, and coming as it does from one of the severest and most fastidious critical journals in Europe, as well as the most able, I think I am justified, without being charged with unbecoming vanity, in feeling proud of such a verdict:

'It is amongst the peasantry that Mr Carleton is truly at home. He tries other characters – rarely, however – and not unsuccessfully; but the Irish peasant is his strong point; here he is unrivalled, and writes like one who had nothing to look out for, to collect by study – to select – to mould – who merely utters what comes spontaneously into his thoughts, from which the language and the sentiments flow as easily and naturally as articulate sounds from the human lips, or music from the skylark. Those who have in early life dwelt among the peasantry, and since forgotten that period in other and busier scenes of existence, meet again in the pages of Carleton the living personages of long past days, like friends returned from a distant land after an absence of many years.

'The primary and essential value of Mr Carleton's works upon Irish peasant life and character,' it proceeds, 'unquestionably consists in this – that they are true, and *so* true to nature; but it is enhanced by a circumstance recently recorded and lamented by Lord Cockburn in reference to Scotland. The living originals are disappearing; some of them have already disappeared. In Ireland, since our author's youth, changes rapid and deep have taken place, which, according to diversity of prejudice, and the other causes that generate diversity of opinion, will be referred to different sources, and brought to illustrate different political and social theories. It is in his pages, and in his alone, that future generations must look for the truest and fullest pictures of those who will ere long have passed away from that troubled land – from the records of history, and from the memory of man for ever. *That field,*' adds the *Edinburgh Review*, alluding to Irish literature, '*in which he stands without an equal among the living or the dead.*'[1]

I have already said that I did not feel comfortable in Murphy's

[1] Dr P. A. Murray, the Maynooth professor already referred to, was the author of the article in the *Edinburgh Review* quoted here.

house. I had nothing that could enable me to fill up my time with the exception of some attempts at poetry. In writing poetry, however, the mind must be more or less at ease. I was young, and my mind – but above all my imagination – was active. In fact, the adventures of Gil Blas were seldom out of my head. It is true I looked upon the incident to which I owed my present situation as something of an adventure, but then it was an adventure so contemptible and beggarly in its character and results, that it rather disgusted me than otherwise. Still, I thought the world was wide, and had room enough for higher and better chances, and I came to the conclusion that it was not by leading the life I was so unprofitably passing, that I could have any opportunity of affording myself the advantages of such chances.

I received my first quarter's salary (three guineas) and went without loss of time to the town of Carrickmacross, where I expended the money in the purchase of some additions to my wardrobe. I came home with only three or four tenpenny bits in my pocket, and sat down to the sickening task which daily devolved upon me. On the evening of my return from making my purchases, I went up to Corcreagh, to pass away an hour or two as best I might. I there met a man named Conway, a gauger whom, as an intimate friend of Keenan's, I had met and known at Glasslough. He was stationed there, and a very scheming vagabond he was. It was said he never paid anyone; as a barefaced sponge, I never saw him equalled. This gauger – Peter Byrne – a suspended priest named Finnigan (who had been curate in my native parish for years, and who was besides a native of the neighbouring town of Carrickmacross) – the sergeant of the military detachment then stationed at Corcreagh, named Pierce Butler, and myself were taking refreshments – I at the solicitation of Byrne, the proprietor of the house. The county of Louth was at that time under martial law, and the unfortunate priest, whose suspension had been caused by an over-zealous devotion to the glass, was at that moment in custody for being out at illegal hours. He was made a prisoner the night before, having been found about two o'clock riding he knew not whither, and was brought to Corcreagh. Peter Byrne, in order to prevent him from being sent to the guardhouse like a common offender, asked Mr Butler, the sergeant, to allow him the privilege of stopping in his house, which was granted. The matter, however, did not end here. I became the poor inoffensive priest's advocate with Butler, who was a good Catholic, and not at all disposed to severity, especially towards a priest of his own religion. Father Finnigan, therefore, slept in Carrickmacross that night a free man.

When the reckoning came to be settled in the course of the evening, Conway, the worthy gauger, said:

'My dear Mr Carleton, will you have the goodness to settle my share of the reckoning until I see you tomorrow? – I haven't a cross in my possession at this moment.'

I complied at once, because I did not know the man, and went home penniless to Pierce Murphy's. As I was at the tavern door about to start, Byrne whispered to me:

'Why the devil did you pay that schemer's reckoning? – you may go whistle for it now.'

All I can say here is, that I was naturally generous, not at all inclined to suspicion, and had little experience at the time. I was now sick of Murphy and his place, indeed so much so, that I resolved to leave at once. As I had gone nearly a month into a new quarter, I asked him to pay me the trifle that was coming to me.

'What,' he replied, 'you are not ashamed to break your engagement, then?'

'I am ashamed to hold such a situation,' said I. 'I am only wasting my time with you, Mr Murphy. I must consult my own interests, and look for something suitable to the education I have received. I'll thank you to pay me the trifle that is due to me.'

'Not a penny,' he replied, 'to any dishonest scoundrel who breaks his engagement – unless the amount of it might assist him to the gallows.'

'Do you call me a dishonest scoundrel?' I asked.

'I do,' said he; 'you're breaking your engagement.'

There was a little green plot that led to the hall door, and was separated from the farmyard by a wall: on this green plot were we standing, within about three yards of the door, when, in the twinkling of an eye, there was only one individual there in an erect attitude. After Murphy's last words I instantly knocked him down and, turning my steps towards Corcreagh, called upon my kind friend Byrne. He and two of his brothers had gone to Dundalk market, but I was resolved to remain there until he should return. I was not much acquainted with the young man whom I found at home. The truth is, he was only on a visit with his brothers. He was by trade a saddler, and had merely come from Dublin to see his relatives.

My object now was to go to Dundalk and consult with my relative Keenan as to what I should do. My expectations were that he would give me an appointment as usher in his school. Still I waited at Corcreagh until Peter Byrne should return; but hour succeeded hour, and no Peter came. I felt then that I was once more entering upon life, and I wondered on what new adventure I should stumble next. At length it grew late – indeed, so late that to walk to Dundalk that night and arrive at Keenan's establishment in anything like decent time, would, I felt, be out of the question. At this moment a hearse and four horses stopped at the door of the tavern, and the driver went in to have some refreshment. After some conversation, he gave us to understand that he had conveyed a corpse to a graveyard at a long distance, the name of which I did not hear. When asked where he was bound for, he replied, 'for Dundalk' – and that moment young Byrne, taking me aside, said:

'Here now is the very thing you want – this hearse—'

'But I beg your pardon,' I replied, 'it is just the very thing I *don't* want, and I hope I shall be able to say so for many a long year.'

'You don't understand me,' said he, laughing 'What I mean is that I'll get this man to give you a seat as a passenger in the hearse to Dundalk. Bring him in and order him a glass or two of whisky, and I shall act as if the treat was yours.'

My sense of the ludicrous, if anything ludicrous can be associated with a hearse, overcame me. I laughed as heartily as he did. I treated the driver to a couple of glasses of whisky, or rather Byrne did so in my name, entered the hearse, shook hands with Byrne, and off we started. Of one fact I could take my oath – that since the first hearse trailed its slow length along, no vehicle of the kind ever went at such a pace until then. A funeral pace, indeed! Why it ought to have appeared, so far as speed was concerned, among the chariot races of the Romans.

At this particular period of time, it so happened that Keenan, who had to my own knowledge been publicly prayed for in every chapel throughout the country, was in a most doubtful state of health, his complaint being a chronic one of the liver. I gave the driver of the hearse directions where to stop – my directions being confined to the mere mention of Keenan's name, and stating that he kept a large classical school somewhere in Dundalk. This was before we entered the town, but the moment I mentioned Keenan's name, the man told me to be easy, he knew the house right well, as who did not. 'I will leave you,' said he, 'at the very door; I know it well – and I'm afeard, poor gentleman, that he'll soon come my way.' He accordingly stopped at the door, and as it was very clear moonlight, he descended and let me out of the hearse.

Now of all men living or dead, who should be standing at his own drawing-room window, looking into the street, but my invalid cousin, the Rev. John Keenan! An old schoolfellow of mine, whom I forgot to mention before, by name Bernard McKenna, was his first classical assistant, and had been his pupil when he kept his school in Glasslough. When I discovered this, which I did that evening, I gave up all hopes of an appointment as usher. McKenna was a young fellow who had read most assiduously – in fact, whose eyes were never off his books by night or by day. I don't think I ever met a better classical scholar; neither Keenan himself nor I were fit to be named in the same day with him. In the course of that evening, Keenan sent for me from his private room, where he received me with a face indicative of anything but kindness.

'I saw your arrival here this evening,' he said; 'you came like a bird of evil omen to pay your visit to me. I suppose you thought there was something significant and prophetic of my state of health in the vehicle you pitched upon to perform your journey.'

I explained the circumstances to him in a very few words, but I could perceive that he took a superstitious view of it.

'William,' said he to me, in a serious, but not very friendly voice – 'it so happens that at this moment I don't want any assistant in my school. If there had been a vacancy indeed, it would have been better for you – as it is, I do not see what I can do for you.'

'You know, sir,' said I, 'that as matters now stand, I can do nothing for myself. I know not to what point of the compass I can turn. I cannot return to my native place, because there I have no home.'

'I think,' he replied, 'you will have to work. There's Owen Traynor, who was with us in Glennon and Glasslough – he is now working on his father's farm like any other of his brothers. You too, I fear, will have to take to the spade and reaping-hook.'

'Not,' said I, 'while I can get a shilling a day – eighteen pounds five a year. I will walk over the country, mile for mile, from one end of it to the other, before I degrade myself to the condition of a day labourer.'

'Many a better man has,' said he. 'Go home – go home – and if you should ever visit me again it must not be in a hearse.'

I left him, and I need scarcely say that our parting was rather cold. I felt that from whatever cause he acted, his reception of me was a very heartless one, and considering the loneliness and dereliction in which I was placed, in a strange town, without a single friend, it was such – considering, too, our close affinity – as proved that he was not the man I had taken him to be. Under the circumstances, his conduct to me was, I consider, cruel and un-Christian.

After leaving him, I inquired for Bernard McKenna, his chief usher, but could not see him. There was a lodging-house within a door or two of Keenan's where I slept that night, and as the proprietors had taken it for granted that I was likely to be a permanent lodger, they did not trouble me for payment. I now bethought myself of what I should do, but could shape out no distinct or definitive object whatsoever. I strolled a good deal through the town, and went to see a large salt-pan where they made salt from sea-water. I asked myself where I should go; but could find no reply. I had not a coin from his Majesty's mint in my possession, yet, at this very moment, I said to myself, 'I will start for Dublin.' I accordingly got upon the Dublin road, by which I mean the road that led to Dublin by Drogheda. In this mood of mind, and with this resolution, I started for the metropolis, without having tasted food that day.

Ignorance of life confers great moral fortitude. I advanced on my journey towards Drogheda with my mind balanced between apprehension and romance. Should I, like Gil Blas, have an adventure? When was I likely to procure my dinner? This last conjecture began to give me some trouble, because I was getting hungry. Still I proceeded, mending my pace, from an apprehension lest I might be obliged to enter Drogheda after night – a possibility which I dreaded very much.

At length, I perceived by the number of cars and carts that met me, as well as by the unsteady and staggering appearance of many foot passengers, that I was getting near the town. The next question was, where should I stop? I was a perfect stranger in the place. At length, I recollected that there was residing in it a clergyman from my native parish, who had been appointed one of the curates at Drogheda. His name was Maginn, I think, but be that as it may, he had a brother a professor of theology in Maynooth College.[1] I had no difficulty in finding out his residence, but alas! only to experience a most woeful disappointment. He was from home – had gone on a visit to his friends in the north,

[1] Probably the Rev. Edward Maginn who afterwards became Bishop of Derry, and whose biography was written by Thomas D'Arcy McGee.

or, in other words, he was then with his relations in my own native parish.

When the servant maid told me this, I asked her if she could direct me to any house where I could stop for the night. She immediately pointed out what she called an eating and lodging-house, where she said I could get a dinner and bed if I wished. She said it was kept by a widow who was remarkable for kindness and charity. As she uttered these words she gave a short 'hem' or cough, the meaning of which I did not at that time understand. I proceeded to the house, which was and is on the left-hand side as you come from Dundalk. I think the season was Lent, for as I entered, I saw nothing on the tables but fish. Conscious of my ignorance in the ways of life, I sat for some time to watch how matters went on, and I perceived that there was no great mystery in it. The men came in, ordered their dinner, and having finished their meal, paid for it at once; others, however, sent out by the servant for either whisky or porter to the next public-house, but in that case it was necessary the money for the drink should be forthcoming. I did not venture on this; I only asked the waitress, who was a woman advanced in years, if I could have a bed there that night; and she replied in the affirmative. 'Then,' said I, 'I shall sleep here tonight.' She looked at me rather with kindness I thought, and said:

'Won't you have anything to drink, sir? We don't keep it ourselves, but there's as good whisky next door as ever was tasted.'

I replied that I didn't drink, but that as I felt fatigued I would go early to bed. I accordingly amused myself with the conversation of the guests, and occasionally reflected upon what the result of this adventure might be. One thing, however, sadly disheartened me; it was clear that of all the termagants in or out of hell, the landlady was the greatest. She had such a thin, unfeeling mouth, such sharp, piercing eyes – actually emitting fire – as if she was in a perpetual state of fury, which was the fact – that I felt anything but at ease. In temper she resembled Pierce Murphy as much as one human being ever resembled another. Many of the

136

guests entered into conversation with me, several invited me to partake of their drink, and others asked me to accompany them to some more respectable establishment, where we could sit and chat without being deafened by such a vociferous din as went on around us. To these persons I apologized with all due civility and kept my seat.

At length the house began to *thin*, as they say; one by one the guests disappeared, and when the time of rest arrived, I asked to be shown to my bedroom.

'Come here, young man,' said the landlady; 'the usage of this house is, that when a stranger wants a bed he must pay for it and his dinner here at the bar. I'll thank you to pay now, and the woman will show you your bedroom.'

Said I, 'You must wait till morning – I have no money about me, but I shall receive some from a friend pretty early.'

'Very well,' she replied, 'but in the meantime I must take care of myself. Biddy, go up, and after he goes to bed, bring me down his shirt. I see he's a swindler,' she added, 'although no one would suspect as much by looking at him. I have met some of his kidney before, though – smooth water runs deep.'

The old woman brought me upstairs, and showed me into a small room with a single bed in it. The poor creature was deeply affected, and expressed herself with a a generous sympathy that went to my heart.

'God help and pity, you poor young man,' she exclaimed; 'it's a cruel thing to see one like you brought to this. I suppose you're *on the world*.'

I wondered where she got the term, and I felt that it was never applied with more melancholy truth.

'I wish to God,' she continued, 'that I had the money about me, because if I had you wouldn't be long without it; but don't let down your heart, dear – if I haven't it now, it'll go hard or I'll make it out in the mornin'. So strip yourself,' said she. 'I'll stand outside the door for a minute – then go to bed, and throw your shirt over upon a chair or anywhere. She'll fiz for this, anyhow,'

137

exclaimed the kind-hearted creature, 'and that she may, I pray God this night, the blackguard skinflint.'

I don't think I ever enjoyed a sounder night's rest during my life. When I awoke the next morning, all the incidents of the preceding day and night rushed back rapidly to my mind. As the reader knows, I had looked upon my first adventure with contempt, as being sadly deficient in dignity; compared with my present, however, it was worthy of a prince. Here was I, a miserable devil, in the hands of an ill-tongued shrew, who, so far from feeling sympathy or humanity, absolutely left me without a shirt to my back. How was was I to live? Where was I to go? Could I proceed to Dublin, to the great metropolis, in this state? Was I to starve in a Christian country? Still, I would not despair. Who could tell but I might find a friend somewhere? There were worse cases in *Gil Blas*. There was no risk of my life here, and in any event, I must only endeavour to pluck up as much courage as I could.

I accordingly dressed myself, but resolved, before I left the house, to appeal in the case of the shirt to the landlady. I did so, but I will not inflict upon the reader the torrent of abuse she poured upon me. The pith of it was – that I ought to feel deeply thankful to her that, instead of paying herself with my shirt for the victuals she was obliged to hand out honest money for, she did not have me taken up and punished for swindling. This startled and alarmed me, because I felt that in one sense she was not far from the truth. If it were not swindling, it looked as like it as anything ever did. She added that if I did not leave the house immediately, she would send for the police.

Here was I now, at large again, and in a strange town, where I knew not an individual. I was, as I had been the day before, not only without my breakfast, but without the means to purchase it. What was to be done? I knew not. In the meantime, I was beginning to lose a great deal of my relish, not only for the adventures of Gil Blas – whom I cursed in my heart – but for my own, which certainly were at strong variance with romance. I recollected, however, that I had one article about me which might possibly be disposable, and I resolved to try it. This was my pocket-handkerchief, which was nearly new and had been handed to me, washed a couple of days before, at Pierce Murphy's house. I accordingly went down to the river, and got on board a ship which was lying there, and having entered into conversation with the sailors, who appeared to be all Drogheda men, I succeeded in selling the handkerchief for two shillings.

Short as my stay had been in Dundalk, I became slightly acquainted with one or two of Keenan's oldest pupils, who had heard through Bernard McKenna, I suppose, that he and I were cousins, and that I was looking for some employment as a teacher. One of these, a very gentlemanly young fellow, asked me would I teach a school. I told him I would be very glad to do so if I could get one to teach; upon this he informed me that a Catholic gentleman, Fitzgerald, of Fane Valley, had built a schoolhouse for the children of his tenantry, and that he would soon require a master. I paid no attention at the time, and the matter for the moment went out of my head. I had now two shillings, however, but my romance and love of adventure were altogether gone, at least for the present. It is wonderful what strength there is in two shillings. I felt full of courage, and said to myself, 'I will not go to Dublin, but I will return and offer myself for this school of Mr Fitzgerald's. I'm tired of adventures.'

A slight turn was now to take place in the tide of my affairs. From being penniless, without a shirt to my back or a breakfast in my stomach, I was soon to become master of eight-and-six-pence. See what it is to be made master of an important political secret, if I may call it so! I bethought me of the fact that I was a Ribbonman, and had never once reflected that the circumstance might be valuable to me. I resolved therefore to try it with the sailors, who seemed beyond doubt to sympathize with me. This I saw by their conduct, inasmuch as it was not because any of them wanted such a handkerchief that they purchased mine, it was because they saw I had no money. There was among them a young fellow who had appeared anxious about the sale of my handkerchief, which, by the way, was purchased by subscription,

139

and to him I resolved to give the sign; this I did by tapping the point of my nose twice with the top of my middle finger. I found four of the men in the ships were initiated, but as the vessels were loaded with grain, which had been imported from England as seed, I found many there who were not sailors, but labourers engaged to remove the oats to the adjoining granaries. To be brief, I left them with the vast sum of eight-and-sixpence in my pocket, which was about to be reduced by two shillings – the price of my pocket-handkerchief, which I asked to re-purchase. The sailors would not, however, listen to such a proposal. The handkerchief was immediately returned to me, we cordially shook hands, and I left them.

I then returned to that portion of the county of Louth with which I was best acquainted, having first secured my 'inner garment' from the landlady of the eating-house. I had scarcely entered, when the poor woman who acted as waitress, gave me a sign to follow her to the back door, and this I had no sooner done than she placed three-and-ninepence in my hand.

'Now,' said she, 'you can pay her, and get your breakfast besides.' Of course I declined her money, assuring her that I was provided.

Much of the happiness we enjoy is comparative. I was now in possession of the eight-and-sixpence, and felt it scarcely possible I could ever want.

I returned from Drogheda to Louth by another road, simply for the sake of variety. I do not think that any man living was ever so fond of the novelty of scenery as I was. I could stand and look upon it for hours. On one thing, however, I was resolved, and that was to practise the utmost frugality in using the money now in my possession. Notwithstanding this resolution, however, I felt a slight touch of the recent romance quietly stealing upon me. Surely my visit to the ships was rather an agreeable adventure, and I might meet others more so. I commenced my frugality and simplicity of food before I left Drogheda that very day; the first thing I did being to purchase a couple of coarse rolls, went to a dairy, got a halfpenny-worth of fresh buttermilk, and made my breakfast; a habit which I practised for years before I came to Dublin and after.

The first town I stopped at after leaving Drogheda was Ardee. I took lodgings for the night in the house of a jolly fellow, who had been for several years a sailor, but had returned to Ardee – which was his native place – where he married a good-looking woman, who possessed not only their present establishment, but some other little property, in the shape of small tenements in the town. The proprietor of this house, which was not only a lodging-house, but a public-house, seemed to me one of the most perfectly happy men I had ever seen. He was constantly singing, and, so far as my ears informed me, perpetually the same song – its burthen was:

> *'And the Ardee dog sent round the grog,*
> *And pushed about the jorum.'*

He appeared to be in a state of the most absolute enjoyment, his countenance lit up with an expression of infinite delight, his clear blue eyes smiling, and every feature of his face animated with the sense of almost ineffable pleasure. He was never sober, nor was he ever drunk, but maintained, as he used to say himself, 'the goolden mane' between them. I was often at his house afterwards, and upon these occasions I became well acquainted with his character. His name was Peter Murray, but no man was a favourite of his who did not call him 'the Ardee dog'.

God help us! How many admirable and original characters are there in life of whom the world neither has nor knows anything – men whom to examine would present a profound and interesting study to him who wishes to become thoroughly acquainted with human nature. They pass away, however, like the phantoms of a dream, and leave no memory or impression behind them. *Qui caveat sano vate!*

From Ardee I returned once more towards Dundalk, but as I was now becoming acquainted with the manners and habits of the people, I became very fond of them, and began to like living among them. For instance, there was a man who kept a public-house, and a most respectable one, on the road between Dundalk and Drogheda – I had crossed the country and once more come out upon that road – and on going along towards Dundalk, I went in to get a glass of porter, feeling rather thirsty after the walk. The proprietor of the house was there – a rare case, because he was a land-surveyor of much business and but seldom at home. His house was not far from Fane Valley – the residence of Mr Fitzgerald – one of the most beautiful of valleys, and almost the only one in Louth. We soon became quite intimate and even confidential. He was a man of fame, and told me that he had corresponded for years, in the mathematical department, with one of those small publications which went among the lower classes at that time – sometimes called *The Lady's Almanack*, and sometimes *The Lady's Magazine* – all of which I had seen hundreds of times.

These little annuals were a singular feature in our literature at that period. They consisted, firstly, of all the matter which constitutes an almanack upon a small scale. After this, they were filled with riddles of every description, rebuses, enigmas, conundrums, charades, and every difficulty of the kind, such as I see our present literature has degraded itself by resuming. There was, however, one department in those little almanacks which I am sorry to say, our later periodicals have not. I allude to the mathematical. The little works I speak of contained several mathematical problems of surprising ingenuity and great difficulty, and were the means of developing many a mathematical genius that never could otherwise have been discovered. The questions in all the departments were inserted one year and answered the next – it could not well be otherwise in an annual publication. My dear friend, the late Professor McCullagh of Trinity College, to whom I dedicated my 'Miser', told me that he first discovered his genius for science by answering these mathematical queries. At the age of twelve years he was able to answer every one of them.[1]

[1] James McCullagh was a Tyrone man, and one of the most remarkable mathematicians of his day. Some of his problems and theories are wonderful. He took his own life, before he was thirty, his mind having given way from over-work in his pursuit of mathematical science.

On hearing the name of the surveyor – it was Moran – I remembered it distinctly. I could therefore entertain little doubt of his being a first-rate mathematician. Up to that day he was a correspondent to *The Lady's Almanack*, and I have little doubt but he owed much of his practice to that very fact.

Chapter XII

Fitzgerald, of Fane Valley – Carleton as a story-teller – Navan – How to wash a shirt – Visit to Clongowes and Maynooth – A bully chastised – Rev. Paul O'Brien – Judy Byrne – Big Magee – Celbridge – Becomes a hedge schoolmaster – On the road to Dublin.

W HEN I alluded to my intention of seeking the mastership of the Fane Valley school, Moran's eye brightened, and he caught at it at once.

'I'll tell you what you must do,' said he; 'in the first place make this house your home, as long as it may suit your own convenience. Go abroad about Fane Valley and make inquiries; ascertain everything you can; and then we will know how to act.'

I did this, but could ascertain very little, and that was not satisfactory. I thought Mr Fitzgerald's steward might, from his situation, know something about it, and it was from him that I gained the only information I received that was worth anything. 'The master,' he said, 'who was engaged was then in some society in Dublin, where they train masters to teach schools.' I did not understand this, and I considered it a poor proof of qualification for such an office, that it was found necessary to teach any master his duties. I had never heard of the Kildare Street Society at the time, and I suppose it must have been to that he alluded. The honest steward, however, gave me the best advice he could; it was to make application to Mr Fitzgerald himself,[1] who knew the truth, he said, and from him I could learn it. On inquiring the best hour to see him, he said after breakfast, or about eleven o'clock.

This was the information I gained, and it was anything but promising. Mr Moran, the surveyor, on hearing this information,

---

[1] Father of Mr Percy Fitzgerald, F S A, author of innumerable books, who was born at Fane Valley in 1834.

agreed with the steward that I should call upon Mr Fitzgerald himself, state my qualifications, and offer myself for the situation. The next morning I was at Mr Fitzgerald's hall-door at the hour suggested to me by the steward; when it was opened, I was asked my business, and of course said I wished to see Mr Fitzgerald. He came up with a pen in his hand, and a more interesting or gentlemanly man I seldom saw. On stating the object of my calling on him, and on hearing that I was a classical scholar, he told me, with a smile, that he should regret seeing a young man so well educated teaching a school like his. I should look for something better, but, under any circumstances, he was sorry to inform me that he had already engaged a master, so that even although disposed to give me the appointment, he could not do so without a violation of his word, and the engagement he had entered into. To this I had nothing to say, so I respectfully raised my hat and took my leave.

This interview closed my expectations in that direction, and I felt that there was no earthly hope for me. Keenan's conduct to me filled my heart with a sense of strong indignation, and I began in fact to regret that I had ever opened a classical book in my life. Why was such a fate attached to me? Every young man I met or spoke to, had a home, a comfortable residence, and friends who felt an interest in him; while I, without any fault of mine, was left homeless, houseless, friendless. Nobody could dream of what I privately felt at the contemplation of my position, and above all of futurity, which was black and lowering before me, without a single gleam on which either the eye or heart could rest. Oh, the bitter tears I have shed in secret, when no eye but that of God Himself was a witness!

I now resolved to go to Dundalk and see Keenan again. A week had elapsed since my interview with Mr Fitzgerald, and during this period I was the guest of Mr Moran, or rather of his family, because he was engaged in his profession several miles from home.

At length I started for Dundalk, but, on reaching the town, I changed my mind and declined seeing Keenan. On arriving there,

I sent for Bernard McKenna, who told me that my cousin's mind was occupied by some prejudice against me; and he thought Keenan felt as if I had disgraced him by the incident of the hearse. Keenan was a very weak-minded man, and to my own knowledge, notwithstanding his education, a good deal tinged with superstition. He was, besides, getting worse in health, and his temper had become snappish and disagreeable to everyone that approached him. Still I thought McKenna might have misrepresented him, or exaggerated his state of mind, from an apprehension lest he might remove him and take me, a near relative, in his place. I accordingly wrote him a few lines, asking him finally whether he could give me any employment in his school or not. To this I received a reply, in three or four lines, stating that he had no employment he could offer me, and recommending me, as before, to take up a spade and work – or perhaps I might get employment as a hearse-driver with some undertaker. I knew very well what he meant as hearse-driver, but was utterly ignorant of what he wished to express by the word 'undertaker', which I had never before heard.

A thought now struck me, originating in a combination of despair and listlessness. The apathy I felt preserved me from utter despair, and the despair, fortunately for myself, took the shape of apathy.

To be brief, I made acquaintances, visited this family and that without invitation, and was received with as much kindness and cordiality as if a deputation had waited on me to go. This not only reconciled me to such a life, but made the time the most agreeable I had yet spent. The neighbouring families began almost to quarrel as to which of them should receive me. The only equivalent I could bestow was the narrative of the old classical legends, which I transmogrified and changed into an incredible variety of shapes. I would have given them Irish legends, and sometimes did, but then the Irish legends did not show the 'larnin' '.

I made one discovery, while leading this extraordinary kind of life, and that was the power of my own invention. It did not indeed strike me very forcibly then, but since that time I have reflected on it with something like wonder. Finding that it would not do to go over the same ground so often, I took to inventing original narratives, and was surprised at the facility with which I succeeded. This new discovery was as great an amusement to myself as it was to my audience. I used to compose these fictions in the course of the day, while walking about, and recite them at the fireside in the evening. I was beginning to enjoy a certain degree of local fame, which constituted me a treasure to whatever neighbourhood I stopped in. The number of people who came to hear me in the evening was surprising, as were the distances they came from. In fact I became a regular *improvisatore*, and was the subject of many a wondering conversation among the people. I had lost all hope in life, and took it for granted that I was then in the highest position which I should ever reach. I had no motive of action, and avoided looking into the distance before me – a distance which to me was a perfect blank.

In this state of mind I was walking one day near Mr Taaffe's, of Smarmore Castle, and turned accidentally into a house on the roadside, which proved to be a school. The master and I entered into conversation; he learned from me that I was very anxious to procure some kind of decent employment. This information I gave him, unaccompanied by any feeling whatever – as a mere matter of course – but to him it suggested an idea which transferred the scene of my operations from Louth to Meath.

'I'll tell you what I'd advise you to do,' said he; 'go to the town of Navan – there is a celebrated Catholic boarding-school there, and it's not unlikely that you might on application get employment as an usher.' The suggestion excited very little hope, but still I felt anxious for a change of scene – I would try a town. Anything would be better than the monotony of the life I led. The season was summer, and I started, immediately after my conversation with Mr Hart the schoolmaster, for the pretty town of Navan. I took a lodging in the house of a man named Sheridan, who kept a regular lodging-house for travelling pedlars – delft men – in fact, for everyone of the multifarious class to which I allude. It was there I became acquainted with a learned tailor named Gaynor, who, although no classical scholar, was one of the most naturally eloquent men I ever met. This tailor had great influence, and was looked up to as a prodigy, and indeed it was well for me that he possessed this influence, because he took me under his patronage and protection. He was also very pious, one of the most sincerely religious men I ever met. He took a singular fancy to me, or rather, I should say that he devoted himself to, and identified himself with, my interests. His table was my table during a great portion of the time I was in Navan, and that was about three months. He enabled me besides to set to rights some little matters in my wardrobe, and never permitted me to be without a few shillings in my pocket.

And now that I have mentioned my wardrobe, the reader may take it for granted that one of the greatest sources of my anxiety was to keep it, or to continue it, as decent as became a young man whom the people looked upon with sincere respect. And this reminds me of a circumstance which occurred about a month before I started for Navan. I was living at that time in the house of a farmer – a comfortable one he was, and as kind as comfortable. There was a small lake, a very small one, not more than two hundred yards from his house; there lived also beside him another family – his cottar's – consisting of an aunt, a niece, and a nephew, a very intelligent young fellow with whom it was a pleasure to converse. I only allude to them for the purpose of stating that it was in their house I first met Miss Edgeworth's inimitable *Castle Rackrent*. The scenery around this farmer's house was sweet, but plain, if I may say so. The family were making their turf in a small bog that was on their own property, and not very far from their house. One day – I think it was the hottest day I ever remember – I perceived that they were all out engaged in the turf-cutting, both males and females. The day before, in walking some distance through the adjoining fields, I discovered a small but clear stream running through a most secluded and lonely spot, about half a mile from any residence of man. A thought then struck me which I kept to myself until the next day – that of the turf-cutting. What I am now relating has reference to a certain portion of my wardrobe. On finding that the family were all from home – engaged at the turf-cutting – I began to rummage through the kitchen, and kept searching about until I discovered a large piece of soap. This I covered with a burdock-leaf, and having placed it in my pocket, I sought the clear and lonely stream I have mentioned. At the spot I selected for the task I proposed, there was on one side a banky eminence of more than twenty feet. I crossed the stream, ascended the eminence, and, on glancing round, could not discern the presence of a human creature. I went down again to the edge of the stream, deliberately stripped myself of my coat and waistcoat, and after looking around once more in every direction – very like a thief or some villain about to commit a crime – I denuded myself of my small clothes, and in an instant stood as a very stout and athletic representative of the prize-ring, concerning which, by the way, I shall have more to say in connection with my own prospects as I go along. In plain terms I took my shirt, my only shirt, off, I put it into the river, took it out again, and having lightly wrung the water out of it, I soaped it thoroughly. I had previously taken off my shoes and stockings, so that I stood in the little stream. I will not go through the whole process, or detail the number of washings and wringings which took place, but at length the task was over. After having wrung the shirt until no drop of water made its appearance, I stretched it out to its natural dimensions, and then spread it on the dry sward, under one of the most scorching suns I ever remember. It dried much sooner than I had expected, so when I thought it safe to put it on, I stretched it out again, and folded up the collar, which I hammered with my hands in imitation of what the washerwomen do before they lay the smoothing-iron to their linen.

Nothing in the shape of good luck remained with me. By Gaynor's advice I wrote to the pious and amiable Bishop of Meath, the Right Rev. Doctor Plunket, soliciting an appointment through him to a situation in Navan School. He very kindly sent my letter to the Rev. Dr O'Reilly, who was the master of the establishment, and who to my own knowledge received it; but he, to my own knowledge also, sent not a single line in reply, although my address was in the letter. I met him afterwards, and thought it only justice to myself to make the necessary inquiries about the matter, and I protest to Heaven that such an ill-bred and contemptible clerical prig I never met. For his haughty and insulting manner to me he deserved to get his nose pulled, and he owed it to his black coat that he did not. I question if I ever felt such indignation – yet such is life: whoever is, or has been, jostled through it as I was, will meet many such characters – men who take pleasure in exhibiting the wanton insolence of a low disposition and a narrow mind towards those who are struggling through the difficulties of the world, while they themselves are contemptibly slavish and obsequious to anyone who stands a single step above them in society.

I have said how Gaynor the tailor befriended me at Navan, but unfortunately he was obliged to remove for a brief period, upon a matter of business, I think, to the town of Mullingar, where he had resided before he came to Navan. Here was I left friendless again, with my prospects in life as dark as usual. Where to go I knew not; but, as in the case of my pilgrimage to Lough Derg, the reader is aware that I went to visit that far-famed locality more from curiosity than devotion, so the idea of a visit to Maynooth seized upon me, a visit to the town in which the great college was to be seen with my own living eyes. I think I was more anxious to see that college than I had been to see Lough Derg itself. I consulted nobody. Indeed, in making my resolutions in life I seldom or very rarely consulted anyone. I think I spent no less than a couple of days on my journey to Maynooth. I don't even recollect the way or ways by which I reached the place. All I know is that I approached it by the little town of Kilcock, and there I stopped for about a week before going farther. I forget the name of the man in whose small but comfortable lodging-house I put up. His son became quite attached to me, and as I was at that candid period of my life anything but close or secretive, he soon became as well acquainted with my history as if he had been my companion step by step through the short period of my eccentric and original wanderings.

Clongowes, the seat of the Jesuits' college, is not many miles from Kilcock. I think it was these learned and reverend fathers who changed the original name of it, which was Castle Browne, to Clongowes.[1] My landlord's son advised me to pay a visit to this now celebrated establishment, which I did, having slept the preceding night in the miserable village of Clane. I sent in a letter written at the very top of my skill – but nothing came of it. The fathers had no vacancy of any kind which they could offer me. During our interview there were six or seven of them present, and as the room was large, they whispered together occasionally in corners. I was treated to a solitary dinner, and when I had finished it, one of the clergymen came in, and laid down something wrapped in a small paper parcel and wished me every success in life. When he went away, I examined the parcel, and found there was fifteen shillings in it. This I was very glad to get, for at that moment my pockets were all but empty.

When I returned to Kilcock, where I slept that night, I resolved to visit Maynooth the next day, and never was a man so thoroughly disappointed on walking through that beggarly-looking and contemptible village, for indeed it is not worthy the name of town. Of course, I stopped in a lodging-house. It was kept by a carpenter, whose name I forget, and to whom I gave an excellent drubbing for his inhuman brutality to his children. From a father to his own offspring, his conduct stood alone, not only in originality, but in a cruelty that was revolting to witness as practised upon any child. At the period of which I now write, the present Duke of Leinster – who had been then recently married – was building a grand saloon, or at least making some large and important addition to his castle, under the management of Mr Carolin, the celebrated builder. His eldest son, whom I knew long afterwards as the Alderman, was then conducting the works for

---

[1] Carleton is guilty of an error here. The *house* was called Castle Browne, having belonged to a well-known Catholic family, the Wogan Brownes, but the *place* was never anything but Clongowes.

his father. Now the house where I lodged in Maynooth was filled with the workmen whom Carolin was obliged to bring from Dublin to Maynooth, in order to fill his contract. I mention this, because most of these men were present at the comical incident I am about to relate – the day was Sunday, and they were all at home. The anti-natural cruelty of this heartless savage – a cruelty which would have deserved a very severe visitation from the cat-o'-nine-tails – consisted in this; he corrected his children for offences which very few other parents would have visited with punishment at all; the poor things naturally wept bitterly; on seeing this, he got a large switch, and, taking the child, placed it standing before him to hear the command, the habitual command, which he insisted on its complying with:

'Come now, sir, commence a loud laugh this minute, or if you don't – do you see that switch?' And he shook it over the trembling creature's head.

This was expecting from nature more than nature could either afford or accomplish, and on the child's failing, he applied the scourge again, attended by a similar command to laugh. Thus the diabolical ruffian proceeded, until the poor child became an object of the greatest compassion. My own impression was that the little fellow, overcome not only in consequence of what he had suffered, but by the damnable task imposed upon him, was about to become insensible – perhaps to die. I accordingly went over and seizing the scourge which his father held in his hand, I attempted to wrest it from him.

'You accursed scoundrel,' said I, 'are you about to murder your own child? – let go the scourge.'

'Do you call me a scoundrel?' he replied; 'take that,' and as he spoke, he aimed a very violent blow at me, which I parried. The fellow was a stout-looking ruffian, and evidently took it for granted that he had the result of the battle in his own hands. I was at that time in the very strength and energy of youth, and felt the villain's cruelty as a powerful motive for determined action. The battle commenced, but as some persons, more peacefully disposed than others, attempted to put us asunder, I called upon the other bystanders to prevent any interference between us, to which they replied, with one voice, that they would suffer nothing of the kind; the fight must go on. I am not about to act the part of a reporter here. It is enough to say that in the course of twenty minutes I had made the fellow so helpless that he could not stand; his eyes were bunged up and his face was frightfully disfigured. In fact he was in the same state to which he had often reduced his own children.

'Now,' said I, 'you admit that you are a beaten man, do you not?'

He made no reply. 'Listen to me,' said I; 'if you don't instantly reply and admit it, by all that's sacred I'll stave you to pieces. Are you not a beaten man?'

'Well,' he replied, 'I am, and d—n you for it.'

'Never mind that,' said I, 'no bad language – be a Christian – but, in the meantime, don't you feel rather comfortable and easy? Come – be merry – and enjoy yourself. Give a good laugh now – a regular mirthful cackle – for, mark me, you have no other means of escaping a second thrashing. Be quick.'

The scoundrel could not even make the attempt. I accordingly seized him by the neck, and kicked him out into the street, leaving him to amuse himself as best he could.

'Now,' said he, when he felt himself at large, 'you immediately leave my house – for another hour you shan't be under my roof.'

'I have no notion of anything of the kind,' said I; 'under no other roof in Maynooth will I sleep but yours.'

'If you go, Mr Carleton,' said one of Carolin's respectable tradesmen, 'a single man of us won't stay in his house;' and it so happened that I lodged nowhere else, so long as I remained in Maynooth. They say that a good action does not always bring its own reward, but although there may be some instances to that effect, the general rule to the contrary is ten thousand to one. During my wandering life I had before that period won little faint glimpses of local fame – upon a very small scale. Here, however, it shot up with a brilliancy that filled Maynooth from

153

one end to the other. I was looked at and admired, and even many hats were raised to me, in a spirit not only of respect but gratitude. I could scarcely understand all this, nor why a private skirmish should have such an effect upon so many. This mystery, however, was soon explained to me, for in the course of the ensuing week I discovered that my customer was the bully of the town, and an insolent tyrant over weaker men than himself.

I had not yet had any communication with the college – what communication could a nameless wanderer like me expect with such an establishment? Still, I was very anxious to see it, both inside and out – I wished to go through the grounds, for instance, in order to ascertain if there was anything in the prospect better than I had already caught a glimpse of. The Professor of Irish at that time was the Rev. Paul O'Brien,[1] to whom I wrote a note, asking him for permission to see the place. He answered me very kindly and went with me himself through the grounds. He was a droll man, a humorist, and full of anecdotes that the dullest intellect could not resist. I mentioned in a preceding portion of this biography, that when I was at school with the fellow named McGoldrick, there was a poor scholar there from some place near Enniskillen named John Quin – and a poor scholar he was in every sense. I saw him at the gate, and he trembled as if he would sink into the earth from an apprehension that I might mention that fact, and consequently lower him in the estimation of his fellow-students. Altogether my opinion of those young gentlemen was just then rather low, though with a good many exceptions. The *curriculum* of their educational course was, however, very limited, but that may possibly have resulted from the state and condition of the Catholic Church in Ireland at that time, and its undefined relation to Government. Greek was not then indispensable, as it is now. In my work upon Ireland, called the *Squanders of Castle Squander*,[2] I have given their *curriculum*, or

[1] Author of an Irish grammar (1809).

[2] It will be observed that Carleton does not call this book a novel. He is wise in describing it as a 'work upon Ireland.' It has less merit than almost anything he wrote. It is not a novel, as it professes to be, but a pamphlet.

the course of their education in the year 1848, at full length, showing that it is both liberal and extensive.

The most original character I met at Maynooth was Judy Byrne, who was fruit-woman to the college. I think she was a woman by mistake, and indeed her whole life seemed to be a proof of that fact. She was a virago of immense size, wore a man's short outside coat over her female apparel, and a man's hat. She had very comfortable lodgings about the centre of the town as you go to the college; her rooms were stored with an incredible abundance of the finest fruit, the fragrance of which was delicious. The freedom of her language went, in cool, brazen assurance, beyond anything ever heard from a woman's lips, whilst at the same time it was irresistible in drollery. She had been during the year of the rebellion what she herself termed – and boasted of – a United Irishman. She never addressed the professors by any other appellation than their surname. For instance, if she met the Professor of Irish, she did not say, 'I hope your Reverence is well today.' Instead of that it was:

'Well, O'Brien, how did you sleep last night? – no headache this morning – eh?'

It was the same with the present Duke of Leinster, whom she used to approach with – 'Well, Fitzgerald, how long are you married now? You look rather pale upon it – no matter – here' – extending her hand – 'give us a tip of your scratcher; but' – whisper – 'don't set Kildare on fire.'

There was also another curiosity then in the college, for whose presence I could not account. This was the celebrated Irish giant, Big Magee, a man – a colossus – who had been exhibited all over the world. I knew him well, because he was the son of a man and woman, both under the middle size, in my native parish of Clogher, whose residence was not more than three miles from my father's. He was a most ingenious man, and his constant occupation was the invention of clocks and watches, of original and strange construction. He told me he was brought to Maynooth to regulate the clocks, but be this as it may, he was a fixture there for some years. At the time I saw him at Maynooth he told me

155

that he had all but discovered 'perpetual motion'. He was the largest object in the shape of man and the most symmetrically made I ever saw.

There was a thin, lively man two or three doors from where I lodged named McDonough – a comic little fellow, but sharp and intelligent. He had been a pedlar, and had carried about soft goods throughout the country. He used to supply the students with handkerchiefs, and was sometimes employed by them to act as their agent in town, whenever they stood in need of anything connected with their wardrobe. This man became acquainted with a female of his own profession, whom he married by appointment in the town of Maynooth, where he immediately took a house and set up in the soft goods business. McDonough was a hospitable soul, and felt an exceedingly friendly interest in me. One cause of his respect for me was the drubbing I gave the ruffianly carpenter who treated his own children with such unnatural barbarity. He was perpetually on the look-out for something that might suit my interest, and so indeed was every respectable inhabitant of Maynooth. At length he heard of something likely to offer very soon in the town of Celbridge, within a couple of miles of Maynooth, where there is probably the most magnificent private residence – that of the Connolly's – in all her Majesty's dominions. I went to Celbridge in quest of employment, and took lodgings in an old house which was then nearly in ruins, although it must have been, once upon a time, the finest house in the town. Here I was engaged by the wife of a gauger to teach two little girls spelling and reading and writing. The husband, whose name I am not sure of, was seldom at home, but when he did come, it was easy to see that he troubled himself about no earthly business whatsoever. He was, however, a perfect gentleman, and of a gentlemanly family. By the way, I think his name was Flood, and that he claimed descent from the celebrated Henry Flood, the great contemporary of Grattan.

In Celbridge there was a man named Gallaher, who kept a very large school, and whose house was every evening the rendezvous of almost every person in the town capable of enter-

156

ing into decent conversation. One of his pupils was son to the man who kept the hotel in the town. He (the pupil) afterwards became one of the proprietors and contributors to the *Satirist* newspaper, and subsequently went to London, where I saw him in the year 1850. He was then a resident in the Temple and the proprietor of a newspaper in which appeared a brief history of my novel of *Willy Reilly*.[1]

It was at Celbridge that, for the first time since I left home, I lost my health – or rather was attacked with some complaint that confined me for three weeks to my bed. During all this time Mrs Flood acted as a mother to me. Every morning her servant-maid came with my breakfast, and in the course of the day with a great variety of delicacies suitable for an invalid. At length I recovered, and on my recovery I found that Mr Flood had been promoted to a higher appointment; this of course occasioned him to remove to a different locality. Mrs Flood, before the family went, enclosed me twice the amount of the salary due to me. She was one of the most amiable and truly pious women I ever met.

Little McDonough called upon me at Celbridge, and told me he thought that something had turned up at last. I asked him what it was, and added that I was quite indifferent on the subject. I felt a fixed presentiment, I said, that nothing worth my acceptance would ever offer, and indeed I am not surprised, after all my disappointments, that I was unable to resist such an impression. I was, however, utterly without experience, and altogether devoid of that common sense which prompts so many, not only to calculate upon their chances of life, but upon the best means of working them out. The truth is, I was to a great extent the victim of a romantic imagination. McDonough brought me home with him. and sent over the way for a man named Madden, a saddler, whose words were to become the oracle of my good fortune. There was,

---

[1] This was John Sheehan, 'the Irish Whisky-Drinker', who was, however, one of the proprietors of the *Comet*, not the *Satirist*. He came from Celbridge originally, as Carleton states, and was a frequent contributor to *Bentley's Miscellany*, *Temple Bar*, etc. He edited *The Bentley Ballads*, 1869, and died in 1882.

in fact, and this was the important revelation, an excellent opening for a school in a place only about three miles off – called Newcastle, in the county of Dublin, and not more than a mile and a half from Hazel-Hatch upon the canal. Madden had some friends there to whom he recommended me, and after due exertion I got a promise of about a dozen or two wretched boys and girls, and the gift of an uninhabited hut – one of the worst that ever covered a human head. In due time the establishment was opened, and I, William Carleton, became the master of a hedge school. Yes, a hedge school – so it must be called, for so it was.[1] But when I bethought me of the hedge schools in which I had myself been educated, of the multitude assembled, of the din arising from the voices of the comic crew around, I felt like a hermit in a wilderness.[2]

Fortunately, there were three or four families in the neighbourhood who sent their sons to me, and so far relieved me from the miserable monotony in which I must have passed my time, among eighteen or twenty half-naked brats, to most of whom I was teaching their alphabet. Of course, like every other hedge schoolmaster, I lived among those farmers, who treated me with singular respect.

This thing, however, was a dead failure: had I been left to depend for my mere subsistence upon the profits of my school, I should have starved. Its income would not have clothed me – and I consequently began to experience once more those droopings of the heart to which I had been so often subjected.

At this time, I was on the eve of a change, such as few

[1] In connection with hedge schools, John O'Hagan's lines will occur to many Irishmen:
'Crouching 'neath the sheltering hedge, or stretched on mountain fern,
The master and his pupils met, *feloniously* to learn!'
[2] The allusion to a hermit in the wilderness reminds one irresistibly of the medieval Irish story, one of the most humorous ever conceived, of the three hermits, who, sick of the clamour of the world, sought peace in the desert. At the end of a year, one remarked, 'It's a fine life we're having here!' After another year a second hermit replied, 'It is.' After a third year had elapsed, the last hermit broke in with – 'If I can't get peace here, I'll go back to the world.'

158

individuals ever underwent. The reader, from what I have written, may naturally take it for granted that, looking at the subject from whatever point human existence in a free country may present, it was impossible that any change could be for the worse. Before I go farther, however, let not the reader suppose that up to the present moment in my narrative, I have detailed every incident in my life. From some of those incidents any man of feeling would shrink with shame, and a bitterness of recollection that often almost drove me into a blasphemous ingratitude for the curse of my very existence. I have gone through scenes which, if related, would strip my narrative or my suffering of all claims to the dignity of ordinary experience. I am speaking now of the past – of all that occurred until I arrived at and left Newcastle.

The reader will now understand the mood of my mind when I found that I could not live in Newcastle. Young as I was, I began to contrast my own fate in life with that of almost every individual I met. A moral gloom appeared to supervene, not only upon the life I led, but upon the general workings of society. My object was to ascertain the causes of things as they appeared to me; but this I could not do. I had no opportunity of making myself acquainted with those works which treat of the moral government of life. I had read nothing but a few odd novels and some classics, and was in every way badly qualified to analyze the progress of the world as it went on. Thinking and reasoning had almost come to a standstill with me. I looked back to my youthful life as a dream – although I was scarcely out of youth at the time. What was I to do now? I had tried everything – I felt that I was progressing downwards. Was there a peculiar fate attached to me? It looked like it – and if so, why? I examined my past life strictly. I compared it with the rules of duty and the aberrations from it to be found in our prayer-books, and I could not charge myself with any crime capable of exciting either sorrow or remorse.

Chapter XIII

Dublin – Dirty Lane – The mountebanks – The beggars at home –
'William Carleton, Ladies' Shoemaker'.

THE last thing I remember about Newcastle is receiving from
the farmers, whose sons I was teaching, the amount of the last
quarter's payment. It came seasonably. My shoes were all but
gone, and I lost no time in going to Maynooth, where I left my
measure with a shoemaker, and in a few days had a new pair
with which I started on my journey to Dublin – in order to seek
my fortune there.

After having paid for my shoes, I started for the great city
with two-and-ninepence in my pocket. Now one would naturally
imagine that after the severe and almost hopeless experience which
my intercourse with life had already given me, it would have been
little short of insanity for any young fellow in my position and
circumstances to take such a step. I myself can only account for it
by the feeling – derived from *Gil Blas* – which urged me on to
ascertain the developments of life, and that with a hope, that after
struggles and adventures, I might, like him, come to a calm and
safe harbour at last. I walked my way into Dublin, and arrived
there in the evening by the great southern road that leads into
James's Street. I had sense enough to know that with the purse
I possessed, I could not think of penetrating into the city beyond
the suburbs; I consequently turned to my left hand, and went
down a street which led I knew not where. I looked into the
windows of the houses as I proceeded – they were all houses of
business – and at length came to one which, from its unpretending
appearance, I thought would suit my limited circumstances. There
was a bill up – *A bed to let* – and I accordingly went in and hired
the bed for that night only. I had taken a penny roll and a glass
of porter before I went in. The roll I got at a baker's, and the

tumbler of porter in a public-house. I slept soundly enough, and awoke the next morning refreshed. When I made my appearance, which was not until near nine o'clock, I was asked by the woman of the house if I would have breakfast. I thought of the capital in my pocket, and felt that I could not afford to take one of *her* breakfasts – which would have cost me perhaps tenpence or a shilling. I said I came to see a friend, and that it was likely I should breakfast and dine with him so long as I stayed in town. I accordingly went out, and had my roll, as was usual with me. My residence here was but short. I afterwards discovered that the name of the street in which I lodged was ominous. It was then called Dirty Lane, but its name has since been changed to Bridgefoot Street. The number of the house was forty-eight – a number on which I perpetually stumbled during my adventures in Dublin.

In the course of the next day I began to look as was but natural, at the proprietors of the house. The landlord seemed to be a simple man, not so far as I could judge, a native of Dublin. His wife was an interesting, handsome young woman, but it seemed to me that they could not have been very long married. At least, there was a mystery in their conduct to each other, altogether different from what I had observed in married life. On my leaving there the first morning, I walked abroad and breakfasted; and, after going from street to street, I returned in the course of the day several times as if to rest myself. On these occasions I saw that three persons – young men – were extremely familiar with my landlady – jested with her, called her by her Christian name of Mary, and made her get them a dinner of rasher and eggs, which, however, they prepared and cooked themselves. I also saw that she was sewing some small dresses that resembled those intended for children's dolls. They left in the evening and took these things with them. Altogether I could understand neither their conduct nor their laughter and grimaces, any more than their unaccountable familiarity with the handsome mistress.

About seven o'clock, the owner of the house asked me to go out and have a walk with him, telling me that he would bring me to a place of amusement which would cost us nothing. Of course I felt very glad to pass the time as agreeably as I could, and I consequently accompanied him. I knew not at that time the streets through which he brought me, although I found them out soon afterwards. We went up Capel Street, and then passed through Mary Street and Henry Street, until we arrived at Moore Street, where, on the right-hand side as you turn up towards the butcher's market, we stopped in a large room where the show of 'Punch and Judy' was about to be exhibited. He brought me forward, and we took our seats among a good many others, awaiting the lifting of the little curtain. At length it rose, and we enjoyed the play together, with a great variety of legerdemain tricks, all of which were perfectly new to me, and some of which threw me into convulsions of laughter. The reader however, may judge of my surprise, when I found that the three fellows who had helped themselves that day to their liberal dinner of rashers and eggs, were the proprietors and actors in the establishment. On our way home, her husband told me that these worthy professionals were his wife's brothers, and that she had been an actress in their drama, until he took her from among them and married her. They were against the marriage, he said, and refused to allow it unless they were remunerated in the sum of fifty pounds as compensation for the loss of her services. Had I known as much of life then as I know now, I might have seen at once that she was not their sister. I think that both her object and theirs was to fleece the fool – for indeed he appeared to be a simple though good-natured booby, altogether guided by her. I stopped with them three nights and two days, strolling through a strange city with, I may say, empty pockets. I knew not a single individual within the compass of the Circular Road. The three brothers were there every day, and dined and drank at her husband's expense. They did not appear to relish me, but they frequently asked me if I would 'stand' something after having been made free of their entertainments. This I would have complied with willingly, were it not that, as my readers are aware, I had sound reasons to the contrary. I had that evening parted with my last coin for my roll and glass of porter, and consequently was in a position which to me had nothing novel in it. In this man's house they went to bed very late, never before eleven or twelve; but on that evening I observed something strange and wilfully disagreeable in their manner towards me. The husband went to his paltry counter after a hint from the wife, and pulling open a drawer, handled some loose halfpence, and asked me if I could oblige him with one and eightpence till tomorrow morning. One and eightpence was two ten-penny bits. I told him I could not; then he asked me for ten pence; but received the same reply. My impression is, that they must have searched my pockets in the course of the night, and discovered my miserable want of cash. He then asked me 'had I no money?' and I was obliged to acknowledge that painful fact, but I told him that I was to get money the next day. It was about twelve o'clock, if not later, and he told me that he felt sorry that he could not allow me to sleep there that night. I said I did not want to occupy a bed, but I hoped he would allow me to sit at the fireside till morning: at this proposal the wife gave a knowing giggle, as if she thoroughly understood some meaning which might be drawn from my words – probably an intention of robbing the house while they were asleep.

'Do you want,' said I, 'to turn me out at this hour of the night in a strange city, and without a single farthing in my pocket? I owe you nothing, but if you will allow me to stop tonight, I will call tomorrow and pay you. You know I could get no bed at this hour, especially as I have no money.'

The man put threepence into my hand, and desiring me to follow him, went to the door of a cellar exactly over the way; at this he kicked, and on its being opened, told me I might pass the night there.

'I am putting you into very respectable company,' said he, 'so be sure and conduct yourself like a gentleman.'

The cellar was very spacious: I should think that the entrance into Dante's Inferno was paradise compared with it. I know and have known Dublin now for about half a century, better probably than any other man in it. I have lived in the Liberty and in every close and outlet in the City of the Panniers,[1] driven by poverty to the most wretched of its localities, and I must confess that the scene which burst upon me that night stands beyond anything the highest flight of my imagination could have conceived without my having an opportunity of seeing it. Burns must have witnessed something of the sort, or he could never have written the most graphic and animated of all his productions – 'The Jolly Beggars'.

The inhabitants of Dublin, and even strangers, are in the habit of listening to the importunities of those irreclaimable beggars whom no law can keep from the streets, of ballad-singers, strolling fiddlers, pipers, flute-players, and the very considerable variety of that class which even now, when we have to pay poor-rates, continue to infest our thoroughfares. What must not the city have been, however, before the enactment of poor-laws? Why, at that period, there existed in Dublin two distinct worlds, each as ignorant of the other – at least, in a particular point of view, and during certain portions of the day – as if they did not inhabit the same country. I have heard many a man of sense and intellect ask, before the establishment of poor-laws, where the vast crowds of paupers passed the night; I never heard the question satisfactorily answered. On that night, however, I found a solution of it, and ever since it has been no mystery to me.

When I got down to the cellar, and looked about me, I was struck, but only for an instant, by the blazing fire which glowed in the grate. My eyes then ran over the scene about me, but how to describe it is the difficulty. It resembled nothing I ever saw either before or since. The inmates were mostly in bed, both men and women, but still a good number of them were up, and indulging in liquors of every description, from strong whisky downwards. The beds were mostly what are called 'shakedowns' – that is, simple straw, sometimes with a rag of sheet, and sometimes with none. There were there the lame, the blind, the dumb, and all who suffered from actual and natural infirmity; but in addition to these, there was every variety of impostor about

---

[1] Carleton has mistaken *cliath* for *cliabh* in the word Ath-cliath (Dublin), which signifies 'The Ford of Hurdles'. *Cliabh* signifies a basket or pannier.

me – most of them stripped of their mechanical accessories of deceit, but by no means all. If not seen, the character of those assembled and their conduct could not possibly be believed. This was half a century ago,[1] when Dublin was swarming with beggars and street impostors of every possible description. This, I understood afterwards, was one of the cellars to which these persons resorted at night, and there they flung off all the restraints imposed on them during the course of the day. I learned afterwards that there were upwards of two dozen such nightly haunts in the suburban parts of the city. Crutches, wooden legs, artificial cancers, scrofulous necks, artificial wens, sore legs, and a vast variety of similar complaints, were hung up upon the walls of the cellars, and made me reflect upon the degree of perverted talent and ingenuity that must have been necessary to sustain such a mighty mass of imposture. Had the same amount of intellect, thought I, been devoted to the exercise of honest and virtuous industry, how much advantage in the shape of energy and example might not society have derived from it. The songs and the gestures were infamous, but if one thing puzzled me more than another, it was the fluency and originality of blackguardism as expressed in language. In fact these people possessed an indecent slang, which constituted a kind of language known only to themselves, and was never spoken except at such orgies as I am describing. Several offered me seats, and were very respectful; but I preferred standing, at least for a time, that I might have a better view of them. While I was in this position a couple of young vagabonds – pickpockets, of course – came and stood beside me. Instinct told me their object, but as I knew the amount in my purse – one penny – I felt little apprehension of having my pockets picked. On entering the cellar, I had to pay twopence for my bed, so that I had just one penny left.

How the night passed I need not say. Of course I never closed my eyes; but so soon as the first glimpse of anything like light appeared, I left the place, and went out on my solitary rambles through the city.

[1] That is, about 1818.

The reader need not expect that I could, even if so disposed, give anything like a detailed account of what I suffered in Dublin, while an obscure stranger. It is a task through which my memory could not carry me – and, what is more, a task from which my heart revolts. Here was I now, with just one penny in my pocket. There was not a single shop open – I had not closed my eyes the preceding night. I knew not where to go, or on what hand to turn. At all events, I turned to my left, and walked up the street into that from which I had turned into Dirty Lane on my entrance into town. I turned to my left again and went on towards town, until I found myself in Castle Street. Going down Castle Street, I accidentally looked at the shops upon my left, and to my surprise, and – need I deny it? – to my hope, I saw over the door of one of them the name – William Carleton, Ladies' Shoemaker. I marked the street, and took its name strongly into my memory.

I can scarcely remember my travels during that morning – scarcely? why, I cannot remember them at all. All I know is, that I bought a roll, and breakfasted upon it. After breakfast, with reverence be it spoken, I kept walking about – found myself in some of the squares, at which, in spite of my miserable and most pitiable position, I could not help wondering. Nothing in the city astonished me so much as the Bank of Ireland and the College. The reader, however, must perceive that I was in a bad frame of mind for admiring anything. Still, the force of novelty is very strong, and I now feel, and have often felt since, how much I was indebted to it upon that occasion.

In this manner I kept wandering about, without an object which could be defined, until probably about twelve o'clock, when, with more difficulty than I apprehended, I contrived, by frequent inquiries, to make my way back to Castle Street. The day was fine, and I walked up and down it two or three times, and glanced once or twice through the windows. At length I went into the shoemaker's shop, and behind the counter saw one of the handsomest and most gentlemanly looking men I ever looked upon. That was my impression then, and it is my impression now after half a century. I approached the counter, and asked if he was Mr Carleton. He replied in the affirmative, and asked me what was my business with him. I paused – I felt the frightful state of destitution in which I stood – I knew not where to find the language I required – I attempted to speak, but could not, and burst into tears. Mr Carleton appeared surprised, and relieved me from much embarrassment by asking the cause of my agitation, upon which I told him I would prefer mentioning it privately, and he accordingly called me over to the other side of the shop, where no one could hear us. I scarcely remember now what my language or the tale it expressed actually was. All I recollect is, that he went to a clerk on the opposite side of the shop and said, 'Give this young man five shillings.'

The value of money and almost of everything is comparative; and I do not think that, from that day until this, I ever felt in its full force the consciousness of what wealth meant. I actually considered myself a wealthy man, and made up my mind under any circumstances never to despair.

I now bethought me of the schools, both classical and English, and looked upon them as the only source of anything like success.

Talking of the schools of Dublin at that time, my readers will feel surprised at a fact which I shall now mention. Only that I am personally aware of this fact, and conscious of placing nothing before the public but the truth, I could scarcely command sufficient courage to make the following statement. I have reason to feel convinced, then, that half a century ago there were nearly as many 'hedge schools' in Dublin as there were of all other classes put together. In other words, that nearly one-half were hedge schools, taught in private rooms by men, who were unworthy to be compared for a moment with the great body of the country hedge schoolmasters of Ireland. They were for the most part, if not illiterate, excessively and barbarously ignorant. Nay more, I knew one instance in which the master actually went round with his scholars, as they used to do in the country, and as I myself did at Newcastle. At this time Dublin, was by no means sufficiently supplied with schools of respectability for the better classes; and for this reason, the hedge schools were crowded, not merely by the poorer children, but by many of the better orders. Education, not only in Dublin, but throughout all Ireland was in a state of shameful and national neglect.

Chapter XIV

'Shooting the moon' – McDonagh, the literary tailor – The tailor's flitting – The designing widow – Carleton tastes wine – A generous gift – The widow's little bill – The circulating library – A new rig-out – Miscellaneous reading – A prediction.

As for me, how I lived I scarcely know – the changes in my state of life and circumstances were so rapid and often so unexpected that no memory could recall them. I need not say that I was frequently driven, by sheer necessity, to run away from my lodgings, or that I was sometimes traced to those in which I took refuge, and their discovery generally occasioned another removal. I remember taking lodgings in the house of a man named William Ridge, a mail-coach guard on one of the northern coaches. He lived in No. 4 Moore Street; and there I met a fellow-lodger named McDonagh, a tailor and a man of letters. He was perpetually writing his life; but as he wrote a vile hand, and was anything but distinguished for spelling, he engaged me to go to the country with him on Sundays – fortunately for me it was summer – where, having seated ourselves in some quiet green field, he produced half a quire of paper, with a pen and ink, and began to dictate his life and adventures, whilst I acted as his amanuensis. I will venture to say that no literary tailor ever felt himself so happy in an amanuensis. He was a little, thin fellow, with intensely black hair, black whiskers and black lively eyes – not at all ill-looking; on the contrary, there was a slight tinge of the gentleman in his appearance and manner. The sad deficiency (simply a want of education) under which the poor fellow laboured was one for which he was not responsible. The great foible of his character, however, was a wish to be looked upon as a man of genius, who had by some unaccountable decree of Providence been placed in a wrong position in life. There is no vanity so incurable as that which arises from the mistake made by a weak mind, when it supposes that it is possessed of intellect. This man had surprising fluency of language – spoke very correctly, and had an excellent accent, as thousands of empty blockheads like him have had before his day and since. Putting all these things together, he took it into his head to consider himself not merely a man of intellect, but a man of genius.

I have just said that he was fortunate in having such an amanuensis, but I must say that the amanuensis was still more fortunate under the patronage of this man of genius. On the first Sunday I perceived that the fluency of language which he possessed in conversation, utterly abandoned him in dictation. He paused – he hesitated – he stumbled; he wanted a particular word here – another there – until he became confused and almost incapable of proceeding. Here he felt the value of his amanuensis. The language in which he was deficient was as free to me as the stream of a summer river. I found the word which he wanted – I saw the drift of what he was about to say – I shaped it in my own language – I proceeded – I gained confidence by degrees. He ceased to be the dictator. I made him give me the simple facts, which I imbued with an easy spirit of fiction – adding, improving, and ultimately inventing with such success, that the poor tailor, when I read over a portion of what I had written, would fly into ecstasies, snap his fingers and dance about like a madman.

After our first day's work was concluded, he said to me on our way home:

'Now, did you imagine me capable of such things? Tell me the truth?'

I looked at him, to ascertain whether his vanity had led him so far as to suppose that *my* work was *his own*.

I replied, 'Many a man does not know the extent of his own genius until he tries it.'

'Yes,' said he, 'yes – that's truth – but listen. So long as you and I reside in the same house you must live at my expense. I have thirty shillings a week with Mr Short, a master tailor in

170

Coghill's Court, off Dame Street, and I will not take your services for nothing; besides – I speak now for your own sake – the thing will improve you. You'll find it a great advantage to understand what genius means.'

'Yes,' said I, 'but I could not think of accepting the kind proposal you make as to my support.'

'Oh, but you must,' said he. 'I have credit with Mrs Ridge – I have been lodging off and on for years with her. When you get something in the shape of employment, you can set all right.'

Such indeed were my circumstances at the moment, that I felt no very strong objection to this proposal.

In this way we lived for about six weeks together, devoting every Sunday to his biography, which was a mere record of the same facts and incidents repeated *ad infinitum*. In the meantime, I owed Mrs Ridge a month's lodging, for which she carved me pretty sharply. This gave me very little trouble, because I took it for granted that my man of genius would come to my assistance for such a trifle, without the slightest hesitation. I never was more mistaken in my life, although when I asked him to take me out of my little difficulty he replied, 'Most certainly – on the day after tomorrow I will settle it.'

Mrs Ridge and I, however, were somewhat surprised on finding that the man of genius did not return that night – nor the next – nor yet the next. In fact he had bolted, upwards of three pounds in her debt; and as a portion of that was incurred for my support, she very naturally turned to me for it. I, as was only natural, seeing my circumstances, took example by the man of genius, and bolted also.

My next change was to Mary's Lane, where I found lodgings with a Mrs Carson, a widow. There were five or six of us – two printers from Enniskillen, who were at work with a Mr Smith, a printer of Mary Street, who was then printing some classical schoolbook. Mrs Carson was extremely kind – indeed so much so that I could not understand it. Of course none of her lodgers boarded with her. She cooked their breakfasts only – for they always dined out – and sometimes made their own tea for them

171

in the evening; for this she charged them a small percentage. She herself seldom breakfasted until all her lodgers had gone out to their employment for the day. I rarely went out until they had all gone, and upon some occasions she became exceedingly kind and complacent. I had had very little experience of women, and none at all of widows, at that period of my life. There is, however, an instinctive feeling in these matters between the sexes – especially in some minds – that guides us to a true conclusion. One day, as I was going out she asked me to breakfast with her the next morning.

'You know,' said she, 'I don't breakfast until all my lodgers go out – so,' she added, smiling rather significantly, 'you know we will have this place to ourselves; but you mustn't take advantage of that, and make love to me.' Then, after throwing out this hint, she rapidly turned to the same subject in a different form. 'Oh, no,' she proceeded, 'you mustn't make love to me while I'm in *this* house and in *this* street. I'm about to remove either to Mary Street or Henry Street. I have made about a hundred and forty pounds, and my intention is to furnish a house, and (with some assistance from my brother) to open a boarding establishment. They tell me it's coining, and nothing else. Now good-bye, but see, remember you're to breakfast with me tomorrow.'

The sagacious and calculating widow was between thirty-five and forty, although she looked younger. Before a week passed after this conversation, I found myself almost at home. Every attention was paid to me. My word was law. Every wish of mine was anticipated, and I found myself a free guest at her table. This state of things did not pass unobserved by my fellow-lodgers, who quizzed me about it to no end. In the meantime, as week succeeded week, and she was working heaven and earth to lure me to a declaration, I happened one day to meet a person who must have known something about my object in life, although I cannot now remember who he was. He told me there was a classical school in French Street, and that its proprietor, a Protestant clergyman, wanted a classical assistant. I immediately returned to my lodgings, where I sat down, and with much care and pains, addressed to him an application for the appointment in the best Latin I could muster. I then called at the school, sent in my letter, and left word with the servant that I would call the next day.

I must observe here, that if ever a man was born to what is called ill-luck, I was, and to this day am, that man. At cards, for instance, I might play for a whole night, and not win more than a couple or three games at the most, although there was not a man living who understood the game better. This has been always my luck in any game that depended on chance.

I called next day to see the proprietor of the school in French Street, sent in my name, and was shown into the parlour. Here I had not remained long, when the clergyman came in, and shook me warmly and cordially by the hand. This reception gave me courage and hope, both however but of short duration.

'I deeply regret, Mr Carleton,' said he, 'that you did not make an earlier application. On the very day before I received your letter, I engaged a gentleman who commenced his duties this morning; a fact,' he added, 'which I almost regret, for your letter is one which I will venture to say neither he nor I could write.'

He then entered into that kind of conversation with me, and made those kind inquiries, which betoken both a friendly and a generous heart. I gave him an outline of my adventures and exertions in quest of employment, and a brief history of my repeated failures, and then took up my hat from a back table, which stood in a little recess in a shadowy part of the room. He seized my hat, and said, 'Don't be in a hurry – sit down a few minutes, I wish to ask you a few more questions,' – and when he said this, he went outside the parlour door into the hall, where he remained five or six minutes, holding my hat as if unconscious that he had it in his hand. On his return, he replaced it on the little table, rang the bell and ordered in refreshments, which consisted of wine, cold meat, and other things, of which we both partook. *Now this was the first occasion on which I had ever tasted wine.* I again got up and went to the hall door on my way out – we shook hands most cordially, and just as I was about to bid him farewell, he said, 'Be careful of your hat, and when you next take it off – look into it. God bless you. Call on me from time to time.'

I was struck by the language he used about my hat, immediately took it off, and found three pound notes in the bottom of it. This act of pure and elevated charity had a most extraordinary effect upon me – it not only affected my moral feelings, but my reason. It sustained and supported me, and filled my mind with a fresh sense of hope, such as I had not felt for many a month before.

I was now a wealthy man, and every one knows that wealth creates independence. I could not close my eyes to the widow's object, and I felt a very uncomfortable sense of degradation at the notion of being tied to such a woman. Accordingly on my return home – that is to say, to Mary's Lane – I asked her to let me know the amount of my bill. She started, and looked at me, in a state of confusion that she could not conceal.

'Surely you are not going,' she said; 'I did everything in my power to make you comfortable – didn't I?'

'Indeed I feel that, Mrs Carson, and I shall never forget your kindness.'

'But where are you going to?' she asked, 'and why do you leave the place?'

'I am going to fill an appointment,' I replied, 'which I have just got in the city of Cork. I must start by the Cork mail tonight.'

'And you wish, of course, to settle,' said she. 'All right! I will produce the bill in a few minutes. Just sit down until I come back.'

At this moment Mr Gartland, my countryman,[1] one of the printers I have referred to, chanced to come in, and I told him that I was going.

'Have you quarrelled?' said he.

'No,' I replied; 'she is only gone to get my bill.'

'I see,' said he; 'but listen – she lured you in to live with her under the hope that you would marry her; but this is an old trick of hers. Now that she finds you are going she will bring you in a bill that will astonish you.'

[1] That is, from his part of the country.

'What am I to do, then?' I asked.

'Ask her,' he replied, 'if she knows a friend of yours, a printer that you knew in Birmingham. The man is her husband, and left her, not without good reason. She produced him a young daughter about five months after their marriage, although that marriage took place when they had been only six weeks known to each other. She knows,' he added, 'or rather, she suspects, that I am acquainted with the fact – and for that reason I shall remain in the room until the bill is settled.'

Mrs Carson was but a few minutes absent, and when she did return, the bill she produced was monstrous. Her countenence was as black as night – she trembled with the combined influence of disappointment and indignation. On looking at the bill I was certainly thunderstruck. Every meal which, in point of fact, she had forced upon me under the pretence of hospitality and kindness, was down to day and date – and at unconscionable terms.

I handed the bill to Gartland, who, on looking at it, brought her into another room, and after about twenty minutes, returned by himself, stating that she was satisfied to receive thirty shillings, instead of four pounds twelve, the original amount.

On that very day, I happened to be walking along Francis Street, and when accidentally on my way towards the Coombe, I observed a bill for lodgings in the window of a house on the left-hand side. I went in to make the usual inquiries, and to my surprise and delight, found myself in a circulating library. I immediately took the bed that was to be let, and paid the amount of the first week (two shillings) in advance, making it a condition that I should be free of the library. To this there was no objection. As usual, and the better to account for the want of a trunk, I told the landlady that I would only lodge with her, but that I boarded in the house of a friend who had no bed to spare.

In the meantime, an astonishing incident occurred to me. I was still in possession of nearly thirty shillings. My wardrobe wanted repair. I need scarcely assure the reader that ever since my arrival in Dublin, I had always resorted to the second-hand market. Now the great second-hand clothes-market – the Monmouth Street of

Dublin – is Plunket Street, which reaches from Francis Street nearly to Patrick Street. Little Mary Street, to which I had just bidden farewell, was another such market, and as it was there that I always dealt, I found myself in Plunket Street for the first time. I was walking along slowly, examining everything of the kind I wanted, when a man, bare-headed, and evidently the proprietor of one of the shops, approached me, and holding out his hand, said, 'Good God! William Carleton, is this you?' I looked at him, and in an instant recognized a brother of one of the most popular characters I ever drew – 'the poor scholar'. If a spirit from the other world had stood before me, I could not have felt more astonished. On my making inquiry as to his presence there, Donnelly told me that the late proprietor of the establishment had been a relative of Mr McArdle, the parish priest of Clogher, who had given him a letter to him. On the strength of that letter, he had trained Donnelly as a salesman until he understood the business, after which he died, having first seen him married to his daughter. There never lived a more generous or a more affectionate man than Donnelly. He insisted on rigging me out from top to toe, gratuitously.

I was now, at least in my own opinion, a very comfortable young fellow. I had a good cheap bed in a snug back room off the parlour, with a whole circulating library for my amusement. It would be useless to attempt anything like a description of my enjoyment. I think I could not have read less than from twelve to sixteen hours a day. I have read from many a circulating library since, but from any approaching this one in character, never. The best and most perfect I ever knew was that kept by Mr Gerald Tyrrell, in a corner house that opened into Lower Abbey Street and Lower Sackville Street. Mr Tyrrell is still alive, and one of the Dalkey Commissioners, but what became of his library I know not. The woman who kept the Francis Street establishment was a widow, a Mrs Richardson, but never upon any occasion did I see her look into a book. Whether it was she herself who collected and arranged the library, I cannot say. I only hope, for the honour of her sex, it was not; because such a mass of obscenity and profligacy was (out of Holywell Street, the Jewish establishment in London) never put together. How booksellers were found to publish the books it is difficult to say, or how they escaped prosecution. There was not a book in the whole library but Mrs Richardson was acquainted with its character, a fact which she never denied.

One of them, for instance, was the *History of Mrs Leeson* – or in other words the history of the infamous Peg Plunkett, who figured during the viceroyalty of Lord Manners, and of whom the anecdote of 'Manners, you dogs,' is yet told. *The History of the Chevalier de Faublas* was also there, and another revolting abomination under the nickname of Aristotle. There was also among them a book which, as a repertory of the antique scandal of the fashionable demireps of that day, would be apt to fetch a good price even now. It was called the *Irish Female Jockey Club*. Only the initials of the names of the characters were given, but so well had they been known to several of the readers, that the names were found pencilled in full on the margins. How so much private scandal was got together, and whether by one or many contributors, it is impossible to say. All I can add is, that the minuteness of the details, and the acquaintance with the localities exhibited by the author or authors, proved those sketches to contain a vast deal of truth – a fact which probably accounted for their escape from prosecution. The curiosity of a young man, added to the fact that they came in my way by accident, must plead my excuse for reading them. Independently of this, the very best of us have a taste for scandal. I dined frequently with my friend Donnelly, the 'poor scholar's' brother, in Plunket Street; but unfortunately, he was carried off by fever in three months after we had resumed our acquaintance in Dublin.

I was now a well-dressed man, and I can assure the reader that a smooth outside, in such a world as this, where outsides are so much looked to, is a strong letter of recommendation to a stranger who has little else to recommend him. What good was my intellect to me when in shabby apparel? What person could discover it in a man with a seedy coat upon his back, when that man was a stranger? We ought not to expect impossibilities. I myself at that time was not conscious of the possession of intellect – although I must confess that there lurked about me, as I have said elsewhere, a vague impression that I was not an ordinary man. This impression prevented me from writing home to my friends, and acted as a justification of the resolution I had come to, of never either writing them a line or returning to my native place, unless I could do so with honour and credit to myself. There were also two other motives; to one of these I have already alluded – I mean Anne Duffy. I wished to distinguish myself in order that *she* might hear of my distinction; at the other the reader may probably smile. As I am on the subject, I shall mention it here, lest I might altogether forget it.

My eldest married sister, Mary, lived (about the period when I, having been set apart for the Church, commenced my Latin) in the townland of a place called Ballagh, remarkable for the beauty of its lough. It was during the Easter holidays, and I was on a visit with her. At that time it was not unusual for a small encampment of the Scotch gipsies to pass over to the north of Ireland, and indeed I am not surprised at it, considering the extraordinary curiosity, not to say enthusiasm, with which they were received by the people. The men were all tinkers, and the women thieves and fortune-tellers – but in their case the thief was always sunk in the fortune-teller.

Now one of these gipsies called on my sister while I was with her, and having been desired to take a seat, she did so, and looking at me, said, turning to my sister, 'Do you wish to have this boy's fortune told?'

'I do,' replied poor, unsuspecting Mary; 'I would be very glad to have his fortune told.'

'Well,' said the other, extending her open hand, 'cross my palm; we can't tell truth unless we receive money.'

This condition was pretty generally known, and the people were prepared for it. My sister accordingly gave her a tenpenny bit; upon which she produced a pack of cards from her pocket, shuffled them repeatedly, and placing them before me, desired me to cut them deeply, as she would have the more information to disclose as to my future fortune. She was cunning enough to draw from my sister, without seeming to have any purpose, all the information she could gain respecting my prospects in life, and so learned that I was intended for the priesthood. The sallow old pythoness lost little time in revealing the oracle of my destiny; I remember the words as distinctly as if I had heard them only yesterday.

'He will never be a priest,' said she, 'he will love the girls too well; but when he grows up, he will go to Dublin, and become a great man.'

This prediction I never forgot, nor was it without influence in urging me into the city.

Chapter XV

In search of a religion – A strange figure – Mrs Ridge's 'uncle' –
Removal to the Coombe – Return of McDonagh – Weyman and
Lablache – Love of the drama – The nondescript, and his brother –
Marsh's library – A glimpse of Maturin.

WHILE lodging in the library I did not forget my business; by
this I mean that I was always on the look-out for something in
the shape of employment. About this time, too, I began to think
a good deal upon the subject of religion. I occasionally went, at
first out of curiosity, sometimes to one church and sometimes to
another; and I was much struck and often very deeply impressed
by what I had both seen and heard. I did not, however, confine
my Sunday visits merely to the churches of the Establishment. I
often went to the Presbyterian places of worship also, but I did
not relish them so well. Even the Methodists did not escape me.
In point of fact, I was resolved to look through them all. If I do
not examine and compare, thought I, how can I form an opinion
as to their relative merits? One doctrine of the Catholic Church
I had sent to the winds long before that period. I allude to
exclusive salvation. Neither logic nor reasoning was required to
enable me to discard it. Common feeling – the plain principle of
simple humanity – was sufficient. This, indeed, was the doctrine
which first taught me to feel the justice of thinking for myself;
and from that moment I felt that I could not much longer hold
the doctrines of a Catholic. This course of thought was not
suggested to me by a human being, and to confess the truth, I was
a Protestant at least twelve months before the change was known
to a human being.

A circumstance now occurred which, I may say, shaped the
destiny of my future life. I was one day as usual going among the
schools – with the old object in view, the seeking of employment.

I knew that, without exertion, employment was out of my reach. I was passing through Peter Street, going towards Bride Street, when on a hall door I saw a brass label on which was engraved in large and legibile letters:

MR KANE'S CLASSICAL ACADEMY

'Here goes,' thought I, 'once more – and I suppose with the same success,' as I knocked. When the door was opened, I asked to see Mr Kane, and was shown into the parlour. In less than a minute a gentleman dressed in black entered. But before I proceed a step farther I must describe him. He was probably near sixty – a large roundish kind of man, and about five feet ten in height. His black costume did not resemble those which I was in the habit of seeing everywhere I went. He wore a black coat, a black waistcoat, black knee-breeches and black stockings, in fact, he was black from top to toe. During all my life I never saw any human being so awkward and ungraceful: but what was this when compared to his face? His complexion was of a dull, dreary red, and his cheeks hung about his face as if they would actually drop off. His eyes at a first glance were large and apparently meaningless, and as for his legs, they would have made the fortune of a chair-man,[1] whilst his fists would have done credit to Tom Cribb the pugilist. This is but a faint sketch of him, indeed it might cause any friend of his, should one chance to see it, to set me down as a corrupt rascal, and who had allowed myself to be bribed into giving him a most agreeable and interesting appearance.

Well, he came into the room – entered into conversation with me – talked with such a spirit of kindness and courtesy, and, as I proceeded to allude to my object, with such thoughtfulness and consideration; his language, too, was so easy – combining in itself the spirit, not only of the gentleman but of the Christian – that I felt an actual charm pervade my heart, and I could almost have thrown my arms about him, and pressed him like a father

[1] The men who carried the sedan-chairs in the last century were mostly Irishmen, and were chosen for their size and strength.

to my breast. He reminded me of those dissolving views, in which some object painful to look upon, passes away, we know not how, and ere we are aware, something in the strongest contrast, and at the same time exquisitely beautiful, takes its place.

After our conversation had nearly closed, and I was about to take my leave of one of the most fascinating men I ever met – 'By the way,' said he, 'a thought strikes me. A friend of mine is master of a very large English school on the Coombe, and I remember that when last I saw him, he asked me if I could recommend a classical tutor for his son. This conversation occurred only a few days ago. I could think of no one at the time; but I will give you his address, and when you call on him, say that it was I who sent you.'

I got the necessary address, and lost no time in calling on Mr Fox, the gentleman in question. I found him a plain, agreeable man, remarkable for common sense, and a benignant spirit. We came to terms at once, and before I left the house it was arranged that I should commence my duty as tutor to his son the next morning. Thus was the ice first broken, after many an unsuccessful and depressing experiment – that often made my heart sick and almost indignant against Providence itself.

In the meantime, Mrs Richardson became troublesome, peevish, and altogether sickening. I could not help observing from time to time, that her temper, from being fretful, was passing to a very opposite condition. She frequently became musical, and sometimes a regular attitudinizer, accompanying the attitudes by winkings and other motions, which to me were perfectly unintelligible. At length, I asked the servant to give me an explanation of her conduct.

'Poor woman,' said she; 'they don't last very long; she takes them only by fits and starts; but at all events *you'll* soon have to leave us – at least for about a month.'

'Why so?' I asked.

'Can you keep a secret?' she inquired.

'Why not,' I replied, 'if it be necessary?'

'Well,' said she, 'listen: there's a wealthy married gentleman from Limerick who comes to Dublin four times every year. He lodges in her rooms upstairs – for you know she owns the whole house. This gentleman brings a lady with him, wherever he gets her, and they stop – that is they sleep – upstairs while he's in town. When this gentleman comes, you must leave the place until he takes his departure. So now make money of that.'

Every word the woman uttered was verified. In the course of a fortnight afterwards, I got notice to travel, and so brief was the notice, that I was not allowed to sleep in the house that night, although it was late in the evening when I learned that I must move. Altogether, I felt very indifferent in the matter, for I was tired of the old wretch, and her periodical fits of maudlin indulgence. I accordingly went over to Moore Street, and slept that night at No. 4, Mrs Ridge's old lodgings. The next morning I got up and dressed myself – all except my coat and boots; neither of these were forthcoming; and on my making inquiries, she very coolly told me that she lent them to an uncle of hers in the next street. When I left her as a lodger I did not imagine that she would consider me her debtor, because McDonagh, the literary tailor, had, in my own hearing, told her that until further notice both my board and lodging should be at his expense; and with this assurance she seemed perfectly satisfied. Upon his subsequent disappearance, without settling either for himself or me, I thought I saw at a glimpse the value of his hospitality, and the sincerity of his friendship. At least, such was my opinion then. On going that night to Mrs Ridge's, I had enough small change to pay for my bed and breakfast next morning, so that I entertained no apprehension of the step she took. She assured me very solemnly, as I have said, that my coat and shoes were with her relative – that she had just got upon them the amount I owed her, and that I might take whatever course I deemed best under the circumstances. I paused, and felt sadly at a loss. In fact I had no friend, and could think of nobody.

'Why don't you write,' said she, 'to the gentleman whose son you are teaching?'

I seized upon this hint, but became alarmed lest such an unusual application might deprive me of my only tuition. Still, turn it over as I might, it was my only chance; and having got Mrs Ridge to furnish me with pen and paper, I gave her a note to the mother of my pupil, who, from all that I could observe of her, was a very amiable and kind-hearted woman. In due time she and Mrs Ridge made their appearance; and in less than ten minutes I was on my way to the Coombe under the friendly guidance of Mrs Fox, the kindest and most motherly woman that ever existed. Mrs Ridge had *not* pledged my clothes.

'Now,' said she, on our way home – 'there is a nice room and a spare bed in our house that are not used by anyone. You had better occupy them; they are lying there empty, and, in truth, will be better for occupation You will oblige us by accepting them; and they will cost you nothing – at all events until you get rich, which I hope will be soon.'

I was not then in a strait waistcoat, and as a natural consequence, received this kind offer with a deep sense of gratitude. I slept at Mrs Fox's that night, and did not take my departure for, I think, two years afterwards. McDonagh, the literary tailor – or, in other words, the man of genius – and I were fated to meet again. I saw him one day on Ormond Quay, when he explained his abrupt and somewhat mysterious disappearance. If the poor fellow told truth – and I think he did – there was no blame to be attached to him. He had received a letter from some part of Connaught, stating that his mother was dying, and that, finding herself near the close of her life, she begged him for God's sake to go to her – to let her see him if only once before she died. It seems the poor fellow scrambled up all the money he could, and arrived just in time to gratify her last wish. I believe all this to have been strictly true, because when he returned to town, he once more resumed his position with Short, the master tailor of Coghill's Court. On that very occasion, he told me that Short wanted a person to instruct his children, a son and a daughter, and he said that if he had known my address he would have acquainted me with the fact before.

184

'Just come with me now,' said he, 'and we'll call upon him.'

We did so, I began to teach Short's children the next evening. For this I had a guinea a month, and in the course of about half a year was one of the best dressed young fellows in Dublin. By this I mean that I was as becomingly and respectably dressed as any man could be – certainly without dandyism or vain and empty nonsense. They say that one good thing seldom comes without another to keep as it were, in countenance.

I return to my journey home with the mother of my first Dublin pupil. My bed was aired, and comfortably made. I slept soundly, and next morning had a message to come down to breakfast. I did so. I was also asked to dine, and under the impression that such invitations would be rare, I accepted that also – and from that day forth, during two years and upwards, I lodged, breakfasted, and dined with that most affectionate family. If I breathed the notion of removing, they became indignant; but, indeed, in the course of a very short time removal was the farthest thing possible from my mind.

The Fox family consisted of the father and mother of my pupil – one of the best and sweetest tempered boys that ever lived – two maiden aunts, a niece, by name Jane Anderson – and her sister Margaret, who was much younger. Old Mr Fox was a most delightful companion; had seen a great deal of the world, and was a personal friend of Grattan. He had a magnificent bass voice, and was one of the celebrated choir of Christ Church, at the head of which was the immortal David Weyman – then considered the most powerful bass in the world, and author of the best work upon choral and cathedral music that we possess.[1] I heard him in Christ Church, but could scarcely believe that musical thunder so deep and terrible could proceed out of human lips. Such was my opinion until I heard that prodigy Lablache,[2] to whose paralysing peal Weyman's thunder was but a squeak.

---

[1] Weyman was vicar-choral of St Patrick's. His *Melodia Sacra* was edited by Dr Smith, and appeared in six volumes in 1844. Weyman died in August 1822.

[2] Lablache, though born in Italy, had an Irish mother.

Lablache was six feet six in height, and more than corpulent in proportion. Such was his weight that, as he approached the footlights, the very floor of the theatre shook, and so powerful was the vibration of his voice, that any side curtains that happened to be down were shaken by his tones. I feel that I have travelled a little out of my way here – but to return.

The evenings I spent in conversation with Mr Fox were delightful. He was full of anecdote connected with Grattan and Flood, and all the other eminent men in the Irish Parliament.

There is nothing more valuable in life than respectable connection. Before long I became acquainted with a Mr Gallaher, who was also a musical man, and the possessor of a magnificent bass voice. He had had a conversation with a Mr Eustace, who kept a very respectable school at No. 2, Lower Buckingham Street, of which I was the subject. Gallaher's father and Mr Fox were not only neighbours, but warm and sincere friends, and it was through their intimacy that I and Mr Gallaher's son became connected. The son at that time held a high situation in La Touche's celebrated bank in Castle Street. The result of Gallaher's conversation with Mr Eustace was an intimation to me, through Mr Gallaher, that Mr Eustace wanted a classical assistant; and the second result was, that I called upon him and was engaged, at the very fair salary of thirty-five pounds a year. Now my readers must admit that this certainly was advancing in the world. In looking back over this portion of my life, I cannot forget my extraordinary delight in witnessing theatrical entertainments. I might now be considered wealthy; but even before this, when I was struggling with penury itself, I have often spent almost my last shilling on the upper gallery – both in Crow Street and Hawkins Street.[1] No man ever enjoyed theatrical representations with greater enthusiasm. This, however, is not at all surprising, because that was precisely the period when the Dublin theatre was in its glory. We had from time to time the Siddonses, Kean

[1] Neither of these houses is now in existence. The Theatre Royal was in Hawkins Street. Two histories of its vicissitudes have been published, one by an anonymous writer, and one by R. M. Levey and J. O'Rorke.

the elder, Miss O'Neil, Young, Macready, and several other celebrities. I could now afford to attend the theatre, and a very regular attendant I was.

One morning, we were sitting in Mr Fox's parlour after breakfast, when a gentlemanly-looking man, whose presence had been expected, entered the room, accompanied by one of the most extraordinary nondescripts I ever beheld. That the person who accompanied or introduced him was a gentleman there could be no doubt. He was calm, collected, and intelligent, if not intellectual in every feature; but, in addition to this, there was an expression of kindness and affection, especially when he looked at the nondescript, which evinced the strong interest he felt in him. Nor was this interest lessened by a smile of good nature which played over his countenance, and which it evidently cost him an effort to keep within the bounds of laughter. The question now is, how shall I attempt to describe the nondescript? Surely, if I fail, the reader will not blame me. Let him, imagine, then, a man about one or two and twenty, with pale, sandy hair, dressed in an outside frieze coat not worth half a crown, worn almost out of all decency; a waistcoat with but one button, old corduroy breeches, open at the knees, stockings, with the heels out, gartered under the knees, clouted brogues white with dust, his coarse shirt unbuttoned at the neck, and free from the restraint of a handkerchief. On entering the room and sitting down, he placed his *caubeen*, the crown of which had fallen in, upon the floor beside him. His hands, which were crusted with black, mouldy dust, he stretched gracefully along his thighs, until his fingers bent over his knees as if to keep the joints steady. His face was, without exception, the most blank and sheepish I ever saw; the eyes, a dull grey, were looking steadily on to the floor before him, unless when spoken to, and then he would give an awkward, timid, side glance, like a man conscious of having been detected in guilt, and hopeless of pardon.

The reader will perceive, or ought, by this time, that business was fast increasing on me – when he learns that this young gentleman was coming to be placed under my tuition and Mr

187

Fox's – under mine for classics, and Mr Fox's for English. His history was that of many, whose families have been brought to desolation and ruin, with the exception probably of a single member, who has been rescued from the common fate by the benevolence of wealthy friends. Such was the fact here. The two individuals before us were brothers, one of them having been a lieutenant in the Peninsular War, and the other, the unfortunate nondescript, one of those individuals who attend a turf-boat on the canal. The reader will now understand why I was able to give the description of his dress with such accuracy. His brother having arranged the terms for his board and education, with Mr Fox and me, brought him out upon a wardrobe expedition, and returned with him, walking more like a piece of machinery than anything else, in a new suit of clothes. In the course of the same evening some additional baggage in the shape of a trunk was brought home by a porter.

The two were strangely separated; while the elder brother was engaged in helping to seal the fate and fortune of Napoleon at Waterloo, the other, as I have said, was attached to a turf-boat on one of the canals. He had never opened a book, but I believe in my soul that such a progress, in the teeth of so much stupidity, was never made by a mortal man. That progress was one of the most striking proofs of what incessant work and unswerving perseverance will do, that ever was witnessed. The family I refer to had wealthy and powerful friends; one of these was the late Mrs La Touche of Delgany. She purchased a commission for the elder brother, provided him with a handsome outfit, and sent him to join Wellington and seek his fortune. He returned, however, without a fortune, but as the young man possessed good sense, and a considerable affection for his brother and sisters, he commenced such a course of classics as enabled him to enter college, and take a degree. At the very time he produced his brother as a claimant for education, he himself held the situation of private tutor in a Wexford family, which had certain historical associations even now well known.

During the time of the younger brother's residence with Mr

Fox, the late James Digges La Touche was secretary to the Sunday School Society for Ireland, an institution which, at that time, when education was scarce, conferred most important advantages upon the country. We were preparing him for an appointment there, and we did so with the greater goodwill and satisfaction as we knew he would get it the moment he had a chance for it. There were no competitive examinations in those days – personal influence did all – and in preparing for it the young fellow rendered us every assistance. At all events, in due time the expected vacancy in the Sunday School Society occurred, and in due time he applied for it and got it.

Everything now went smoothly with me. I was attending Mr Eustace's school in Lower Buckingham Street as a classical assistant. I was also attending Short the tailor's children every evening in Coghill's Court – and I was attending Armstrong, the turf-boat man, and Mr Fox's son, without the slightest inconvenience with respect to time.

At this period I became acquainted with a gentleman named William Sisson, who, in consequence of some dreadful accident, lost the greater portion of one leg and thigh; but so admirably was this replaced, that to an ordinary eye he looked like a man afflicted only with slight lameness. He was deputy librarian of Marsh's almost unknown library in St Patrick's Close. This was the first public library I had ever seen, and I wondered at the time how such an incredible number of books could be read, or, which comes to much about the same thing, how a sufficient number of men of letters could be found to read them. I read there for two seasons, and during all that time I never saw so many as half a dozen avail'ng themselves of that noble institution. Of the two whom I met there, one is still living – Dr Travers, lecturer on Medical Jurisprudence, I think, in Trinity College – and the other was the late Rev. Thomas Shore.

Maturin had not only been a reader there, but wrote the greater portion of several of his novels on a small plain deal desk, which he removed from place to place according as it suited his privacy or convenience. And now that I have mentioned Maturin, the fact reminds me of a visit I paid him a little before the period of which I am writing. I had read several of his novels in Mrs Richardson's library, his tragedy of *Bertram* included, and as I knew he lived in York Street, I resolved, under some pretext or other, to pay him a visit, that I might satisfy myself as to what a man of genius could be like. I accordingly called at his house – which was on the left-hand side as you go from Aungier Street to the Green[1] – and was admitted. At that time I had read so little of the habits or the personal appearance of men of genius, that I knew not what inference to draw from his. He was dressed in a very slovenly manner – a loose cravat about the neck – was in slippers – and had on a brown outside coat much too wide and large for him. Altogether he appeared to be an irreclaimable sloven. After motioning me to a seat, and allowing me a reasonable space to explain the cause of my visit, he asked me was there anything in which he could oblige me. I replied that I was anxious to enter Trinity College, but that I did not feel myself in a position to do so.

'In other words,' said he, 'you are not able to pay the fees. In that case, then, I would recommend you to read for a sizarship.'

'But then I might fail,' said I.

'Then,' he replied, 'you have only to try it again – or, hold!' said he, 'I think you could be got in as a non-demurrent pensioner.'

Of course we had more conversation than I am now detailing, during which he would become abstracted, as it were, for a moment, and raise his open hand as if he were about to say, 'Hush! I have an image!'

After having left him, I would, had I possessed the experience which I do now, have pronounced him to be as vain a creature as ever lived. He was a thin man, not ill-looking, with good eyes, and when wrapped up in the brown overcoat resembled a man to whom some person, larger in size than himself – seeing that

---

[1] Stephen's Green.

his wardrobe was at a low ebb – had generously thrown a half-worn suit, until something better might happen.[1]

[1] Maturin's works, notwithstanding the high opinion of Scott and Byron, are almost entirely forgotten. His *Melmoth, the Wanderer* has been most often reprinted. It is a powerful, but gloomy story. His tragedies were no less popular than his novels.

Chapter XVI

Love re-asserts itself – Mortimer and Samuel O'Sullivan – Matrimonial notions – Transformation of the nondescript – James Digges La Touche – Appointed to a clerkship – High treason against the Sunday School Society – Marriage – Thomas Parnell – Ambition to enter TCD – Notice to quit – Reinstatement.

I NOW found that I was progressing as favourably as could be expected, as the phrase of the sick-room has it; but at the same time, a new element took possession of me – although the reader will probably condemn me for associating it with anything like novelty, inasmuch as I may appear to be merely going over the same ground which I travelled with the miller's daughter for my lodestar. In other words I was once more in love, and with as pretty a girl as Anne Duffy; and that was Jane Anderson, my present wife.

My readers, I repeat, may say that they can discover nothing novel in a second love, and yet I can assure them with truth, that the two passions as they existed in me, had scarcely any resemblance to each other. In the first instance, I fell in love with Anne Duffy when I was a mere boy, not fifteen years of age. Anne Duffy I loved at a distance – we never spoke during the course of my love – and although she possessed a healthy bona fide existence, yet to me she was nothing but the ideal spirit of beauty. The power of the imagination illustrates the feeling of love in a young heart, especially under circumstances similar to those of Anne Duffy and me, and throws an ethereal charm over first love – a charm that can never be felt during any subsequent engagement of the heart, however powerful or intense. That love is the only one which re-opens to us for the first time the gates of that paradise from which the whole human race has been so long expelled. That I admit the full force of the *charm* I allude to in my first love is only a truthful record of what I felt, but my love for Jane Anderson, although it had less poetry in it, yet had more of that reality which is sanctioned by the heart rather than the imagination. In Anne Duffy's case my love was *a first impression*, and first impressions, under circumstances similar to ours, can never be removed.

The notion of entering college had been of late beginning to set strong within me. Who knows but that the distinction of which I sometimes had dim dreams might yet be realized? Who knows but that I might yet become the Gil Blas of Ireland? It is, indeed, extraordinary to think how a love of fame often lurks, almost unknown, in the human heart, like the first indistinct emotions of love.

The school kept by Mr Fox was one of Erasmus Smith's, and with the exception of the classical schools on that magnificent establishment, was one of the highest and most valuable. I don't think it brought him in less than three hundred a year. This school was in the parish of St Catherine's, in the Coombe. The Protestant clergyman of the parish was the Rev. William White-law, who had succeeded as rector his brother,[1] one of the authors of Whitelaw and Walsh's *History of Dublin*. He was one of the most amiable men I ever knew, and in virtue of his official duty as visitor to the school, I had frequent opportunities of meeting him. He was the first Protestant clergyman I ever dined with in Dublin. The Rev. Samuel O'Sullivan – then a resident master in college – was his curate, and brother to Mortimer O'Sullivan, rector of Killyman, in the diocese of Dromore.[2] I have heard

[1] The Rev. James Whitelaw was born in Co. Leitrim about 1749, and died 4th February, 1813. The *History of Dublin* referred to is still valuable, though Dr J. T. Gilbert's work has superseded it.

[2] These two brothers were born in the South of Ireland, and were originally Catholics. They wrote many books, which were extravagantly praised by their Protestant friends. They were very able men, and Mortimer will be chiefly remembered as the cause of Moore's *Travels of an Irish gentleman in search of a religion*, to which Mortimer replied by a *Guide to an Irish gentleman in search of a religion*. Moore makes delicious fun of him in his 'Fudge' poems.

many eloquent men, but a more eloquent man than Mortimer I never heard.

I now began to read for college, and took Mr Armstrong, my pupil, into the course. I had also prepared him in book-keeping, which I studied for the occasion, and had put him through the three 'sets' when the vacancy in the office of the Sunday School Society, for which both he and we were looking out, actually took place. As Mrs La Touche of Delgany was his friend and patroness, I need scarcely add that he was immediately appointed. He still, however, continued to board at Mr Fox's. I have stated that something I felt no difficulty in bearing, from my past experience, began to act as an obstruction to those literary distinctions which I felt awaited me in college. In other words, Cupid interfered both with literature and ambition. I never was a man who looked far before me – what man of impulse ever does! I consequently made several attempts to gain a place in the heart of Miss Jane Anderson, but as I was obliged to feel, with only indifferent success. I could not get her to understand me. I now feel that I was, without exception, the most ridiculous blockhead that ever lived. I kept hinting, and insinuating, and shaping small oracles, which no human being could understand, and that with a face that seemed better adapted for a death-bed repentance than for a lover disclosing the tender passion. It mattered not; although slow, I was sure – yet I scarcely have to thank myself for the security. I also threw out hints to the lady's aunt, who received them with more good humour than I relished, because the matter was above all others one on which a man would decline being laughed at. At length, the aunt uttered one serious sentence, which brought me to reflection.

'I think, William,' said she, 'it would be time enough for you to think of marrying a wife when you feel yourself able to support one.'

This was a home-thrust which no armour could resist, and I felt it for the time like a death-blow. Three months now went on, and I was neither better nor worse. Armstrong, although he had got the appointment, still, like a sensible fellow, remained under my tuition in the classics, because it was his brother's object that he should enter college, a design which was ultimately accomplished.

It is not to be supposed that I lay upon my oars here, especially as the prospect of the wife remained in the background as an incentive to action. Ever since I became a lover, I gave up like a true Irishman all notion of collegiate distinction.

I have mentioned the fact that a Mr Gallaher held an advanced situation in La Touche's bank. He was not only an eminent accountant, but a first-rate musician. For instance, he was engaged as singing master to Santry Charter School, where he attended three times a week; for this he was well paid. The Government money was liberal in those days, without much inquiry as to its application, or rather the object of its application.

Armstrong's case was a proof to me of a principle which has not been much understood. It is this, that we are not to form an opinion of minds upon which neglect and poverty have operated in early life, from their first exhibitions under instruction. Let us consider the mind of the individual like the body of a sick man recovering after illness – it is weak, and can do very little of itself until strengthened by medicine, and such nutrition as is suitable to its condition. By following judicious regimen, it gradually advances from weakness into strength, and exhibits, in the course of the treatment applied to it, the principle which not only developed its cure but established its natural strength. My pupil, who, when first placed under me, scarcely knew his right hand from his left, began to feel and exhibit an activity of intellect which surprised me. In simpler words, his mind, his intellect, grew strong under cultivation. Nobody could now imagine from his language, his conduct, and his whole manner, that he was the mere block which I had seen him on his first appearance. He knew he was of a respectable family, and on mingling with respectable persons in society, he gained self-confidence and a very becoming spirit of independence. He was not, however, a man capable of warm attachments – or I think of much gratitude – but at all events, it was arranged between us that whenever a vacancy in the

Sunday School Society should occur, he would let me know. Months, however, went on, with no prospect of a vacancy, and still I was making every effort to advance myself – though without much prospect of success. The only thing in my favour that occurred in the meantime, was an additional tuition procured for me by Gallaher. He had a sister, a widow, and I was engaged to educate her children, who attended me at Mr Fox's house.

At length, I received intelligence through my pupil that there was a vacancy in the Sunday School Office, and I lost no time in setting to work. I immediately waited upon Gallaher, who mentioned the matter to the secretary, James Digges La Touche. That gentleman told him that I ought to lose no time in sending in my papers, adding that of course it was the first step I ought to take. Matters went on quietly for about a week, when Gallaher brought me a communication – I took for granted it was from the secretary himself – that it would be a proper step for me to visit him some morning at his residence, *Sans Souci*, beyond Donnybrook. I accordingly paid an early visit, and on reaching the house was shown into a very fine library, in which there were some first-rate editions of the classics. A splendid edition of the Delphin was then, I think, in course of publication in Paris. He found me looking into one of the volumes, and observed, 'Oh, you are a classical scholar, Mr Carleton?'

I said I knew something about classics, that they had constituted my favourite study, and that I had still some notion of entering Trinity College, but that I had many points to consider before I could come to a determination on the subject.

He very kindly asked me to breakfast, but on my assuring him that I had breakfasted before I left home, he desired me to amuse myself among the books, adding that after breakfast he would give me a seat into town in his gig.

I cannot describe what I felt; my heart was in a tumult. I could read nothing – I could think of nothing but the one event. On that day the committee was to sit – on that day my fate was to be decided. That day, indeed, I felt to be an important one to me. I had already consulted Miss Anderson's aunt as to our marriage, and she said that, provided I got the appointment I was seeking, she on her part would offer no opposition. The reader may now form some notion of what I felt at such a crisis. Hope, however, was paramount, although Mr La Touche never opened his lips upon the subject of my appointment. Surely, if he had not intended to advocate my claim he would not have sent for me, neither would he have so publicly identified himself with me as to give me a seat into town in his gig. On going home I knew not how to pass the time. It was early when I got there, and the first thing I found was a note, without any signature, directing me to call on James Ferrier, Esq., Christ Church Place.

After I had waited a few minutes, Mr Ferrier came in, entered into conversation with me very briefly upon the duties of the situation, and stated that he was then on his way to join the committee, to whom he would make a favourable report. I thought there could be very little doubt in the matter after the incidents of that morning, and it is unnecessary to say that I went home fully confident of my success. I knew that when Armstrong would return from the office, I was certain to hear the truth, and hear it I did, through a note from the amiable Mr Boyd, the under secretary to the society, by which I was informed that my appointment had that day been made, at an opening salary of sixty pounds a year – the hour of morning attendance nine o'clock, the departure at evening five.

Here was I now living in a family, where neither bed, board, nor washing cost me sixpence, with a salary of sixty pounds a year. It is true I lost my appointment with Eustace, the teacher – but I retained the others, which, although small, were not at all to be overlooked by a young fellow plunging into life. The only objection against me, on my ascertaining the duties of the office, was the fact that I did not write a good hand. This, however, by care and assiduity, and the greatest possible attention to the subject, I gradually overcame with such success that I was complimented by Mr La Touche himself, who said that the improvement was extraordinary.

The notion of entering college now once more returned to my

mind. I thought it a hardship that I should be nailed to a counter, as it were, for the remainder of my life, whereas, by entering college, I might gain a profession, and become a more important member of society. In the meantime, as my chief object in gaining the recent appointment was to secure as my wife the girl to whom I was so deeply and devotedly attached, I lost no time in bringing about the important event in which my whole happiness consisted. I know not whether the generality of men feel the force of that happiness with such power, and fulness, and enthusiastic tenderness as I did. I told my wife, I remember, that I then knew what the honeymoon meant, but I added that it must be painful, especially to thinking men, to reflect that there was nothing sweeter than honey.

I have often thought that man's life is divided or separated into a series of small epics; not epics that are closed by happiness, however, but by pain. Here was I now, according to the usual sense and meaning of the epic, left after a life of awful struggles and heart-breaking trials, in a state of perfect happiness. My wife and I lived with our friends, as contented a young couple, and as free from care, as ever existed. It was never proposed to us to remove to another residence, now that we had means of supporting ourselves. Armstrong and I were in the same office – both went there together, and both returned home together, and indeed we felt ourselves extremely comfortable. There is, however, a providence in everything if it could be only seen. Had I, for instance, entered college, it is impossible to say what the result might have been; had I still remained, fagging away as a clerk in a Sunday School Society, upon a small and limited salary, I might have been there still, but who ever would have heard of my name? Would that name ever have been honoured by its association with the literature of my country – or by the important accessions which I have made to that literature? Under any circumstances, I thought it was no harm to resume my classics, a step which I was urged to take from the following circumstances. My predecessor in the office had also taken up the notion as to entering college – a notion which he ultimately carried out, and left the society at the very moment, it was urged against him, when he had become thoroughly conversant with its business. Another before him, again, was removed because it was ascertained that he too was preparing himself for college – although he offered to pledge himself most solemnly that he would never enter college, or leave the society, so long as they were satisfied with his services and his efficiency in the discharge of his duty. And now my intention of entering college came to the ears of one member of the committee – Thomas Parnell, brother of the late Sir Henry Parnell, County of Wicklow. He said the clerks were making the society a mere stepping stone to promote their own interests in life, and that the moment their services became valuable to the society, they left it. Now the fact is, the matter was not worth contest. The business of the society was so plain, simple and uniform, that a boy of twelve or fourteen years, after a little practice, could discharge the most difficult duties of it. Thomas Parnell, however, was very difficult to be satisfied with anything that did not depend upon some original suggestion of his own. He walked through these religious societies, like a perturbed spirit, making every office unhappy into which he entered.

He was a tall, heavy-faced man, with a lounging gait, who seemed not to know how to dispose of his time; and I know that every clerk in the Sunday School Office stood in the relation of a slave to him, except myself. For instance, he would glide in just about five o'clock, the hour appointed for the close of our business – take a seat upon one of the stools, and remain there probably for an hour and a half. I need scarcely add, that while he kept his position on the stool, not a clerk would leave his desk. This occurred repeatedly, in fact, it was a habit of his, because the Sunday School was his pet society.

At this precise time, it had got abroad that I was preparing for college, and the truth is, I was reading hard. The significance of this observation will be shortly seen. One evening, Parnell came in at the hour of five, as before, and we all turned round to our desks as if to resume business. He sat there in solemn silence for at least three-quarters of an hour, when, fretted and irritated by conduct so inconsiderate and unfeeling, I deliberately settled my papers – locked my desk – took down my hat, and making him a respectful bow, took my way home. The very next evening, the same scene was repeated, but on this occasion, when the clock struck five, he said:

'Carleton, as your time appears to be so valuable to you, you may go home.'

'I never go home, sir,' I replied, 'until the hour for closing comes – and I am not aware that we are expected to stay beyond that hour. Nine in the morning and five in the evening were the hours named in our instructions.' I accordingly bowed to him most respectfully as before, and took my departure. Armstrong, who, as the reader knows, lived in the house with me, did not reach home for an hour or upwards after me; he, with the rest, did not possess spirit to act with independence. I will not forget the observation he made to me, at his solitary dinner after his return from the office.

'Take my word for it,' said he, 'you ought to lose as little time as possible in looking out for another situation. Your doom is sealed with us – and that's the opinion of the whole office.'

I could not take such a severe view of the matter as that, because at the time, I did not know the man, but still I had my apprehensions.

It was about the third or fourth day after that, or perhaps a week, when one of the committee, by name Vicars Boyle, father or brother to the present most respectable banker of College Green, Alexander Boyle, came into the office, and after chatting awhile with Mr Boyd, our able under secretary, lounged round and came over to me. I felt flattered by this attention, and looked upon it as a distinction in its way. He entered into conversation with me – told me he had heard that I was a good classical scholar, and asked me if it were true that I was preparing myself to enter college. I replied that a good deal of that depended upon circumstances over which I had no control – but that nothing would gratify me more than to take college honours.

'You would, in other words, have no object to become a Fellow,' he added, smiling. I have often felt since that this notion of entering college after my marriage was wild and chimerical.[1]

About a month now elapsed, during which time we never saw Tom Parnell's heavy face. I was getting on very agreeably – I felt the world no trouble to me. My wife had prevailed on me to give up all notions of college distinctions – a sacrifice I would have made for none but herself – for still – still – still the idea of distinction kept moving before me in the distance, and luring me on to something, indeed vague and indefinite, but possessing such an interest for me as I cannot describe. In the meantime, I was as happy as any young man in my position of life could wish to be.

One day, about a month or six weeks after the visit of Mr Boyle to me – it was the day on which our committee met every week – the business had been concluded – when a Mr Johnston, who generally attended the committee – there was some name for his office which I forget – came up with the committee book under his arm and said to me, with an honest depth of feeling which could not be misunderstood:

'Mr Carleton, I am deeply distressed by the intelligence I am forced to communicate to you – I wish from my soul it had devolved on anyone else.'

My friend Armstrong sat at the desk, on the left-hand side next to mine, and the moment Johnston spoke, the warning, or prophecy, which he had uttered on the evening alluded to, flashed upon me. We looked at each other, and he shook his head in a spirit of despondency which I felt to be too just. Johnston proceeded:

'The committee,' said he, 'no longer require your services, Mr Carleton, and you are no longer a clerk in this office.'

'But, Mr Johnston,' said I, 'this requires an explanation. Why am I removed from my situation, without any charge having

[1] The Fellows are of course precluded from marrying. Late last century a great scandal arose in Dublin through charges made by Theophilus Swift, a satirist, to the effect that the Fellows were evading the rule. The end of it was that Swift and a Fellow were imprisoned for libelling one another.

been preferred against me? Have I exhibited either incapacity or neglect? Have I done anything to entitle me to such treatment? You who manage the proceedings-book ought to know.'

'It is not my business,' said he, 'to pass any opinion upon the proceedings of the committee – I am merely their registrar. I do not think myself bound to do more than record these proceedings, and that you know is my duty.'

'Well,' I replied, 'there is one thing clear, that I must have been guilty of some act or acts which bring me under their censure.'

'This much I will say,' replied kind-hearted Mr Johnston, 'that there is no charge of incapacity brought against you.'

'Well,' I replied, taking up my hat, 'my only remedy now is to see Mr La Touche, by whose influence I was appointed.'

'Do not go as yet,' said he, 'I am going – you know that on every committee day, when he does not attend, I bring him over the book that contains the register of the proceedings.'

I felt that he was right, and I felt besides that he was sincerely my friend.

I need not enter into the details of this affair, for although it was a matter of the deepest importance to me at the time, it may not be so to the reader. It is enough to say, that when I waited on Mr La Touche on that same day, subsequent to Mr Johnston's official visit, he said with a firm and indignant eye:

'Mr Carleton, we will not discuss this matter here – my office is not the place for it – only mark me – *return to your duty.*'

'But how can I do so,' I replied, 'after having been dismissed?'

'It is shameful,' he proceeded, forgetting himself in the genuine indignation of the moment; 'your only fault is, that you were preparing yourself to enter Trinity College and qualify yourself for a higher, and probably a more distinguished, position in life than could be found by a young man of intellect in our office. I remember that on the morning you were out with me at *Sans Souci*, you expressed a wish to enter college, so that, at all events, you treated us candidly since the very commencement. Now,' said he, 'return to your usual duties in the office, and say that you do so by my authority.'

Mr La Touche, in consequence of the pressure of public duty upon him as a banker, found it impossible to attend every meeting of the Sunday School committee. On the next occasion, however, he made it a point to be present, and at the meeting I was re-appointed to my situation. Mr Boyd, the assistant-secretary, who still holds that situation in the society, cannot forget the circumstances I am relating.

No man ever felt the sense of triumph with a more exultant spirit than I did on this occasion. I looked upon that triumph as ultimate. I may as well, however, relate here the grounds on which I was removed from my clerkship, although I think the reader may very readily anticipate them.

Two clerks, my predecessors in the same society, had availed themselves of their appointments in it to enter college. It seems they were very able men, and of course succeeded in gaining high honours during their college course – they then left the society, and fresh, untrained hands, forsooth, were called in to struggle through the intricacies of the business that was placed before them. Parnell, the fat spectre of the societies, was the moving spirit against these respectable and talented men, as he was against me. There is nothing more simple than the business of these societies – as I have already stated. Parnell wished to make it appear that my preparations for college were made furtively, and without the knowledge of the society. At the meeting of the committee which restored me to my situation, Mr La Touche, who attended expressly on my account, contradicted the intention imputed to me of preparing for college in an underhand manner – so did honest Vicar Boyle, who, after this very serious charge against me by Tom Parnell, had been desired by Mr La Touche to speak to me on the subject, and to observe if he could perceive any reluctance on my part to disclose my intentions on that point.

Chapter XVII

AFTER having given up all notion of entering college, I took, in the evenings during my leisure hours, to the amusement of writing short essays upon different subjects, after the manner of Addison in *The Spectator*. The rapidity with which I wrote these astonished myself; but as my judgment was far from being matured at the time, how could I, a poor obscure creature, ever dream that such productions were worth notice! Still, I brought some of them to William Sisson of Marsh's library, and he actually appeared to be thunderstruck by them. I had several essays upon different subjects – some serious and some humorous – all of these I left with him, because, being ignorant of everything connected with literature at the time, I really knew not what to do with them.

No man living ever felt a warmer interest in my fortunes than William Sisson. He had obliged Archbishop Magee in matters connected with the library, and made his Grace a very warm friend of his. I have said that he had, in consequence of a dreadful accident, lost almost the whole thigh and leg on one side. The medical gentleman who performed the terrible operation necessary to the safety of his life was the late Surgeon Kirby, of Harcourt Street. The latter was one of the most able and intellectual men I ever met. He was possessed of the highest and most accomplished literary tastes.

When I had been about six months in the Sunday School Society office, the sedentary life (from nine a.m. till five p.m.) brought on a complaint for the treatment of which Kirby was celebrated. In fact he was the Butcher or the Colles of his day.[1]

---

[1] Two celebrated Irish surgeons in the early part of the century, Abraham Colles (1773–1843) being the better known.

He also had read my essays, and expressed such an opinion of them that he advised me to bring out a weekly periodical like *The Spectator*, stating that he would subscribe one hundred pounds to it, and also see what he could do among his friends. All this was very flattering, but I had not courage to undertake it. It would indeed be strange if I had.

I believe I may appeal to all those who know me upon the subject of vanity. I do not think it ever has been said, or ever will be said, that I am a vain man, remarkable for literary assumption and self-conceit. So far from this, I may state that my friends have brought charges of the very opposite description against me, for instance, that I seemed to undervalue myself, and that I did not assert the position to which my talents had elevated me. There is a good deal of truth in the latter charge. Beyond the fact of having secured fame, I seldom gave myself any further trouble about the matter. I introduce these observations here to meet any charge of vanity which may be brought against me for the statement I am now about to make, especially when that statement has personal reference to myself. At that period, then, of which I write (A.D. eighteen hundred and twenty), I think after I had written a good number of essays, both serious and comical, which had been privately circulated among literary people by my friends, most of whom, if not literary themselves, were persons of taste and education, a small undercurrent of that kind of reputation which goes about in a private way was attached to my name. I was often spoken of as 'that clever young fellow Carleton, who wrote Jeremy Baddleback', for such was the name of a humorous essay I had written, my first effort at representing a *character*.

I was now nearly six months married, almost the same period of time in my situation, and not at all in a capacity to enter into speculations which would require money, and which, besides, were so uncertain in their results. My wife, besides, was beginning to appear 'as ladies wish to be who love their lords'.

Thus was I comfortable enough; and I was satisfied also that my salary was a rising one. Gallaher, I have stated, was in the habit of going twice a week to teach music to the children of

Santry Charter School. He always, it seemed, went there in a hack car, for which he paid nothing, being allowed the expenses; but be this as it may, he happened to call at my office about four o'clock one day, and asked me to accompany him. At this time I had never seen Santry – or a Charter School – and I said to Mr Johnston, 'Mr Gallaher, a very particular friend of mine, wishes to give me a drive to Santry – it's something before the closing of the office, I know – but the truth is I have nothing here to do, and I would wish very much to go.'

Of course he consented at once, and I was on my way downstairs, when whom should I meet coming up but the 'skeleton' of all the religious offices, Thomas Parnell. He gave me a peculiar and inquisitive look, but passed on. Gallaher and I spent a very agreeable evening at Santry, and although we had music and supper, we reached home at an early hour. The master of the school was a serious and evidently religious man, but there was nothing about him that was not kind and hospitable. Gallaher lived in Cork Street, and I in the Coombe, within fifty yards of the entrance to Cork Street. We were at home about ten o'clock.

My position in life, notwithstanding my essays, seemed now to be fixed. Parnell had tried his strength and was beaten. In spite of all his influence. I held my situation, and was master of my desk in the office. Two or three weeks, however, went on, and nothing happened worthy of observation, until one day that the committee had closed their weekly meeting, when the registrar, Mr Johnston, came up as usual from the committee-room below stairs, and said:

'Mr Carleton, I am sorry to bring you bad news a second time; you have this day been removed from the situation you have held here.'

'Why, Mr Johnston, I thought this matter had been definitely settled. What is the charge now?'

'The same as before,' he replied, 'with the addition that you are in the habit of leaving the office at irregular hours, and not returning until it is closed.'

I felt at once that this lying charge had its origin in my visit to

Santry – because I knew that from the first day I entered the office as a clerk, until that moment, no similar case on my part had ever occurred. If it were an offence, it was my first and only one.

'Well,' said I, 'this case is as clear, so far as I am concerned, as the other was. I must only state it once more to Mr La Touche.'

'I am very sorry,' said he, 'that such a step is now not within your power. Mr La Touche left home on Friday last for France or Italy, and is not expected to return for two months. The committee,' he added, 'have voted you an additional quarter's salary.'

I felt hopeless indeed, and on looking at him I saw at a glance how deeply the poor fellow entered into all my feelings. The door of the next room, which belonged to one of the other societies, was open, and Johnston went over and looked in; he beckoned to me to join him, as there was no one in the room.

'What I am about to say, my dear Carleton, I mention in the strictest confidence. There was a very angry scene about you a while ago – James Ferrier was strongly against the step that has been taken; so were most of them, and Parnell would have failed, had he not threatened at once, not only to resign, but altogether to withdraw himself from the society. This, you know, would be a serious loss to us, inasmuch as, one way with another, he is worth upwards of a thousand per annum to us. His word in the religious world carries everything with it – especially with a certain class of religious people.'

I had nothing for it, therefore, but to submit; this I was forced to do, and with a very bad grace I did it. That day was quarter day, in other words, the day on which we received our salary and all the consolation I had was, that instead of fifteen pounds I received thirty.

I began now to reconsider my relation to Providence.

Why were my hopes, when they seemed firm and permanent, perpetually dashed from my grasp? Was I worse than other men? I was not conscious of any crime; I felt that I was naturally benevolent and disposed to serve my fellow-creatures so far as I could. Why then did ill-fortune and human enmity in the shape

207

of my evil genius, Tom Parnell, thus dog my heels. Even Tom Parnell himself was not without his enemies, but he stood beyond their reach. His harsh conduct to me on this occasion actually crept abroad, within certain limits, to the disadvantage of his character.

Here was I again, once more upon the world, with blank prospects. What was I to do? On what hand to turn? Mrs Carleton's uncle had lost his health, and with his health his temper. He was peevish and snappish, and unmanageable by either reason or feeling. On hearing of Parnell's first attempt to remove me from the Sunday School Society, and also of its failure, he felt quite at ease, especially as he had James Digges La Touche on his side. On the second occasion, however, when he found that Parnell had carried his point, he became rather uneasy; but at this time he was ill. Taking his whole character in at a glance, he was a man guided by results, not by truth. He took me to task, therefore, upon the subject of my second dismissal, and argued from that fact a justification of the first. It was in vain that I placed clearly before him the circumstances connected with both facts – in vain that I adduced the receipt of a quarter's salary, as a kind of admitted compensation for the injustice which was done me.

'I am very glad,' said he, 'that they have given it to you – you must leave this house – I am unable to support you any longer.'

'You have supported me much longer than most men would,' I replied, 'and I am deeply thankful to you for it; but did you ever witness an act on my part with which you could find fault? Has not my conduct been that of a correct, moral, and sober man ever since we met – ever since I came under your roof?'

'Begone,' said he, 'you shall not remain here another night.'

'I don't intend it,' I replied. 'Jane, my dear, get your things – I will go for a car – and when I return with it we can go.'

I accordingly went for a car to take away our baggage, but judge of my surprise, when, on returning with it, I found my wife locked up in what we used to call our own room. There she was under lock and key, and a strong protest on the part of her uncle that he would not permit her to accompany me. I was about to break open the door, but her aunt whispered me not to feel any uneasiness; that the moment this exhibition of temper disappeared, as it soon would, his natural disposition would return, and all would be well. She entreated me to leave the matter in her hands, and I did so.

'Call,' she said, 'at your usual hour – nine or ten tonight – and you will find everything quiet and peaceable.' My wife whispered me to the same effect through the door, and I left them without any apprehension. On returning that night, you may judge, kind reader, of what I felt on discovering that I was locked out, and, unless by scaling the wall, could not by any possibility make my entrance. The house was a long, large, two-storey house, in the centre of a court, in which was a garden and three large grass-covered platforms. I scaled the wall that led into the back entrance, and knocked at the back door, but found that exclusion was the order of the night. I knew that the window of our room, if played upon by gravel, would enable me to communicate with my wife – but in one thing I was mistaken. A bed had been made up for her in the room where her aunt and uncle slept, yet although that had a window opening backwards, I could not approach it, because there was a wall between me and the other portion of the back court. I knocked, indeed, at the kitchen door, which opened into that part of the backyard where I stood, but could receive no reply. I shouted and called, but to no purpose. I bethought me of how I was to get out of the yard, over the wall of which I came in assisted by two men passing, who had helped me up. I had not long to wait, however, for in an instant old Fox, accompanied by half a dozen watchmen, bolted into the backyard and pounced upon me. I simply knocked them down as fast as they approached me; I did more – I rushed into the passage that led to the hall – then upstairs to our room, which I found locked – then into my wife's uncle's sleeping-room, from whence I brought my weeping wife, with her arms about my neck kissing me most affectionately, and entreating me to take her with me. I was in the upper gallery when about a dozen watchmen came rushing up the stairs to arrest me. I immediately placed my wife in the same room from which I had taken her, and turned upon them in such a state of frenzy as I had never before experienced. To make a long story short, I beat them. They were not able to achieve the landing by the staircase, and they had no other means of reaching me. They then sent for firearms, but Mrs Fox whispered a word or two into my ear, which rendered me as meek as a lamb. I had forgotten my wife's condition, and what the result of further noise or outrage might possibly be, and I accordingly surrendered myself, and was brought away to the watch-house, where I remained for the rest of the night. The next morning, when I was brought before the magistrate, I discovered that he was a gentleman whom I had met at dinner at the house of the Rev. William Whitelaw, the rector of the parish.

The magistrate's office, or, in other words, the police-court, was then somewhere off James's Street. Old Fox, who was at that time near eighty, was punctual in his attendance, and so was his amicable wife, who came for the purpose of establishing goodwill between us. Fox, however, was a man who never could restrain his temper, unless he was allowed to carry everything his own way. When the case came on, he was called upon to speak but never was there such a failure – in fact, his charge was nonsense, and a complete mass of contradiction, without either force or effect. When the magistrate, whose name I cannot now recall, asked me what reply I had to make, Mrs Fox, in a few calm words, made the matter quite plain by simply giving the facts as they occurred. She stated that ever since our marriage, and before it, I had lived with them, that they had allowed us a room to ourselves, where we slept, and that, in every other respect, we were members of the family, and boarded at their table. Also, that it had not been my wish to return to their house that night, but she had extorted a promise from me to do so, as she hoped every angry feeling would pass away in the course of the day, and that all would be peace as usual.

I simply corroborated what she said in a very few words – but in all my life I don't think I ever heard so severe, so terrible a rebuke, as old Fox received from the magistrate. I will not repeat it here. The respectable old man has long gone to a better world than this, and many a time afterwards did he express the deepest sorrow for his conduct on that memorable occasion.

I have been somewhat particular about this scene, because that last night was a memorable one to my wife and me. We took our departure from the Coombe the next day; my wife went to reside with her mother, and I took lodgings in an eating-house almost opposite to her.

I have mentioned William Sisson as one of the kindest friends I ever had. As the acting librarian of Marsh's library, he was in the habit of coming into contact with a great number of reading and literary men, with all of whom he was very anxious to make me acquainted. One of these, a quiet, unassuming clergyman, but a first-rate scholar, was a resident master in college, curate of St Andrew's, secretary to the Association for Discountenancing Vice – which had an office at Mr Watson's, the religious bookseller in Capel Street.

Sisson had shown him some of the prose sketches I have referred to; with these he was so much struck, that he asked Sisson to introduce me to him. He was curate, as I have said, of St Andrew's parish, and after service every Sunday he took a cup of coffee in the house of Mr Hamill, the parish schoolmaster, whose residence is on your left-hand side as you approach the church on the way to Cork Street. I accordingly called on him one Sunday after service, and was shown into the little room above stairs, which was always set apart for him while taking his coffee. Here I found him, and presented my note of introduction from Sisson. My reception was extremely kind; a second cup and saucer was produced, and from that day forward I occasionally dropped in at coffee time, and paid him a visit, which was a very pleasant one to me.

At this time the Protestant clergymen throughout Ireland depended almost altogether upon the Association for Discountenancing Vice for the supply of schoolmasters. This was generally known, and the consequence was, that those men who were anxious for such situations, either in Dublin or the country, had their names registered upon a 'teachers' list', for unless the teacher was sanctioned by the society, he had no chance of being appointed to the school.

I need not say, or rather, the reader shall soon learn, what a fortunate thing it was for me that I made the acquaintance of Dr Wilson. He told me at once, openly and without either wavering or hesitating, that I ought to make literature my profession. That might be true, and it certainly made somewhat more clear the dim and distant stars of future distinction which, from time to time, I saw in the darkness before me.

In the meantime, I had no employment. My mother-in-law, though a respectable, was not a wealthy woman. That she was affectionate there could be no doubt, but that she was narrow-minded and ignorant on many points of ordinary life there could be as little. Her daughter – my wife – had now been some months with her, and no mother since the creation of woman ever loved a daughter with more affection than she loved her – still, she could not understand why a young fellow going about in the dress of a gentleman, should not be able to support his wife. At the very time I write of, she had a small sum in the funds which had been left her by a cousin in the north. The whole family came from Belfast to Dublin, where they settled.

My mother-in-law possessed that sort of northern sharpness, both of feeling and observation, which is to be found nowhere in Ireland outside Ulster. Now I detest this; it is a blot upon my native province, and the consequence was, that she and I never pulled well together. My wife was living with her, and I was living upon a scale of frugality in point of food – in fact, in point of everything – that pressed upon my diminishing purse, in spite of my self-denial, with a sense of exhaustion which made my heart sink. During this time, I lived upon rolls and milk, never tasting either meat, spirits, or malt drink in any shape, and only anxious to extend the little money I had as far as it could go.

This day, on which I am proceeding with the humble records of my life, is the third of November; on this day, in the first year of our marriage, while my wife was lying in a bed off one of the

212

upper rooms, was she delivered of our daughter Mary Anne – our first-born. The day was Sunday, and although the gratifying event had taken place, there was not a single soul visible from whom I could ask a question. The absence of my wife occasioned me to feel some suspicions, because I knew that during the last week her confinement was daily expected. I went quietly upstairs, and on entering my wife's bedroom, I found her lying with a smile of triumph on her face, and our first-born lying on her left arm soundly asleep.

Don't imagine that I am about to describe the novelty of the sensations which filled my heart. I saw, it is true, the sweet, innocent, and unconscious features of the little angel, and looked upon them until my heart softened, and expanded, and melted, and during this examination the eyes of my wife were fixed upon me with an expression of perfect happiness. After a few moments I wiped the tears from my eyes, and stooped:

'Ah,' said the mother, 'you are going to kiss her; there, she is awake.'

'No, Jane,' I replied, 'you are mistaken – it is not she I am about to kiss' – and I pressed my lips to hers again and again, until her emotions warned me to consider the very delicate state of her health. Having composed her, I took the first-born up in my arms, and if the young seraph had any reason to complain of the want of kissings and huggings the fault was not mine. In short, the fact of her birth had altogether placed me in a new state of feeling. I looked upon the world as if I had been under the influence of a dream – a happy dream – but on reflecting that I now stood for the first time in a new character, that of a father, and that this was but the beginning of a fresh responsibility, which every year would call upon me to meet, I felt divided between a feeling of happiness and care: care was perhaps pre-dominant, because, young as I was, I had been taught such lessons as few had ever been forced to learn.

The reader will perceive that fate – a fatality – ever attended upon me, and that no glimpse of happiness or good fortune ever fell in my way, without an accompaniment of something that was calculated to check any feeling of enjoyment that might accompany the good fortune.

My first-born child was sent to me at a time when I had not ten shillings in my pocket. How was I now to live? Again was I to search life for that which I was never destined to obtain – anything in the shape of permanent employment. I must consult my friends. My friends! Why, after all, I had no friends, with the exception of William Sisson. On stating the position in which I stood, he asked me to go and live with him, until something could be done. He lodged at the time with a Mrs Taylor, who kept a combined female boarding school and female day school. Sisson had a good deal of property in Sandymount, and was landlord of the very house which Mrs Taylor occupied. He had a drawing-room and two bedrooms.

My object was now of course the old one – to get employment – and, on consulting Sisson, I told him that I was perfectly sick of Dublin.

'I wish,' said I, 'that I could get a school under some of these societies in the country, where I could live retired from the tumults and disappointments of life. I have no ambition now.'

'Yes,' he replied, 'you have and must; you are not conscious of the powers of your own intellect.'

'Well,' I replied, 'let me get quietly to the country – and when removed from the cares of life, perhaps I may have a better opportunity, in quiet and solitude, to call upon whatever intellectual powers I possess – but at present my most anxious wish is to conduct a school in the country – a school with such a salary as I can live upon. That, at present, is the height and extent of my ambition.'

'Well,' said he, 'my poor fellow, there is something in that. Your mind, when relieved of embarrassments, might gain new strength, and there is little doubt but that relief from difficulties and care would give your intellect that full play which is, I think, all that it requires. A school in the country is the very thing you want – and in this you are very fortunate. Go to our friend Wilson.'

Life is a scene of network. One friend becomes a link between one and another, and in this manner our interests become gradually intermingled in the great web of existence. I called upon Mr Wilson, expressed the same sentiments to him which I had communicated to Sisson. He, however, was a deeper thinker and an older man than Sisson. After hearing me express the sickness of heart which my struggles in Dublin had occasioned me to suffer, he said:

'In one sense I cannot blame you, but there is another view of the subject which I for one cannot overlook. As sure as I live you possess talents which will yet distinguish you, but only on that chance or condition of life which may force you to reside in the city. Go to the country – settle down into the character of a common schoolmaster – and every hope worthy of cherishing in your life is lost.'

'But,' I replied, 'if I possess the talents which you are kind enough to attribute to me – may not the leisure and quiet of a country life enable me, as I told Mr Sisson, to ascertain whether they exist or not. I repeat that I am sick of Dublin life, and I shall never rest until I find myself in a position to leave it.'

'Well,' said he, 'upon this subject I perceive you are immovable. I am constantly written to, in consequence of my position here, to find masters for such country schools as you seek. Call on me from time to time – say once a week – and, meanwhile, leave me your address.'

'Write to Sisson,' said I, 'Marsh's Library; I am there almost every day.'

In about ten days afterwards, Sisson handed me a note which he had received from Wilson. The contents of it were as gratifying as they were unexpected. There was a situation vacant in his own office, and of course he felt very anxious that I should not lose a moment in applying for it. I did so, and although there were only three candidates, yet I had not a chance. Everything depended on the handwriting, and on that occasion I became so disturbed and nervous that my writing, when contrasted with that of my competitors, rendered it impossible I should succeed.

215

Mr Wilson was very sorry for this. 'See what it is,' said he, when I called to know the result, 'to write a good hand – it is the handwriting that is chiefly wanted here. Don't go,' he added, 'I have received a letter from the Rev. Mr Newland, curate of Mullingar. There is a master wanted there – I know he is a man you would like – and who would like you. He possesses literary tastes and has lately written a very able pamphlet on the Church, which he has dedicated to Dr Elrington, son of the late provost. The latter, unless he takes a wealthy college living, will be likely to succeed his father in the provostship. Mr Newland's father, Abraham Newland, is the master of the celebrated school in Aungier Street, and he himself is an accomplished scholar.'[1]

[1] He became Dean of Ferns in 1842, and died about 1862.

Chapter XVIII

Gough's *Arithmetic* – Mullingar – A contributor to *Westmeath Guardian* – A remarkable veteran – The 93rd regiment – Wellington Guernsey – The military riot.

T H I S was precisely the man I wanted. It was at once agreed upon that Mr Wilson should write to Newland, and in the course of a few days I had a letter from that gentleman, requesting me to call upon his father in Aungier Street, in order that I should submit myself for an examination as to my qualifications. I accordingly did so, and had a very fortunate escape from rejection, inasmuch as old Abraham, though utterly ignorant of classics, considered himself one of the sharpest arithmeticians of his day, a notion, however, which wanted corroboration. I had not been long in the parlour, when a back door opened, and in came a man about sixty, wearing a loose, grey surtout, a slate in one hand, and a Gough[1] in the other – exactly in his school costume. He certainly did not overwhelm me with compliments, but treated me much like a servant, who was seeking for some domestic appointment in the family. He handed me the slate and cutter, and, pointing to a chair, requested me by a bow to take a seat.

'I suppose, Mr Carleton,' said he, 'you are a good arithmetician?'

'Well, Mr Newland, I do know *something* about it, and that is all I wish to say. Pray whose arithmetic do you teach?'

'Gough's,' he replied.

'Gough's,' I exclaimed, with astonishment. 'Surely it is not possible that you are teaching the system of a man who for years has proved himself to be ignorant of the doctrine of proportion! I thought I should have found Thompson here, not Gough – but indeed, Mr Newland, I did expect to have met you with Homer

---

[1] Gough's *Arithmetic* was largely used in Ireland.

217

or Virgil in your hand, and not with such a schoolboy's book as Gough's *Arithmetic.*'

'Oh, then, you are a classical scholar, Mr Carleton?'

'Yes,' I replied, assuming an air of offended dignity. 'I believe it is admitted that I am classical scholar, sir.'

'Oh, Mr Carleton,' said he, 'I beg a thousand pardons. I shall write to my son by this day's post, and you may rest assured that my letter to him will close the transaction precisely as you yourself could wish it.'

I did not go to Mullingar for some days afterwards, but Mr Newland had learned through his father that I was a classical scholar, and the father, with whom I was a favourite, eagerly besought his son to overlook that fact, for it was his opinion that, notwithstanding my knowledge of classics, I might make a very good English teacher.

The son, who possessed a great deal of natural humour, enclosed me a copy of this paragraph from his father's letter, at which we had many a hearty, good-natured laugh afterwards.

I need not deny, from a principle of false modesty, that I believe my kind and warm-hearted friend, Henry Newland, looked upon my letter as far above the average expected in those days from a man who was only a candidate for a parish school. The couple of letters he wrote to me, immediately before my journey to Mullingar, were such as might be supposed to pass from one gentleman to another. As a proof of this, he requested to know by what conveyance, and day, and hour I should reach Mullingar, that he might be able to meet me on my arrival. I took a fancy to travel by the canal from a mere feeling of novelty.

On our arrival there, he met us at the canal station house, then kept by a man past ninety, of whom, before I leave Mullingar, I shall have a few words to say. It was out of the question that Mrs Carleton could dine with strangers that day, especially with our first-born in her arms – but it was obvious to me at a glance, that Newland had expected and made provision for this. He had already provided lodgings for us in the house of a broken-down, but respectable merchant named Atkins, and had also his own private car to convey us, either to our new lodgings or his own house – which was the rectory – to dine. After leaving Mrs Carleton at our lodgings, he insisted that I should dine with him. I could not refuse such marked civility, and I accordingly accompanied him to the parsonage where he lived. The Rev. Mr Robinson, the rector, lived with his son a couple of miles from town, and Mr Newland in his absence occupied the rectory. Mr Newland had some gentlemen from Tullamore at dinner that day, and altogether we spent a very pleasant evening.

When I went down to Mullingar, there was no school house, and on this account Mr Newland, with his usual good sense and foresight, secured a large room in the house we lodged in – a circumstance which added very much to the convenience of both myself and my wife. We now set to work. The next day but one, our school opened to about sixteen or eighteen of the most wretched-looking creatures – boys and girls – I ever laid my eyes upon. 'And this,' thought I bitterly, 'is, after all my struggles and hopes, what I have come to.' It was a melancholy position, and when I went down stairs to our private rooms – a sitting-room and a bedroom – and expressed myself more fully to my wife, she acted nobly, both in language and bearing.

'Surely,' she said, 'it is not on *this* day – the very first – that you ought to express an opinion, or to form one either, of your situation. Surely you must wait until you see how matters will turn out. We have food to eat, and the shelter of a house over us, and how many are there in the world who have neither one nor the other.'

'But it is a sad thing, Jane, to be pushed to such a comparison as that. I am not sure that we have much bread to eat, for my purse is very low.'

The poor woman – woman! why, she was not nineteen at the time – the poor child, I should rather say – was about to make some reply, when a girl, who was sent to us by Mr Atkins, the landlord, to do whatever rough-and-ready jobs we required, until a regular servant should be engaged – ran upstairs saying there was a message from Mrs Kidd for us.

We were certainly at a loss – who was Mrs Kidd? What could the message be?

'Well,' said I, 'I have the use of my limbs and of my tongue, and I shall soon know.' I went down stairs to the hall, and found a stout young fellow standing there, with an immense plucked turkey in one hand, and a ham corresponding in both size and weight in the other.

'There's some potatoes here, too, sir,' he said, 'in this sack – but if you will show me where I'm to fetch them to, I will bring them down.'

There could not have been less than four or five stone of potatoes, but the varlet was stout, and in a few minutes I found my empty garrison provisioned for upwards of a week at least. I asked who Mrs Kidd was, and got a reply to the effect that she owned the *Westmeath Guardian*. I would have felt completely in the dark here, had I not learned, the very day before, that there was a newspaper of that name published in the town. I afterwards knew the proprietor of it very intimately, as well as his admirable wife, who, *sub silentio*, had the credit of being the editor. I wrote a good many articles for the *Westmeath Guardian* while I was there – so did Mr Newland. One of mine was on Goldsmith, and I wish I had it now.

My wife's remonstrance with me, on the day we opened our *establishment*, was the first intimation I ever had of the excellent good sense and capacity for business which she possessed. As I have said, she was not nineteen – and had never endured the struggle or trials of life so as to teach her what severe experience meant, yet she spoke with the spirit and feeling of a woman who had spent half a life among the conflicts of the world.

Of course I called upon Mrs Kidd to thank her for the valuable, and I might have added suitable, presents which she so kindly sent us. I then saw her and her worthy husband for the first time. They asked us to dine with them on the next Sunday, and in such a kind and hospitable spirit, that it was impossible to refuse. Little Harry Wilton, too, the proprietor and conductor of the excellent hotel there, was equally kind and equally hospitable.

Indeed, I don't think I ever had my foot in so generous and hospitable a town. The number of presents I received, both in eatables and drinkables, was incredible, and there was nobody to make use of them but myself and my wife, and our servant girl. There was a wealthy family named Troy, whose children attended the school, but upon what basis the said family calculated the powers of ours in wasting food I know not. All I can say is, that scarcely a week passed, during which we did not receive from them more presents, in fowl and eggs alone, than three households like ours could consume.

When I had been in Mullingar for about two months, my wife began to lose her health. A second daughter was born to us, and as the school increased far beyond expectation, she was quite unable to meet with proper effect the weighty duties of her portion of it. The number of pupils had increased so much beyond all calculation, that we were obliged to take a waste house, which had the character of being haunted, and whose only recommendation was its spaciousness, for it was damp and fœtid. I never felt such a detestable and abhorrent change as it occasioned, and the only circumstance that reconciled me to it was the fact that an admirable new schoolhouse, together with a handsome residence for the master and mistress, were at the time in a considerable state of advancement between the canal and the town. I am reminded here, especially by my allusion to the canal, of an anecdote which I promised the reader some time back. It is a strange one, almost comically so, if we dare indulge in mirth upon such an occasion, especially after reading the Old Testament. There was a servant of the Canal company, who had lived in the station house, if my memory serves me, since the first opening of the canal at Mullingar. I have seen the man hundreds of times, and I must say, that during a long intercourse with life, I have never seen such another. To me, who even then did not know myself, or what my anxiety to discover character meant, or how to account for the impression which its exhibition made upon me, this man was a study. In many senses he was a remarkable man – first as to his age. He was, at the time I knew him, in his ninety-fourth year, a fact for which he could produce the most satisfactory proof; and he was never known to taste anything stronger than milk or water. In fact, he belonged altogether to a bygone generation. During his ninety-four years, he was never known to wear a cravat about his neck, or a pin in the collar of his shirt. That shirt, winter and summer, lay open – so did his whole breast, which, together with the neck, presented one of the most healthy scarlets I ever witnessed. I have said that he never tasted anything stronger than water; to this I may add, that during the term of his patriarchal life, he had never suffered one day's illness. There was not a wrinkle in his face, or a white hair in his head. His eye was as the eye of nineteen or twenty, his voice free and firm, as though it belonged to the same date. In stature he was about the middle size – without bend or stoop – and yet, strange as it may appear, you could not avoid, on looking at him, the consciousness that he was one of the oldest men you had ever seen. There was, besides, a peculiarity of expression in his face which rendered it utterly impossible that you could mistake him for another. Now this man of ninety-four took it into his head, while I was in Mullingar, to marry. It is true he had the reputation of having some money – a fact of which there was no doubt – but be that as it may, his little station house had an air of comfort in it that you could rarely see about Mullingar, which was then – whatever it may be now – one of the most slovenly towns in the three kingdoms. Yes, he took it into his head to marry, and he did marry a girl, who was well known to be only in her nineteenth year. She was a sweet, modest-looking girl, remarkable for quiet, good sense; nobody could look upon her without a feeling of instant and well-deserved respect.

Many observations were made upon this strange marriage, which I will not report here. It is enough to say that the newly-married couple appeared quite contented and happy, until, in the course of six months or so, people began to talk again. So they talked, and so time passed until, at the expiration of nine months, the midwife presented the worthy station-master with a fine young son – his own born image. The fact created a sensation.

For six weeks after the event, the house was visited every day – presents were brought both to husband and wife. Even ladies in their carriages went to see them – and I myself, after having had this singular history ringing in my ears for at least a fortnight, went also to pay them a visit. I did so. Never have I seen one human creature such a living image of another, as the young son was of the old father. The resemblance was astonishing, and the more so when we consider their relative ages – the one an infant of only a few months and the other close upon a century.

While I was at Mullingar, the Ninety-Third Scotch Regiment was stationed in the barracks, which are a little more than a quarter of a mile out of the town. What was the cause of the quarrel I know not, but the townsfolk and the kilts carried on an irregular warfare that ended in one of the most dreadful scenes I ever witnessed. The Ninety-Third had a library, which, indeed, might truly and without metaphor be called a circulating one. It was kept by one of the sergeants, who had two sons at my school, and who obliged me from time to time by the loan of any books I may have taken a fancy for. I had also the two sons of Quartermaster Guernsey, as kind and as hospitable a man as ever lived. His wife, too, was not only a perfect lady, but a woman of genius. She was a first-rate amateur artist, and had a painting of the decollation of John the Baptist, for which she was offered two hundred guineas; but she preferred, she said, to leave it as an heirloom to her family. She was also a first-rate musician. Many a pleasant evening I spent with them, and little did I imagine then that the stupid and sickly boy who was under my instructions, should become almost an 'Admirable Crichton' afterwards – but so it was. Quartermaster Guernsey's two sons were named respectively Wellington and Forbes – Wellington being the elder. When with me he was dull, heavy, and apparently possessed of the greatest disrelish for education. This, however, was easily accounted for – the poor boy had a tendency to blood to the head and did not appear likely to live twelve months. He was subject to such bleedings at the nose as I never witnessed in any boy of his age. I have known them to last in my school upwards of an hour and a half – in fact until we were obliged to send for Doctor Middleton, who lived next door, by whose skill and attention we were enabled to send him home. This strange boy afterwards recovered his health, but not while with me, and became the inheritor of his mother's manifold talent. He distinguished himself as a composer of music, and went to the Crimean War, where his distinction was more eminent. After his return, I think he obtained a liberal pension as a reward for some military discovery he had made.[1] The reader sees now that I was in the habit of going up very frequently, during the summer evenings to the Mullingar barracks — a very fortunate circumstance for myself as the event proved.

One thing impressed itself deeply upon the whole town and neighbourhood — the soldiers of the Ninety-Third were repeatedly waylaid, and brutally beaten, on their way both to and from the barracks, but principally on their way home at night. These attacks, too, were conducted with such secrecy and skill, that the soldiers found it impossible to trace the authors of them. One soldier was killed at the canal watering-place, and not the slightest mark could be traced of the murderer or the murderers. The inquest upon the body of the soldier was attended with such a spirit of triumph and derision on the part of the people, as was calculated to try both the temper and the patience of the Ninety-Third to the very uttermost extent. At all events, matters seemed to subside for a little; the season was autumn, and it was not unusual to see the soldiers going in groups of four or five, to the outlets of the surrounding neighbourhood, to enjoy a stroll, from which it was afterwards recollected they never returned until after dusk. One evening, about a week after these excursions had ceased, the great body of the Ninety-Third Regiment rushed from the gates of the barracks, in a state of fury and violence which could not be understood. Every man was armed with a heavy cudgel cut in the neighbouring woods of Knockdrin, and

---

[1] Wellington Guernsey was born in Mullingar on June 8th, 1817, and died in London on November 13th, 1885. He composed much music, and the words of many songs, besides arranging Irish melodies. His most popular air is 'I'll hang my harp on a willow tree'.

calculated to effect terrible mischief in the hands of such stalwart and enraged men. On leaving the barracks, they took their way directly to the town, where they divided themselves into two parties, each in a state of ungovernable fury and vengeance. At first, and before the Highlandmen were seen, the inhabitants of the distant parts of the town, impressed by the noise and tumult, took it into their heads that it was a rising of Ribbonmen, who were about to burn the town. They were soon undeceived, however – for in a short time, such a scene presented itself as had never been witnessed in a state of civil society. The Scotchmen committed such slaughter right and left, as they went along, as could under no circumstances be understood. Every civilian they met was knocked down, and for the most part thrashed into insensibility by these furious men, with their huge and heavy cudgels. The streets of Mullingar were strewn with what were apparently dead bodies. Windows were smashed to atoms – those who ran to the doors to ascertain the cause of the outrage were either knocked senseless inside, or dragged outside and smashed down without mercy. William Kidd, the proprietor of the *Westmeath Guardian*, was standing, or rather leaning, across the half door of his office, when he received two or three blows of a cudgel on the naked head, which confined him to his bed for upwards of a fortnight, and, indeed, occasioned some serious apprehension for his life.

Startled by the noise, I ran down to my own hall door, outside of which I had no sooner taken my place, than three powerful fellows, who were coming down the centre of the street, started across with the purpose of beating me down. This they would have done, were it not for a voice which shouted out to them – 'Hauld your hauns – that gentleman disna belang to them' – and the words were scarcely uttered, when the librarian from the barracks was at my side, just in time to protect me from their violence.

'For God's sake go in, Mr Carleton,' said he, 'and you may thank God that I happened to be passing at the time – only as you hope for mercy don't mention my name.'

I lost no time in bolting in, and took very good care that I did not make my appearance until after the soldiers had returned to their barracks.

The punishment these men inflicted on the people was dreadful; they made no distinction – innocent and guilty were treated with equal ferocity – and, indeed, for nearly three weeks afterwards the town of Mullingar was more like a hospital than anything else. A strong complaint was transmitted to the War Office; an investigation was held, and the decision come to resembled the good sense of a man who cuts off his nose to vex his face. The sentence from the Commander-in-Chief was, that the town of Mullingar should no longer be a military station for his Majesty's troops.

A beggarly staff of veterans merely was left to take care of the barracks. Sir John Buchan and his whole regiment were ordered to some other station, and the market of Mullingar presented a mere skeleton of what it used to be. The inhabitants of the town held a banquet of triumph on the occasion, a fact which caused a great deal of drollery among those who were indifferent to either party. The notion of the sapient citizens congratulating themselves on having deprived the town of an important source of income was, for a long time, a standing joke against them.

Chapter XIX

Clothing the naked – Sir Boyle Roche's bird – Rev. Dr Robinson –
The Rochforts – Election humours – Carleton arrested for debt –
Mullingar Gaol – The suspended priest – The popular idea about
them – Dublin again – Carlow school – Kilkenny coal.

THIS *is* a strange world; at least I have found it so. During my
residence at Mullingar, I received a visit from a friend, who had
been to see some of his relatives in Tullamore, named Pierce, I
think. He was a clever, romantic, unsettled kind of man, but at
the same time generous even to folly. Upon the day he arrived,
I was about to purchase the materials for a suit of clothes, as I
never wished to appear shabby. Upon looking at him, I observed
with regret that the poor fellow, though unquestionably with the
appearance of a gentleman, stood seriously in need of a renovated
wardrobe. I asked him the cause of this, and his reply was
evidently a very true one.

'Well,' said I, 'I am going to buy a suit of clothes for myself;
but for that I am laying down ready money – come with me, and
if the shopkeeper gives me credit, I will rig you out as well as
myself – I might pass,' said I, 'but you stand rather much in need
of a change, Andrew.'

The proprietor of the establishment felt great pleasure in
obliging me, and I desired him to send the materials up to Mr Lee,
the principal tailor in town.

It was just at this time that I received a message from Mr
Newland, requesting to see me. He had finished a pamphlet – and
an able one it was – upon the state of the Established Church in
Ireland. That period, and indeed every period, was always
pervaded by private theological strife, and this was conducted
with a bitterness which was utterly unaccountable. The Established Church at that time resembled Parliament. It had its two

parties, one, we will suppose, representing the government side, and the other the opposition. When I look back upon their by-battles now, I feel surprised at the earnestness and bitterness with which they fought and contested unimportant trifles. Mr Newland did me the honour of reading a page or two of the pamphlet in question – the pamphlet, indeed, which made him Dean of Ferns – until at length he came to one sentence – which was as follows:

'We are attacked not only from without, but also from within.'

'Surely you will change that,' I observed.

'Why should I change it?' he asked

'Excuse me,' said I simply, 'because – with every respect for you – it is not common sense.'

'How do you prove that?' said he.

'Why,' said I, 'because to make it so, like Sir Boyle Roche's bird, you must be in two places at a time. You say that you are attacked from without – now you know that if you are attacked from without you must be within. Then you say we are attacked not only from without, but from within – now don't you see that you cannot be attacked from within, unless you are without? Why,' said I, 'you have left yourself no *locus standi*, you must be hovering in the air – although I question if even that position would justify the figurative expression in question.' It is very strange, but I could not succeed in changing his opinion on the subject.[1]

'The reason why I have sent for you,' he said, 'is to say, that on next Sunday I preach my farewell sermon to my flock – I am leaving the parish and going to the county of Wexford.'

Newland's departure fell very heavily upon me. I generally spent a couple of evenings every week with him, and I told him, at our separation, that it was not my intention to remain in the parish after the change. On the Sunday he preached his farewell sermon there were very few dry eyes in the church; mine at least were wet.

I have as yet had but little occasion to speak about the rector

---

[1] This is not wonderful.

of the parish, the Rev. Dr Robinson. He was a remarkable old man, much stricken in years, and much more in the most pitiable distress and embarrassment. After Mr Newland had gone, he and I were thrown more together, as a matter of necessity, than we had been. I have said that when the school became too large for the room which Mr Newland had taken at Mr Atkins' – who was a retired tanner – the duty of taking an appropriate house was thrown upon me. This circumstance, as matters turned out afterwards, left me responsible for the rent. I took the house, and although I stated candidly that I took it for the purpose of converting it partly into a parish school and partly into a residence for myself, yet that seemed a matter of indifference to the proprietor, who, I suppose, considered me a sufficiently safe mark for the rent.

I never met in my life a more perfect old gentleman than Mr Robinson. For some years past he had not resided at the rectory. He was past all official and parochial labour, and lived with his son a couple of miles from Mullingar, a little to the left of the beautiful lake of Belvidere. His history was a peculiar one, indeed, and contained a great deal of what I may term practical romance. A fine property to the south, I think, of Mullingar, belonged to two wealthy brothers named Rochfort, who stood high among the gentry of the country – one of them being Lord Belvidere. The houses of the brothers had been built very near to each other, but as almost every one knows how often family feuds and implacable resentments which have their source in the adjustment of property, the reader need not feel surprised when I assure him that these two brothers looked upon each other with a feeling worthy of having its origin in hell itself. As a proof of this, I shall relate a short anecdote not very creditable to the old Irish gentry of the country. The house of one of these brothers was right opposite to that of the other; the view from it was delightful, and this was too much of a good thing for one brother to enjoy, especially as the other could put a curtain over the prospect, and shut out the view, either of the landscape or the house. He accordingly built a wall of sufficient height and length for his purpose, and deprived his worthy relative of one of the finest landscapes in the county of Westmeath. He, moreoever, put his action upon an even disgraceful footing; 'he could not bear to look upon the very house in which his brother lived.'

In the good old times the county of Westmeath was never represented except by a Rochfort. The candidates' speeches on the hustings were a proverb, both for their shortness and good sense. They were generally drunk when they came to address the electors, but as the speech was not only a proverbial, but a hereditary manifestation of the eloquence of the Irish hustings of that day, it became such a delightful treat to the electors that they insisted on hearing it word for word, as it had descended to them from their predecessors, and woe betide the man who, guided by common sense and a liberal education, attempted to transgress the original form. The predecessor to the man whom we are about to introduce, upon the occurrence of a general election, having received a better education than any preceding member of the family, and having also improved his mind and experience by travel, attempted, on presenting himself, to address them as a gentleman ought; the scene became tumultuous – he was hissed off – they would not hear him. His friends got about him, and said he had made a cursed mistake, and that if he did not set himself right at once, they would vote for his opponent, because they would regard him as having abandoned the principles of his family. On making his second appearance under better instructions, he addressed them as follows: 'D—n your souls, you affectionate blackguards, am'n't I here before you with devil a political feeling about me but the gout, bad luck to it.' He was returned by a large majority.

The Rev. Mr Robinson was agent to the last of the Rochforts who had been member for the county of Westmeath, and the history of their friendship would have made a good subject for a novel. They were in Trinity College together, but were unacquainted, until the incident which I am about to relate occurred. Rochfort had a quarrel with a powerful young fellow, who, availing himself of his physical strength, though in his own rooms, gave Rochfort, who was slight and by no means a match for him, a very severe beating. At this moment, and when Rochfort had been placed in quite a helpless state on a sofa, Robinson came in, and having learned, from some other students present, the unmanly conduct of Robinson's opponent, instantly charged the latter with his cowardice, and on receiving insolent language from the bully, he set to work and left him lying incapable of raising hand or foot. Robinson and Rochfort, although both resident students of college, had never before met; but the events of that day made them friends for life. When Rochfort came into his fine estate, his agent had just died; but as he had never forgotten the interests of his friend, he not only made him his agent, but bestowed upon him the living of Mullingar, of which he was the lay patron.

Now comes a sequel to the story.

For many a long year, Mr Robinson was the agent to the Rochfort property; and for many a long year did he get together such a sum of money as would have made him and his independent. He devoted himself to other means of increasing his fortune, but they were honest and legitimate means – through the public funds. Still, the friendship between the agent and the landlord held firm. Such, however, is life – Rochfort, who was a profligate in expenditure, took steps to acquire money without either the consent or knowledge of his agent. His motive, however, was honourable. This was repeated time after time, until it became impossible to conceal the fact from Mr Robinson any longer. The latter was a poor man when he became agent to the property of Mr Rochfort; gradually, and by slow degrees, he became a man of considerable wealth. Rochfort was now in a wretched plight – in fact, on the point of ruin. Legal proceedings were taken against him, and on what hand was he to turn? We need not say – his guardian angel, or rather he who would have been his guardian angel if he could – was with him. He owed the property he possessed to the kind and grateful spirit of his friend and benefactor – could he now desert him in his day of trouble?

Alas, there was more than one day of trouble; many a day of

trouble came, and in no instance did ever the noble-minded agent abandon his friend until, after a series of struggling years, they found themselves both beggars.

Don't let the reader dare to doubt this; it is no fiction. I give their names; any man doubting it might as well doubt the fact Nelson's Pillar stands beside the Dublin Post Office.

While Mr Newland was at Mullingar he always paid me my salary. After his departure, I had no one to look to, except Mr Robinson. He came in every day, as I have said, to transact business – with a class of persons on whom no one could look without feeling that they were creditors. He carried a large green bag filled with bank notes, and a second filled with silver. I had been now close upon two years at Mullingar, but I had got tired of the house I was living in. My wife, too, was losing her health, and I felt annoyed about my responsibility for the rent, as well as by a note or two I had received from the shopkeeper to whom I owed the price of a coat for the friend to whom I have referred. With great difficulty, I continued to get the rent paid, but the state of my own health, and that of my wife and infant children, satisfied me that a longer residence in that damp, cold house, filled with draughts as it was, would have been death to us. My chief object now was to get out of Mullingar altogether. I accordingly wrote to my friend Mr Wilson, of Capel Street, requesting him to find for me, if possible, a situation which would afford me and my family more personal comfort. I received a letter from him stating that he had put my name down, and that he would acquaint me with the first comfortable thing that offered.

I now lived a quiet but rather dissatisfied life – I could not at all admire the scenery about Mullingar. Newland was gone, and Robinson I only saw about money matters. I had among my scholars two sons of a Mr Murray, who had purchased the Mullingar Hotel from Harry Wilton, and except my instructions to them, I detested the duties of the school altogether. In fact I was sick of both Mullingar and it, and came to the resolution of giving Mr Robinson notice that I was about to resign my situation. When I went to the parsonage, where for an hour or two he transacted his daily business, and knocked, the door was not opened as usual, and on looking through the parlour window, I noticed the servant maid peeping out: on seeing me she came and opened the door, with a great deal of caution.

'What is the matter?' I asked.

'There's bailiffs about the place, sir,' she replied.

'Well,' said I, 'I won't see him now – but I will write to him.'

This was in summer, and in the course of the evening I was lounging in the house of a man named Barber, a watchmaker, in whose shop some of the most respectable citizens were in the habit of meeting and chatting in the evenings. After a tolerably long and pleasant conversation, I turned down the street on my way home, when, without either preface or apology, I was arrested by two bailiffs, who immediately marched me, or were about to march me, down to the gaol. They would not even allow me to go home and inform my wife of what had happened; and when I attempted to do so, they laid violent hands upon me, one of them giving me a punch on the shoulder which was considered by everyone who saw it as a most unjustifiable assault. I could not restrain my fury at such wanton brutality, and as a very natural consequence, I knocked them both down. Barber, a most powerful man, came out, and prevailed on me to go quietly with the bailiffs, and indeed it was well for them that he did, or they would have received severe punishment at the hands of the assembled crowd, by whom they were detested, as two of the most consummate ruffians that ever disgraced even *their* profession. One of them I got dismissed through John Charles Lyons, the magistrate of Ladistown, brother-in-law to the late Mr Tuite of Sonna.

After all, I must say that there was a good deal of dramatic incident in my life. I was conducted to the gaol, the governor of which was a gentleman named Fulding. Barber and some others of the more respectable neighbours accompanied me. Now it so happened that Fulding's children were my private pupils; by this I mean, that although they came to my school as a public and free one, yet their education was liberally paid for by their father.

233

On entering the prison, I asked to see Fulding, and in the course of a few minutes he presented himself. He appeared to be greatly affected by what had happened, and after dismissing the bailiffs he brought me into his private room, and having ordered some brandy and water, and learned the simple facts, he said, 'Don't be uneasy – you know that as far as I can make you comfortable I will do so. It's nothing – you will be out in a few days. Ah,' said he, 'what is your case? A soap bubble' – whisper – 'do you know whom I have in safe custody?' From what I had seen that day at the rectory, and also from what I had heard on other occasions, I at once suspected the truth. I merely bowed my head and pointed significantly to the rectory.

'Right,' said he, 'and I am sorry for it; there is not a man in the parish, Catholic or Protestant, who will not feel as we do.'

As that was my first visit to a gaol, I felt anxious of course to be placed as they say upon the debtor's side, because I had read enough about gaols to know what that distinction meant.

'Debtor's side – God bless your soul,' said he, 'there is no such thing here. We manage that in the best way we can, and a difficult affair it is. At this moment I have only one room in which, if you wish to avoid the criminals, I can put you. One of the occupants is a droll, vulgar, farmer who is very wealthy, and yet he's a debtor. The other is a man who is in for a crime against the state – in fact, a state prisoner. You see I am anxious to do you honour.'

'But as to our friend,' I said, 'I hope you will make him comfortable.'

'He lodges with myself,' said he, 'and tomorrow, if you are in here so long, you'll dine with us.' He then brought me to my appointed place, and having shaken hands with me at the door, left me.

On entering I found two men sitting there, one of whom I instantly recognized. He was a degraded priest, or what is termed a 'couple-beggar'.

Among the Catholic clergy – who are probably, without exception, considering the natural restraints under which they labour, the most moral class of men on God's earth – it is some-times, but indeed rarely, necessary that the judicial hand of episcopal authority should punish them. When a Catholic priest falls, he himself appears to feel that his fall is hopeless, like that of Lucifer – 'never to rise again'. When the duties required from the individual are of a high, pure and lofty character, and that the position, in a spiritual and moral sense, is also elevated, the fall is then terrible. It is more – it is a dark and maddening descent, which fills the fallen man with utter recklessness of all shame and decency, if not of salvation itself. Indeed, I may say that the degradation to which such men sink, and the open hardihood with which they set public opinion at defiance, is the strongest proof of the inward tortures which they suffer. In the great majority of cases, the melancholy cause of their fall is an excessive indulgence in liquor, and it unfortunately happens too often that, notwithstanding their degradation by their bishop, the compas-sion of the affectionate people for them is a strong temptation after their fall. The belief of the lower classes, is that after having once received full ordination, neither bishop, primate, nor Pope himself, can deprive a priest of his of the spiritual authority. The only length to which ecclesiastical power is supposed to be cap-able of going is to deprive him of the official authority of exercis-ing it. As to anything else, the people say that he possesses the full right of conferring the sacraments. After all, I am inclined to think that the people are right, even in a theological view – '*Tu es Sacerdos in eternum secundum ordinem Melchisedech.*' 'Thou art a priest for ever, according to the Order of Melchisedech.'

On entering the room allotted to me, I found this man was to be one of my companions, a circumstance for which I felt very much obliged to my friend Fulding. In truth, he and I might almost have been termed acquaintances. We had met repeatedly in the streets of Mullingar, through which he was in the habit of tottering in a state of the most helpless intoxication. He would sometimes seize me by the hand and address me in Latin. His crime was the marriage of a Protestant and Catholic, and as it was a case in which there was property concerned, he had been

235

prosecuted upon a statute dug up from the penal laws; while it became perfectly well understood afterwards that the poor fellow knew no more about the property involved than I did.

At all events, between him and Bob Gansey the farmer, I was exceedingly amused. He was the most harmless creature I ever met, and what was more, had a touch of the gentleman about him, and a considerable sense of humour, being also a good classical scholar. There is one thing about the Roman Catholic people of Ireland for which they deserve the highest honour, namely, the affection and respect with which they treat their priesthood. No man, living or dead, ever had a better opportunity of witnessing this than I had. They will treat a suspended priest with as much respect as if he never had been suspended. They do so because they know that on a future occasion, by amendment of life, he may have the suspension removed; a circumstance which occasionally occurs. This man's life was a peculiar one. He was not three days in Mullingar gaol, when the fact became known, not only throughout the neighbourhood, but the whole parish – and the adjoining ones. No one could believe the number of clandestine marriages he performed, unless, like me, they had been in the same prison with him. Fulding had strict orders to prevent his having access to liquor, but he might as well have attempted to deprive him of air. Independently of this, however, no marriage party – however small – ever came to him without bringing whisky. That was a condition, independently of the fees, which varied according to the circumstances of the bride and bridegroom. The prison yard was never without two or three of his messengers – they were generally slips of girls from ten to fourteen. Altogether he was treated with great indulgence, and in spite of his degraded state he occasionally exhibited manifestations of melancholy – especially in the morning – which no man with a feeling heart could look upon without compassion.

I was detained in this prison longer than I expected. Poor Mr Robinson was also an object of compassion although under a different view, and in a different position, and I myself had the consolation to hear from my wife that an execution had been put into my house, and that not the value of sixpence was left under my roof. Newland was gone – Mr Robinson could do nothing – and I could do nothing. The only friend I had outside was a Captain Hill, who, in addition to some other public employments, was an inspector of prisons, or at least of Mullingar prison. He called on me one day, and asked to know the amount of the debt for which I was in; and on the evening but one afterwards, he called again and produced a receipt from my creditor. My wife and our two infants had been taken into the house of a kind-hearted neighbour, named Moffat, whose son, a fine boy, had been at school with me. He and Mrs Moffat treated her and them with every possible kindness and attention. We started for Dublin by the canal the next day, and arrived safely in town. Mrs Carleton, in compliance with her mother's wish, stayed with her, and I with my old friend her uncle on the Coombe.

Our stay in Dublin was not a long one. In the course of three weeks, through the exertions of Mr Wilson, my ever kind friend, I was appointed to a school in Carlow, similar to that which I had left in Mullingar. The rector was the Rev. George Vernon; his curate was the Rev. Mr Jameson, who kept a classical boarding school. I am not sure to this moment whether it was a diocesan establishment or not, but this I do know, that the attendance was both numerous and respectable. Mr Vernon was a nephew of the late Sir Charles Vernon, who had been master of the ceremonies in Dublin Castle. In kindness and personal respect for me he was a second edition of dear Newland. Carlow school was a very large one. I was engaged to teach only the boys – the female school having been conducted by a Mrs Adams. The 'apartments' into which I and my wife were put, consisted of one small room about fourteen feet by ten, and the coals allowed us were of that vile and unhealthy description to be found in some of the coal-mines which lie between the counties of Carlow and Kilkenny. One fourth of them was sulphur, and every morning we could perceive the cream of that sulphur, so white and thick under the door, that we have often scraped it up with a knife in quantities as large as a pigeon's egg. In fact the place was not habitable; not only we ourselves, but our children, became ill, and I found that to live there was only another word for death.

Here ends Carleton's autobiography. His manuscript embraces only the period indicated in his own narrative, in which it will be seen that he has minutely traced each step of his early career, and has graphically described his privations and disappointments. A few incidents, however, he has left untouched. It is known, for example, that he once seriously thought of enlisting in the army, and with that view wrote a letter in Latin to the commander of a regiment in whose vicinity he happened to find himself, explaining his forlorn situation, and asking to be allowed to join. The officer, surprised and touched, wrote a kindly letter in reply, dissuading the future novelist from entering the ranks, and enclosing a sum of money to help him on his wanderings. It is also said that Carleton, in the course of his recurrent quests for employment, on one occasion entered the shop of a bird-stuffer and asked for work. The tradesman, doubting the capacity of the raw countryman, asked him what he usually stuffed birds with. 'Potatoes and meal,' was the innocent reply. Carleton did not secure the position in that bird-stuffer's establishment.

It almost swallowed the bottle as well, so eager was it to get the stuff down.

Farewell to the Hammer
A Shankill Boyhood
John Young Simms
Pbk, 144pp, illustrated, £4.95

A fascinating story of growing up, amidst horses, trams, cobbles and pig's feet, in the Hammer district of Belfast's Shankill Road at the height of the Great Depression.

"Each tale swells in the mind, like grain in water, until the reader finds it necessary to pause, savour its taste, and go back over it again before moving the short distance to the next..." *Sam McAughtry*

The Most Unpretending of Places
A History of Dundonald, County Down
Peter Carr
Pbk, 256pp, illustrated, £7.95

"Sparkles with compelling detail... one of the most impressive local histories available for any locality on this island, north or south."
Linenhall Review

"One word could suffice to describe this book, magnificent! ...I cannot praise it too highly. Well illustrated with photographs, studiously annotated without over-loading the text, a questioning of sources, a good index and the courage to express opinions of a controversial nature. This is what local history is all about." *Irish News*

Gape Row

Agnes Romilly White's classic comedy

Pbk, 200pp, £4.95

Can Jinanna escape the poorhouse? Will young Johnny Darragh jilt Ann? Will Mary get saddled with the awful Andy John McCready? Or will Happy Bill, the wayside preacher, nip in first and win them all for God?

A boisterous, rich, nostalgic book which immerses the reader in the cheerful chaos of everyday life in a small Irish village on the eve of the First World War.

"Captures the spirit of early twentieth century rural Ulster better than any painter of photographer could." *Sunday News*

"masterly... the dialogue goes to one's head like wine." *The Observer*

NEVER!

Fascinating Facts about Ireland

Michael Smith

Pbk, 93pp, illustrated, £3.50

Did you know ...that the only Irishman to be offered the Papacy refused it? ...that an Irish ship discovered the ghostly wreck of the *Marie Celeste*? ...that the first casualty of the Irish Civil War was a Free State sniper, smashed over the head with a teapot by an elderly Dublin woman? ...or that the skull of a Corkman is the most sacred relic of the Ashanti tribe of West Africa?

All is now revealed in this illustrated collection of amusing, amazing and arcane facts relating to Ireland and the Irish.

"jam-packed with all sorts of scarcely believable, probably useless, but nonetheless fascinating gems of information." *The Wicklow People*

The medieval purgatory on Lough Derg was believed to be one of the two entrances to Hell, Mount Etna on Sicily being the other.

Blackmouth & Dissenter
John M. Barkley
Pbk, 192pp, illustrated, £7.95

In this engaging memoir, which will delight his admirers and offer his detractors no comfort, Dr. Barkley, 'without doubt one of the most influential Irish Churchmen of the second half of the twentieth century', writes of his life and the experiences that formed him, lacing his narrative with some astringent criticism of contemporary Irish Presbyterianism.

"An enthralling, delightful story covering a broad canvas of Irish Presbyterianism from Malin to Mallusk over eighty years." *Derry Journal*

A Harp of Fishbones
Russell Walton
Pbk, 128 pp, illustrated, £4.95

Twenty-seven tales of mystery, passion, intrigue and enchantment, some of the most beautiful – and most powerful – Irish and European folk tales, fairytales, and legends to have been written on the theme of harping, along with colourful reminiscences of some of the great Irish harpers, explanatory commentaries, and a bold, iconoclastic introduction by the compiler, Russell Walton.

"Harpers will love these stories, but this is not just a collection for connoisseurs, it will delight all kinds of readers, and touch anyone who has a feeling for music." *Derek Bell*

Stealing behind Murphy, he seized him by the hair of his head...

The storm became so ferocious people thought the end of the world was at hand.

The Night of the Big Wind

Pbk, 158 pp, illustrated, £4.95

The extraordinary story of one of Ireland's greatest natural disasters, the Big Wind of 1839, re-created from contemporary sources, and set in the context of the folk beliefs of the time. Includes an Ireland-wide A–Z of storm damage, and new sections on the storm's meteorology, and the part that religion and the supernatural played in attempting to explain it.

"An enthralling, gripping read" *Belfast News Letter*

"Written in a way which will appeal to everyone, whether an historian, or just an ordinary person who enjoys a good read" *Roe Valley Sentinel*

Two Centuries of Life in Down 1600-1800

John Stevenson

Pbk, 508pp, illustrated, £3.95

Pirates roaming the coast, clerics being paid in beer, shopkeepers issuing their own coinage, French and Spanish money in daily circulation, hanging a man for stealing a chisel...

In **Two Centuries of Life in Down 1600-1800**, John Stevenson brings this forgotten world to life, familiarising us with its customs, tastes and values, and subtly drawing the reader into the lives of a wide variety of its people, from the drunken Viscount and the dowager with servant trouble, to the small farmer facing eviction. The result is something of a tour de force, a book of vast range and daring, and one of the great landmarks of literary County Down.

"no dry-as-dust academic work this, but a wonderful source for local historians, and a marvellous read for anyone who is interested in County Down..."
W.A. Maguire, Keeper of Local History, Ulster Museum.

Available from bookshops, or directly from the publishers.
If ordering, please add £1 for postage and packaging.